PERSONAL MEMOIRS

OF

P. H. SHERIDAN.

VOLUME II.

P H Sheridan
Lieut General

PERSONAL MEMOIRS

OF

P. H. SHERIDAN.

GENERAL UNITED STATES ARMY.

IN TWO VOLUMES.

VOL. II.

NEW YORK:

CHARLES L. WEBSTER & COMPANY,

1888.

PRESS OF
JENKINS & McCOWAN
NEW YORK

PERSONAL MEMOIRS OF
P.H. SHERIDAN
VOL. 2

By P.H. Sheridan
Originally Published in 1888 by Charles L. Webster & Company

©1998 DSI digital reproduction
First DSI Printing: 1998

Published by **DIGITAL SCANNING, INC.**
Scituate, MA 02066
www.digitalscanning.com

Trade Paperback ISBN: 1-58218-103-9
Hardcover ISBN: 1-58218-186-1
eBook ISBN: 1-58218-034-2

DIGITAL SCANNING
& PUBLISHING

Digital Scanning and Publishing is a leader in the electronic republication of historical books and documents. We publish our titles as eBooks, as well as traditional hardcover and trade paper editions. DSI is committed to bringing many traditional and little known books back to life, retaining the look and feel of the original work.

CONTENTS.

VOLUME II.

CHAPTER I.

CHAPTER VIII.

CHAPTER IX.

CHAPTER X.

CHAPTER XI.

CHAPTER XII.

CHAPTER XIII.

CHAPTER XIV.

CHAPTER XV.

CHAPTER XVI.

CHAPTER XVII.

CHAPTER XVIII.

CHAPTER XIX.

CHAPTER XX.

ILLUSTRATIONS

VOLUME II.

LIST OF MAPS.

VOLUME II.

PERSONAL MEMOIRS

P. H. SHERIDAN.

VOLUME II.

CHAPTER I.

ORGANIZING SCOUTS - MISS REBECCA WRIGHT - IMPOR-
TANT INFORMATION - DECIDES TO MOVE ON NEW-
TOWN - MEETING GENERAL GRANT - ORGANIZA-
TION OF THE UNION ARMY - OPENING OF THE
BATTLE OF THE OPEQUON - DEATH OF GENERAL
RUSSELL - A TURNING MOVEMENT - A SUCCESSFUL
CAVALRY CHARGE - VICTORY - THREE LOYAL
GIRLS - APPOINTED A BRIGADIER - GENERAL IN
THE REGULAR ARMY - REMARKS ON THE BATTLE.

WHILE occupying the ground between Clif-
ton and Berryville, referred to in the
last chapter of the preceding volume, I felt
the need of an efficient body of scouts to collect information regarding the enemy, for the
defective intelligence-establishment with which
I started out from Harper's Ferry early in
August had not proved satisfactory. I there-

1

fore began to organize my scouts on a system
which I hoped would give better results than
had the method hitherto pursued in the department, which was to employ on this service doubtful citizens and Confederate desert-
ers. If these should turn out untrustworthy,
the mischief they might do us gave me grave
apprehension, and I finally concluded that those
of our own soldiers who should volunteer for the
delicate and hazardous duty would be the most
valuable material, and decided that they should
have a battalion organization and be commanded
by an officer, Major H. K. Young, of the First
Rhode Island Infantry. These men were disguised in Confederate uniforms whenever necessary, were paid from the Secret-Service Fund in
proportion to the value of the intelligence they
furnished, which often stood us in good stead in
checking the forays of Gilmore, Mosby, and other
irregulars. Beneficial results came from the plan
in many other ways too, and particularly so when
in a few days two of my scouts put me in the
way of getting news conveyed from Winchester.
They had learned that just outside of my lines,
near Millwood, there was living an old colored
man, who had a permit from the Confederate
commander to go into Winchester and return
three times a week, for the purpose of selling

vegetables to the inhabitants. The scouts had sounded this man, and, finding him both loyal and shrewd, suggested that he might be made useful to us within the enemy's lines; and the proposal struck me as feasible, provided there could be found in Winchester some reliable person who would be willing to co-operate and correspond with me. I asked General Crook, who was acquainted with many of the Union people of Winchester, if he knew of such a person, and he recommended a Miss Rebecca Wright, a young lady whom he had met there before the battle of Kernstown, who, he said, was a member of the Society of Friends and the teacher of a small private school. He knew she was faithful and loyal to the Government, and thought she might be willing to render us assistance, but he could not be certain of this, for on account of her well-known loyalty she was under constant surveillance. I hesitated at first, but finally deciding to try it, despatched the two scouts to the old negro's cabin, and they brought him to my headquarters late that night. I was soon convinced of the negro's fidelity, and asking him if he was acquainted with Miss Rebecca Wright, of Winchester, he replied that he knew her well. Thereupon I told him what I wished to do, and after a little persuasion he agreed to carry a letter to her on his next marketing trip. My message was prepared by writing it on tissue paper, which was then compressed into a small pellet, and protected by wrapping it in tin-foil so that it could be safely carried in the man's mouth. The probability of his being searched when he came to the Confederate picket-line was not remote, and in such event he was to swallow the pellet. The letter appealed to Miss Wright's loyalty and patriotism, and requested her to furnish me with information regarding the strength and condition of Early's army. The night before the negro started one of the scouts placed the odd-looking communication in his hands, with renewed injunctions as to secrecy and promptitude. Early the next morning it was delivered to Miss Wright, with an intimation that a letter of importance was enclosed in the tin-foil, the negro telling her at the same time that she might expect him to call for a message in reply before his return home. At first Miss Wright began to open the pellet nervously, but when told to be careful, and to preserve the foil as a wrapping for her answer, she proceeded slowly and carefully, and when the note appeared intact the messenger retired, remarking again that in the evening he would come for an answer.

On reading my communication Miss Wright was much startled by the perils it involved, and hesitatingly consulted her mother, but her devoted loyalty soon silenced every other consideration, and the brave girl resolved to comply with my request, notwithstanding it might jeopardize her life. The evening before a convalescent Confederate officer had visited her mother's house, and in conversation about the war had disclosed the fact that Kershaw's division of infantry and Cutshaw's battalion of artillery had started to rejoin General Lee. At the time Miss Wright heard this she attached little if any importance to it, but now she perceived the value of the intelligence, and, as her first venture, determined to send it to me at once, which she did with a promise that in the future she would with great pleasure continue to transmit information by the negro messenger.

Miss Wright's answer proved of more value to me than she anticipated, for it not only quieted the conflicting reports concerning Anderson's corps, but was most important in showing positively that Kershaw was gone, and this circumstance led, three days later, to the battle of the Opequon, or Winchester as it has been unofficially called". Word

*"SEPTEMBER 15, 1864.

"I learn from Major-General Crook that you are a loyal lady, and still love the old flag. Can you inform me of the position of Early's forces, the number of divisions in his army, and the strength of any or all of them, and his prob-

to the effect that some of Early's troops were under orders to return to Petersburg, and would start back at the first favorable opportunity, had been communicated to me already from many sources, but we had not been able to ascertain the date for their departure. Now that they had actually started, I decided to wait before offering battle until Kershaw had gone so far as to preclude his return, feeling confident that my prudence would be justified by the improved chances of victory; and then, besides, Mr. Stanton kept reminding me that positive success was necessary to counteract the political dissatisfaction existing in some of the Northern States. This course was advised and approved by General Grant, but even with his powerful backing it was difficult to resist the persistent pressure of those

---

able or reported intentions? Have any more troops arrived from Richmond, or are any more coming, or reported to be coming?

"I am, very respectfully, your most obedient servant,

"P. H. SHERIDAN, Major-General Commanding.

"You can trust the bearer."

———   "SEPTEMBER 16, 1864.

"I have no communication whatever with the rebels, but will tell you what I know. The division of General Kershaw, and Cutshaw's artillery, twelve guns and men, General Anderson commanding, have been sent away, and no more are expected, as they cannot be spared from Richmond. I do not know how the troops are situated, but the force is much smaller than represented. I will take pleasure hereafter in learning all I can of their strength and position, and the bearer may call again.

"Very respectfully yours,

*   *   *   *   *

MISS REBECCA M. WRIGHT

whose judgment, warped by their interests in
the Baltimore and Ohio railroad, was often con-
fused and misled by stories of scouts (sent out
from Washington), averring that Kershaw and
Fitzhugh Lee had returned to Petersburg, Breckenridge to southwestern Virginia, and at one
time even maintaining that Early's whole army-
was east of the Blue Ridge, and its commander
himself at Gordonsville.

During the inactivity prevailing in my army for
the ten days preceding Miss Wright's communication the infantry was quiet, with the exception of
Getty's division, which made a reconnoissance to
the Opequon, and developed a heavy force of the
enemy. at Edwards's Corners.   The cavalry, however, was employed a good deal in this interval
skirmishing - heavily at times - to maintain a
space about six miles in width between the hostile lines, for I wished to control this ground so
that when I was released from the instructions
of August 12 I could move my men into position for attack without the knowledge of Early.
The most noteworthy of these mounted encounters was that of McIntosh's brigade, which captured the Eighth South Carolina at Abraham's
Creek September 13.

It was the evening of the 16th of September
that I received from Miss Wright the positive in-

formation that Kershaw was in march toward Front Royal on his way by Chester Gap to Richmond. Concluding that this was my opportunity, I at once resolved to throw my whole force into Newtown the next day, but a despatch from General Grant directing me to meet him at Charlestown; whither he was coming to consult with me, caused me to defer action until after I should see him. In our resulting interview at Charlestown, I went over the situation very thoroughly, and pointed out with so much confidence the chances of a complete victory should I throw my army across the Valley pike near Newtown that he fell in with the plan at once, authorized me to resume the offensive, and to attack Early as soon as I deemed it most propitious to do so; and although before leaving City Point he had outlined certain operations for my army, yet he neither discussed nor disclosed his plans, my knowledge of the situation striking him as being so much more accurate than his own.*

The interview over, I returned to my army to arrange for its movement toward Newtown, but while busy with these preparations, a report came

---

*[Extract from "Grant's Memoirs," page 328.]

"**Before starting I had drawn up a plan of campaign for Sheridan, which I had brought with me; but seeing that he was so clear and so positive in his views, and so confident of success, I said nothing about this, and did not take it out of my pocket * *."

to me from General Averell which showed that
Early was moving with two divisions of infantry
toward Martinsburg. This considerably altered
the state of affairs, and I now decided to change
my plan and attack, at once the two divisions remaining about Winchester and Stephenson's depot, and later, the two sent to Martinsburg; the
disjointed state of the enemy giving me an opportunity to take him in detail, unless the Martinsburg column should be returned by forced
marches.

While General Early was in the telegraph office
at Martinsburg on the morning of the 18th, he
learned of Grant's visit to me; and anticipating activity by reason of this circumstance, he
promptly proceeded to withdraw so as to get
the two divisions within supporting distance of
Ramseur's, which lay across the Berryville pike
about two miles east of Winchester, between
Abraham's Creek and Red Bud Run, so by the
night of the 18th Wharton's division, under
Breckenridge, was at Stephenson's depot, Rodes
near there, and Gordon's at Bunker Hill. At
daylight of the 19th these positions of the Con-
federaie infantry still obtained, with the cavalry
of Lomax, Jackson, and Johnson on the right of
Ramseur, while to the left and rear of the enemy's
general line was Fitzhugh Lee, covering from

Stephenson's depot west across the Valley pike to Apple-pie Ridge.

My army* moved at 3 o'clock that morning. The plan was for Torbert to advance with Merritt's division of cavalry from Summit Point, carry the crossings of the Opequon at Stevens's and Lock's fords, and form a junction near Stephenson's depot, with Averell, who was to

---

*Organization of the Union Forces, Commanded by Major-General Philip H. Sheridan, at the Battle of Winchester (or the Opequon), Virgina, September 19, 1864.

Headquarters Escort:
Sixth United States Cavalry, Captain Ira W. Claflin.

Sixth Army Corps:
Major-General Horatio G. Wright.

Escort:
First Michigan Cavalry, Company G, Lieutenant William H. Wheeler.

First Division:
(1) Brigadier-General David A. Russell.
(2) Brigadier-General Emory Upton.
(3) Colonel Oliver Edwards.

First Brigade:
Lieutenant-Colonel Edward L. Campbell.
Fourth New Jersey, Captain Baldwin Hufty.
Tenth New Jersey, Major Lambert Boeman,
Fifteenth New Jersey, Captain William T. Cornish.

Second Brigade:
(1) Brigadier-General Emory Upton.
(2) Colonel Joseph E. Hamblin.
Second Connecticut Heavy Artillery, Colonel Ranald S. Mackenzie.
Sixty-fifth New York (1), Colonel Joseph E. Hamblin.
(2), Captain Henry C Fisk.
One Hundred and Twenty-first New York, Captain John D. P. Douw.
Ninety-fifth and Ninety-Sixth Pennsylvania,* Captain Francis J. Randall.

* Guarding trains, and not engaged in the battle.

move south from Darksville by the Valley pike. Meanwhile, Wilson was to strike up the Berryville pike, carry the Berryville crossing of the Opequon, charge through the gorge or cañon on the road west of the stream, and occupy the open ground at the head of this defile. Wilson's attack was to be supported by the Sixth and Nineteenth corps, which were ordered

THIRD BRIGADE:

(1) Colonel Oliver Edwards.
(2) Colonel Isaac C. Bassett.
Thirty-seventh Massachusetts, Lieutenant-Colonel George L. Montague.
Forty-ninth Pennsylvania, Lieutenant-Colonel Baynton J. Hickman.
Eighty-second Pennsylvania, Colonel Isaac C. Bassett.
One Hundred and Nineteenth Pennsylvania, Lieutenant-Colonel Gideon Clark.
Second Rhode Island (battalion), Captain Elisha H. Rhodes.
Fifth Wisconsin (battalion), Major Charles W. Kempf.

SECOND DIVISION:

Brigadier-General George W. Getty.

FIRST BRIGADE:

Brigadier-General Frank Wheaton.
Sixty-second New York, Lieutenant-Colonel Theo. B. Hamilton.
Ninety-third Pennsylvania, Lieutenant-Colonel John S. Long.
Ninety-eighth Pennsylvania, Lieutenant-Colonel John B. Kohler.
One Hundred and Second Pennsylvania, Major James H. Coleman.
One Hundred and Thirty-ninth Pennsylvania, Major Robert Munroe.

SECOND BRIGADE:

Colonel James M. Warner.

Lieutenant-Colonel Amasa S. Tracy.*
Second Vermont, Major Enoch E. Johnson.
Third and Fourth Vermont, Major Horace W. Floyd.
Fifth Vermont, Captain Addison Brown, Jr.
Sixth Vermont, Captain Martin W. Davis.
Eleventh Vermont (First Heavy Artillery), Major Aldace F. Walker.

* " Superintended a portion of the line."

to the Berryville crossing, and as the cavalry gained the open ground beyond the gorge, the two infantry corps, under command of General Wright, were expected to press on after and occupy Wilson's ground, who was then to shift to the south bank of Abraham's Creek and cover my left; Crook's two divisions, having to march from Summit Point, were to follow the Sixth and

THIRD BRIGADE:
Brigadier-General Daniel D. Bidwell.

Seventh Maine, Major Stephen C. Fletcher.
Forty-third New York, Major Charles A. Milliken.
Forty-ninth New York (battalion), Lieutenant-Colonel Erastus D. Holt.
Seventy-seventh New York, Lieutenant-Colonel Winsor B. French.
One Hundred and Twenty-second New York, Major Jabez M. Brower.
Sixty-first Pennsylvania (battalion) (1), Captain Charles S. Greene;
                        (2), Captain David J. Taylor.

THIRD DIVISION:
Brigadier-General James B. Ricketts.

FIRST BRIGADE:
Colonel William Emerson.

Fourteenth New Jersey (1), Major Peter Vredenburgh.
                     (2), Captain Jacob J. Janeway.
One Hundred and Sixth New York, Captain Peter Robertson.
One Hundred and Fifty-first New York, Lieutenant-Colonel Thomas M. Fay.
Eighty-seventh Pennsylvania, Colonel John W. Schall.
Tenth Vermont (1), Major Edwin Dillingham.
                   (2), Captain Lucius T. Hunt.

SECOND BRIGADE:
Colonel J . Warren Keifer.

Sixth Maryland (1), Colonel John W. Horn.
               (2), Captain Clifton K. Prentiss.
Ninth New York Heavy Artillery, Major Charles Burgess.
One Hundred and Tenth Ohio, Lieutenant-Colonel Otho H. Binkley.
One Hundred and Twenty-second Ohio, Colonel Wm. H. Ball.
One Hundred and Twenty-sixth Ohio (1), Lieutenant-Colonel Aaron W. Ebright,
                          (2), Captain George W. Hoge.

Nineteenth corps to the Opequon, and should they arrive before the action began, they were to be held in reserve till the proper moment came, and then, as a turning-column, be thrown over toward the Valley pike, south of Winchester.

McIntosh's brigade of Wilson's division drove the enemy's pickets away from the Berryville crossing at dawn, and Wilson following rapidly

Sixty-seventh Pennsylvania, Lieutenant John F. Young.
One Hundred and Thirty-eighth Pennsylvania (1), Colonel Matthew R. Mc-
Clennan.
(2), Major Lewis A. May.

ARTILLERY BRIGADE:

Colonel Charles H. Tompkins.

Maine Light, Fifth Battery (E), Captain Greenleaf T. Stevens.
Massachusetts Light, First Battery (A), Captain Wm. H. McCartney.
New York Light, First Battery (1), Lieutenant William H. Johnson.
(2), Lieutenant Orsamus R. Van Etten.
First Rhode Island Light, Battery C, Lieutenant Jacob H. Lamb.
First Rhode Island Light, Battery G, Captain George W. Adams.
Fifth United States, Battery M, Captain James McKnight.

NINETEENTH ARMY CORPS:

Brigadier-General William H. Emory.

FIRST DIVISION:

Brigadier-General William Dwight.

FIRST BRIGADE:

Colonel George L. Beal.

Twenty-ninth Maine (1), Major William Knowlton.
(2), Captain Alfred L. Turner.
Thirtieth Massachusetts, Captain Samuel D. Shipley.
One Hundred and Fourteenth New York, (1) Colonel Samuel R. Per Lee.
(2) Major Oscar H. Curtis.
One Hundred and Sixteenth New York, Colonel George M. Love.
One Hundred and Fifty-third New York, Colonel Edwin P. Davis,

through the gorge with the rest of the division, debauched from its western extremity with such suddenness as to capture a small earthwork in front of General Kamseur's main line; and notwithstanding the Confederate infantry, on recovering from its astonishment, tried hard to dislodge them, Wilson's troopers obstinately held the work till the Sixth Corps came up. I followed Wilson

SECOND BRIGADE:
Brigadier-General James W. McMillan.
Twelfth Connecticut (1), Lieutenant-Colonel Frank H. Peck.
(2), Captain Sydney E. Clark.
One Hundred and Sixtieth New York, * Lieutenant-Colonel John B. Van Petten.
Forty-seventh Pennsylvania, Colonel Tilghman H. Good.
Eighth Vermont, Colonel Stephen Thomas.

THIRD BRIGADE: †
Colonel Leonard D. H. Currie.
Thirtieth Maine, ‡ Captain George W. Randall.
One Hundred and Thirty-third New York, Major Anthony J. Allaire.
One Hundred and Sixty-second New York, Colonel Justus W. Blanchard.
One Hundred and Sixty-fifth New York (six companies), Lieutenant-Colonel Gouverneur Carr.
One Hundred and Seventy-third New York, Major George W. Rogers.

ARTILLERY:
New York Light, Fifth Battery, Lieutenant John V. Grant.

SECOND DIVISION:
Brigadier-General Cuvier Grover.

FIRST BRIGADE:
Brigadier-General Henry W. Birge.
Ninth Connecticut, Colonel Thomas W. Cahill.
Twelfth Maine, Lieutenant-Colonel Edward Iisley.
Fourteenth Maine, Colonel Thomas W. Porter.
Twenty-sixth Massachusetts, Colonel Alpha B. Farr.

* Non-veterans of Ninetieth New York attached.
† Detached at Harper's Ferry, and not engaged in the battle.
‡ Non-veterans of Thirteenth and Fifteenth Maine temporarily attached.

to select the ground on which to form the infantry. The Sixth Corps began to arrive about 8 o'clock; and taking up the line Wilson had been holding, just beyond the head of the narrow ravine, the cavalry was transferred to the south side of Abraham's Creek.

The Confederate line lay along some elevated ground about two miles east of Winchester, and

Fourteenth New Hampshire (1), Colonel Alexander Gardiner.
(2), Captain Flavel L. Tolman.
Seventy-fifth New York (1), Lieutenant-Colonel Willollghby Babcock.
(2), Major Benjamin F. Thurber.

SECOND BRIGADE:
Colonel Edward L. Molineux.
Thirteenth Connecticut, Colonel Charles D. Blinn.
Eleventh Indiana, Colonel Daniel Macauley.
Twenty-second Iowa, Colonel Harvey Graham.
Third Massachusetts Cavalry (dismounted; Lieutenant-Colonel Lorenzo D. Sargent.
One Hundred and Thirty-first New York, Colonel Nicholas W. Day.
One Hundred and Fifty-ninth New York, Lieutenant-Colonel William Walter-mire.

THIRD BRIGADE:
(1), Colonel Jacob Sharpe.
(2), Lieutenant-Colonel Alfred Neafie.
Thirty-eighth Massachusetts, Major Charles F. Allen.
One Hundred and Twenty-eighth New York, Captain Charles R. Anderson.
One Hundred and Fifty-sixth New York (1), Lieutenant-Colonel Alfred Neafie.
(2), Captain James J. Hoyt.
One Hundred and Seventy-fifth New York (three companies), Captain Charles McCarthey.
One Hundred and Seventy-sixth New York, Major Charles Lewis.

FOURTH BRIGADE:
Colonel David Shunk.
Eighth Indiana, Lieutenant-Colonel Alexander J. Kenny.
Eighteenth Indiana, Lieutenant-Colonel William S. Charles.
Twenty-fourth Iowa, Lieutenant-Colonel John Q. Wilds.
Twenty-eighth   Iowa, Lieutenant-Colonel Bartholomew W. Wilson.

extended from Abraham's Creek north across the Berryville pike, the left being hidden in the heavy timber on Wed Bud Run. Between this line and mine, especially on my right, clumps of woods and patches of underbrush occurred here and there, but the undulating ground consisted mainly of open fields, many of which were covered with standing corn that had already ripened.

ARTILLERY:

Maine Light, First Battery (A), Captain Albert W. Bradbury.

RESERVE ARTILLERY:

Captain Elijah D. Taft.

Indiana Light, Seventeenth Battery, Captain Milton L. Miner.
First Rhode Island Light, Battery D, Lieutenant Frederick Chase.

ARMY OF WEST VIRGINA.

Brigadier-General George Crook.

FIRST DIVISION:

Colonel Joseph Thoburn.

FIRST BRIGADE:

Colonel-George D. Wells.

Thirty-fourth Massachusetts, Major Harrison W. Pratt.
Fifth New York Heavy Artillery, Second Battalion, Major Caspar Urban.
One Hundred and Sixteenth Ohio, Lieutenant-Colonel Thomas F. Wildes.
One Hundred and Twenty-third Ohio, Captain John W. Chamberlin.

SECOND BRIGADE:*

Lieutenant-Colonel Robert S. Northcott.

First West Virginia, Lieutenant-Colonel Jacob Weddle.
Fourth West. Virginia, Captain Benjamin D. Boswell.
Twelfth West Virginia, Captain Erastus G. Bartlett.

THIRD BRIGADE:

Colonel Thomas M. Harris.

Twenty-third Illinois (battalion), Captain Samuel A. Simison.
Fifty-fourth Pennsylvania (1), Lieutenant-Colonel John P. Linton.
(2), Major Enoch D.Yutzy.

*Guarding trains, and net engaged in the battle.

Much time was lost in getting all of the Sixth and Nineteenth corps through the narrow defile, Grover's division being greatly delayed there by a train of ammunition wagons, and it was not until late in the forenoon that the troops intended for the attack could be got into line ready to advance.   General Early was not slow to avail himself of the advantages thus offered him, and my

Tenth West Virginia, Major Henry H. Withers.
Eleventh West Virginia, Lieutenant-Colonel Van H. Bukey.
Fifteenth West Virginia, Major John W. Holliday.

SECOND DIVISION:

(1) Colonel Isaac H. Duval.
(2) Colonel Rutherford B. Hayes.

FIRST BRIGADE:

(1) Colonel Rutherford B. Hayes.
(2) Colonel Hiram F. Duval.

Twenty-third Ohio, Lieutenant Colonel James M. Comly.
Thirty-sixth Ohio (1), Colonel Hiram F. Duval.
(2), Lieutenant-Colonel William H. G. Adney.
Fifth West Virginia (battalion), Lieutenant-Colonel William H. Enochs.
Thirteenth West Virginia, Colonel William R. Brown.

SECOND BRIGADE:

(1) Colonel Daniel D. Johnson.
(2) Lieutenant-Colonel Benjamin F. Coates.

Thirty-fourth Ohio, (battalion,) Lieutenant-Colonel Luther Furney.
Ninety-first Ohio (1), Lieutenant-Colonel Benjamin F. Coates.
(2), Major Lemuel Z. Cadot.
Ninth West Virginia, Major Benjamin M. Skinner.
Fourteenth West Virginia, Lieutenant-Colonel George W. Taggart.

ARTILLERY BRIGADE:

Captain Henry A. Du Pont.

First Ohio Light, Battery L, Captain Frank C. Gibbs.
First Pennsylvania Light, Battery D, Lieutenant William Munk.
Fifth United States, Battery B, Captain Henry A. Du Pont.

chances of striking him in detail were growing less every moment, for Gordon and Rodes were hurrying their divisions from Stephenson's depot across-country on a line that would place Gordon in the woods south of Red Bud Run, and bring Rodes into the interval between Gordon and Ramseur.

When the two corps had all got through the

CAVALRY:
Brigadier-General Alfred T. A. Torbert.

ESCORT:
First Rhode Island, Major William H. Turner, Jr.

FIRST DIVISION:
Brigadier-General Wesley Merritt.

FIRST BRIGADE:
Brigadier-General George A. Custer.

First Michigan, Colonel Peter Stagg.
Fifth Michigan, Major Smith H. Hastings.
Sixth Michigan, Colonel James H. Kidd.
Seventh Michigan, Major Melvin Brewer.
Twenty-fifth New York, Major Charles J. Seymour.

SECOND BRIGADE:
Colonel Thomas C. Devin.

Fourth New York (1), Major August Hourand.
(2), Major Edward Schwartz.
Sixth New York, Major William E. Beardsley.
Ninth New York, Lieutenant-Colonel George S. Nichols.
Nineteenth New York (First Dragoons), Colonel Alfred Gibbs.
Seventeenth Pennsylvania, Major Coe Durland.

RESERVE BRIGADE:
Colonel Charles R. Lowell, Jr.

Second Massachusetts, Lieutenant-Colonel Casper Crowninshield.
Sixth Pennsylvania,* Major Charles L. Leiper.

* At Pleasant Valley, Md., and not engaged in the battle.

cañon they were formed with Getty's division of the Sixth to the left of the Berryville pike, Ricketts' division to the right of the pike, and Russell's division in reserve in rear of the other two. Grover's division of the Nineteenth Corps came next on the right of Ricketts', with Dwight to its rear in reserve, while Crook was to begin massing near the Opequon crossing

First United States, Captain Eugene M. Baker.
Second United States (1), Captain Theophilus F. Rodenbough.
           (2), Captain Robert S. Smith
Fifth United States, Lieutenant Gustavus Urban.

SECOND DIVISION:*

Brigadier-General William W. Averell.

FIRST BRIGADE:

Colonel James N. Schoonmaker.

Eighth Ohio (detachment), Colonel Alpheus S. Moore.
Fourteenth Pennsylvania (1), Captain Ashbell Duncan.
           (2), Captain William W. Miles.
Twenty-second Pennsylvania, Lieutenant-Colonel Andrew J. Greenfield.

SECOND BRIGADE:

Colonel Henry Capehart.

First New York, Major Timothy Quinn.
First West Virginia Major Harvey Farabee.
Second West Virginia, Lieutenant-Colonel John J. Hoffman.
Third West Virginia, Major John S. Witcher.

ARTILLERY:

Fifth United States, Battery L, Lieutenant Gulian V. Weir.

THIRD DIVISION:

Brigadier-General James H. Wilson.

* From Department of West Virginia.

about the time Wright and Emory were ready to attack.

Just before noon the line of Getty, Ricketts, and Grover moved forward, and as we advanced, the Confederates, covered by some heavy woods on their right, slight underbrush and corn-fields along their centre, and a large body of timber on their left along the Red Bud, opened fire from their

FIRST BRIGADE:

(1) Brigadier-General John B. McIntosh.
(2) Lieutenant-Colonel George A. Purington.

First Connecticut, Major George 0. Marcy.
Third New Jersey, Major William P. Robeson, Jr
Second New York, Captain Walter C. Hull.
Fifth New York, Major Abram H. Krom.
Second Ohio (1), Lieutenant-Colonel George A. Purington.
(2), Major A. Bayard Nettleton.
Eighteenth Pennsylvania (1), Lieutenant-Colonel William P. Brinton.
(2), Major John W. Phillips.

SECOND BRIGADE:

Brigadier-General George H. Chapman.

Third Indiana (two companies), Lieutenant Benjamin F. Gilbert.
First New Hampshire (battalion), Colonel John L. Thompson.
Eighth New York, Lieutenant-Colonel William H. Benjamin.
Twenty-second New York, Major Caleb Moore.
First Vermont, Colonel William Wells.

HORSE-ARTILLERY:

Captain La Rhett L. Livingston.

New York Light, Sixth Battery,* Captain Joseph W. Martin,
First United States, Batteries K and L, Lieutenant Franck E. Taylor.
Second United States, Batteries B and L, Captain Charles H. Peirce.
Second United States, Battery D, Lieutenant Edward B. Williston.
Second United States, Battery M,† Lieutenant Carle A. Woodruff.
Third United States, Batteries C, F, and K,† Captain Dunbar R. Ransom.
Fourth United States, Batteries C and E,† Lieutenant Terence Reilly.

* At Sandy Hook, Md., and not engaged in the battle.
† At Pleasant Valley, Md., and not engaged in the battle.

whole front. We gained considerable ground at first, especially on our left but the desperate resistance which the right met with demonstrated that the time we had unavoidably lost in the morning had been of incalculable value to Early, for it was evident that he had been enabled already to so far concentrate his troops as to have the different divisions of his army in a connected line of battle in good shape to resist.

Getty and Ricketts made some progress toward Winchester in connection with Wilson's cavalry, which was beyond the Senseny road on Getty's left, and as they were pressing back Ramseur's infantry and Lomax's cavalry Grover attacked from the right with decided effect. Grover in a few minutes broke up Evans's brigade of Gordon's division, but his pursuit of Evans destroyed the continuity of my general line, and increased an interval that had already been made by the deflection of Ricketts to the left, in obedience to instructions that had been given him to guide his division on the Berryville pike. As the line pressed forward, Ricketts observed this widening interval and endeavored to fill it with the small brigade of Colonel Keifer, but at this juncture both Gordon and Rodes struck the weak spot where the right of the Sixth Corps and the left of the Nineteenth should have been in conjunction, and succeeded in checking my advance by driving back a part of Ricketts's division, and the most of Grover's. As these troops were retiring I ordered Russell's reserve division to be put into action, and just as the flank of the enemy's troops in pursuit of Grover was presented, Upton's brigade, led in person by both Russell and Upton struck it in a charge so vigorous as to drive the Confederates back in turn to their original ground.

The success of Russell enabled me to re-establish the right of my line some little distance in advance of the position from which it started in the morning, and behind Russell's division (now commanded by Upton) the broken regiments of Ricketts's division were rallied. Dwight's division was then brought up on the right,. and Grover's men formed behind it.

The charge of Russell was most opportune, but it cost many men in killed and wounded. Among the former was the courageous Russell himself, killed by a piece of shell that passed through his heart, although he had previously been struck by a bullet in the left breast, which wound, from its nature, must have proved mortal, yet of which he had not spoken. Russell's death oppressed us all with sadness, and me particularly. In the early days of my army life he was my captain and friend, and I was deeply indebted to him, not only for sound advice and good example, but for the inestimable service he had just performed, and sealed with his life, so it may be inferred how keenly I felt his loss.

As my lines were being rearranged, it was suggested to me to put Crook into the battle, but so strongly had I set my heart on using him to take possession of the Valley pike and cut off the enemy, that I resisted this advice, hoping that the necessity for putting him in would be obviated by the attack near Stephenson's depot that Torbert's cavalry was to make, and from which I was momentarily expecting to hear. No news of Torbert's progress came, however, so, yielding at last, I directed Crook to take post on the right of the Nineteenth Corps and, when the action was renewed, to push his command forward as a turning-column in conjunction with Emory. After some delay in the annoying defile, Crook got his men up, and posting Colonel Thoburn's division on the prolongation of the Nineteenth Corps, he formed Colonel Duval's division to the right of Thoburn. Here I joined Crook, informing him that I had just got word that Torbert was driving the enemy in confusion along the Martinsburg pike toward Winchester; at the same time I directed him to attack the moment all of Duval's men were in line. Wright was instructed to advance in concert with

Crook, by swinging Emory and the right of the Sixth Corps to the left together in a half-wheel. Then leaving Crook, I rode along the Sixth and Nineteenth corps, the open ground over which they were passing affording a rare opportunity to witness the precision with which the attack was taken up from right to left. Crook's success began the moment he started to turn the enemy's left; and assured by the fact that Torbert had stampeded the Confederate cavalry and thrown Breckenridge's infantry into such disorder that it could do little to prevent the envelopment of Gordon's left, Crook pressed forward without even a halt.

Both Emory and Wright took up the fight as ordered, and as they did so I sent word to Wilson, in the hope that he could partly perform the work originally laid out for Crook, to push along the Senseny road and, if possible, gain the valley pike south of Winchester. I then returned toward my right flank, and as I reached the Nineteenth Corps the enemy was contesting the ground in its front with great obstinacy; but Emory's dogged persistence was at length rewarded with success, just as Crook's command emerged from the morass of Red Bud Run, and swept around Gordon, toward the right of Breckenridge, who, with two of Wharton's brigades, was holding a line at right angles with the Valley pike for the protection of the Confederate rear. Early had ordered these two brigades back from Stephenson's depot in the morning, purposing to protect with them his right flank and line of retreat, but while they were *en route* to this end, he was obliged to recall them to his left to meet Crook's attack.

To confront Torbert, Patton's brigade of infantry and some of Fitzhugh Lee's cavalry had been left back by Breckenridge, but, with Averell on the west side of the Valley pike and Merritt on the east, Torbert began to drive this opposing force toward Winchester the moment he struck it near Stephenson's depot, keeping it on the go till it reached the position held by Breckenridge, where it endeavored to make a stand.

The ground which Breckenridge was holding was open, and offered an opportunity such as seldom had been presented during the war for a mounted attack, and Torbert was not slow to take advantage of it. The instant Merritt's division could be formed for the charge, it went at Breckenridge's infantry and Fitzhugh Lee's cavalry with such momentum as to break the Confederate left, just as Averell was passing around it. Merritt's brigades, led by Custer, Lowell, and Devin, met from the start with pronounced success, and with sabre or pistol in hand literally rode down a battery of five guns and took about 1,200 prisoners. Almost simultaneously with this cavalry charge, Crook struck Breckenridge's right and Gordon's left, forcing these divisions to give way, and as they retired, Wright, in a vigorous attack, quickly broke Rodes up and pressed Ramseur so hard that the whole Confederate army fell back, contracting its lines within some breastworks which had been thrown up at a former period of the war, immediately in front of Winchester.

Here Early tried hard to stem the tide, but soon Torbert's cavalry began passing around his left flank, and as Crook, Emory, and Wright attacked in front, panic took possession of the enemy, his troops, now fugitives and stragglers, seeking escape into and through Winchester.

When this second break occurred, the Sixth and Nineteenth corps were moved over toward the Millwood pike to help Wilson on the left, but the day was so far spent that they could render him no assistance, and Ramseur's division, which had maintained some organization, was in such tolerable shape as to check him. Meanwhile Torbert passed around to the west of Winchester to join Wilson, but was unable to do so till after dark. Crook's command pursued the enemy through the town to Mill Creek, I going along.

Just after entering the town Crook and I met, in the main street, three young girls, who gave us the most hearty reception. One of these young women was a Miss Griffith, the other two Miss Jennie and Miss Susie Meredith. During the day they had been watching the battle from the roof of the Meredith residence, with tears and lamentations, they said, in the morning when misfortune appeared to have overtaken the Union troops, but with unbounded exultation when, later, the tide set in against the Confederates. Our presence was, to them, an assurance of victory, and their delight being irrepressible, they indulged in the most unguarded manifestations and expressions. When cautioned by Crook, who knew them well, and reminded that the valley had hitherto been a race-course - one day in the possession of friends, and the next of enemies - and warned of the dangers they were incurring by such demonstrations, they assured him that they had no further fears of that kind now, adding that Early's army was so demoralized by the defeat it had just sustained that it would never be in condition to enter Winchester again. As soon as we had succeeded in calming the excited girls a little I expressed a desire to find some place where I could write a telegram to General Grant informing him of the result of the battle, and General Crook conducted me to the home of Miss Wright, where I met for the first time the woman who had contributed so much to our success, and on a desk in her school-room wrote the despatch announcing that we had sent Early's army whirling up the valley.

My losses in the battle of the Opequon were heavy, amounting to about 4,500 killed, wounded, and missing. Among the killed was General Russell, commanding a division, and the wounded included Generals Upton, McIntosh and Chapman, and Colonels Duval and Sharpe. The Confederate loss in killed, wounded, and prisoners about equaled mine, General Rodes being of the killed, while Generals Fitzhugh Lee and York were severely wounded.

We captured five pieces of artillery and nine battle-flags. The restoration of the lower valley -from the Potomac to Strasburg - to the control of the Union forces caused great rejoicing in the North, and relieved the Administration from further solicitude for the safety of the Maryland and Pennsylvania borders. The President's appreciation of the victory was expressed in a despatch so like Mr. Lincoln that I give a *fac-simile* of it to the reader, This he supplemented by promoting me to the grade of brigadier-general in the regular army, and assigning me to the permanent

command of the Middle Military Department,
and following that came warm congratulations
from Mr. Stanton and from Generals Grant,
Sherman, and Meade.

The battle was not fought out on the plan in
accordance with which marching orders were
issued to my troops, for I then hoped to take
Early in detail, and with Crooks force cut off his
retreat. I adhered to this purpose during the early
part of the contest, but was obliged to abandon
the idea because of unavoidable delays by which
I was prevented from getting the Sixth and Nineteenth corps through the narrow defile and into
position early enough to destroy Ramseur while
still isolated.   So much delay had not been anticipated, and this loss of time was taken advantage
of by the enemy to recall the troops diverted to
Bunker Hill and Martinsburg on the 17th, thus
enabling him to bring them all to the support of
Ramseur before I could strike with effect. My
idea was to attack Ramseur and Wharton, successively, at a very early hour and before they could
get succor, but I was not in condition to do it till
nearly noon, by which time Gordon and Rodes
had been enabled to get upon the ground at a
point from which, as I advanced, they enfiladed
my right flank, and gave it such a repulse that to
re-form this part of my line I was obliged to recall

"Cypher"

Executive Mansion.

Washington, Sep. 20 , 1864.

Major General Sheridan
Winchester, Va

Have just heard of your great victory. You have been your own officer man so far, and I am strongly inclined to come up and see you.

A. Lincoln

31

the left from some of the ground it had gained. It was during this reorganization of my lines that I changed my plan as to Crook, and moved him from my left to my right. This I did with great reluctance, for I hoped to destroy Early's army entirely if Crook continued on his original line of march toward the Valley pike, south of Winchester; and although the ultimate results did, in a measure vindicate the change, yet I have always thought that by adhering to the original plan we might have captured the bulk of Early's army.

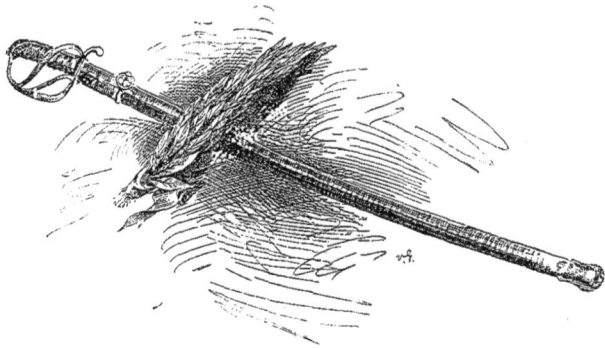

CHAPTER II.

THE night of the 19th of September I gave orders for following Early up the valley next morning - the pursuit to begin at daybreak - and in obedience to these directions Torbert moved Averell out on the Back road leading to Cedar Creek, and Merritt up the Valley pike toward Strasburg, while Wilson was directed on Front Royal by way of Stevensburg. Merritt's division was followed by the infantry, Emory's and Wright's columns marching abreast in the open country to the right and left of the pike, and Crook's immediately behind them. The enemy having kept up his retreat at night, presented no opposition whatever until the cavalry discovered him posted at Fisher's Hill, on the first defensive line where he could hope to make any serious resistance. No effort was made to dislodge him, and later in the day, after Wright and Emory came up, Torbert shifted Merritt over toward the

Back road till he rejoined Averell. As Merritt moved to the right, the Sixth and Nineteenth corps crossed Cedar Creek and took up the ground the cavalry was vacating, Wright posting his own corps to the west of the Valley pike overlooking Strasburg, and Emory's on his left so as to extend almost to the road leading from Strasburg to Front Royal. Crook, as he came up the same evening, went into position in some heavy timber on the north bank of Cedar Creek.

A reconnoissance made pending these movements convinced me that the enemy's position at Fisher's Hill was so strong that a direct assault would entail unnecessary destruction of life, and, besides, be of doubtful result. At the point where Early's troops were in position, between the Massanutten range and Little North Mountain, the valley is only about three and a half miles wide. All along the precipitous bluff which overhangs Tumbling Run on the south side, a heavy line of earthworks had been constructed when Early retreated to this point in August, and these were now being strengthened so as to make them almost impregnable; in fact, so secure did Early consider himself that, for convenience, his ammunition chests were taken from the caissons and placed behind the breastworks. Wharton, now in command of Breckenridge's division - its late commander having gone to southwest Virginia-held the right of this line, with Gordon next him; Pegram, commanding Ramseur's old division, joined Gordon. Ramseur with Rodes's division, was on Pegram's left, while Lomax's cavalry, now serving as foot-troops, extended the line to the Back road. Fitzhugh Lee being wounded, his cavalry, under General Wickham, was sent to Milford to prevent Fisher's Hill from being turned through the Luray Valley.

In consequence of the enemy's being so well protected from a direct assault, I resolved on the night of the 20th to use again a turning-column against his left, as had been done on the 19th at the Opequon. To this end I resolved to move Crook, unperceived if possible, over to the eastern face of Little North Mountain, whence he could strike the left and rear, of the Confederate line, and as he broke it up, I could support him by a left half-wheel of my whole line of battle. The execution of this plan would require perfect secrecy, however, for the enemy from his signal-station on Three Top could plainly see every movement of our troops in daylight. Hence, to escape such observation, I marched Crook during the night of the 20th into some heavy timber north of Cedar Creek, where he lay concealed all day the 21st. This same day Wright and Emory were moved up closer to the Confederate works, and the Sixth Corps, after a severe fight, in which Ricketts's and Getty were engaged, took up some high ground on the right of the Manassas Gap railroad in plain view of the Confederate works, and confronting a commanding point where much of Early's artillery was massed.   Soon after General Wright had established this line I rode with him along it to the westward, and finding that the enemy was still holding an elevated position further to our right, on the north side of Tumbling Run, I directed this also to be occupied. Wright soon carried the point, which gave us an unobstructed view of the enemy's works and offered good ground for our artillery. It also enabled me to move the whole of the Sixth Corps to the front till its line was within about seven hundred yards of the enemy's works; the Nineteenth Corps, on the morning of the 22d, covering the ground vacated by the Sixth by moving to the front and extending to the right, but still keeping its reserves on the railroad.

In the darkness of the night of the 21st, Crook was brought across Cedar Creek and hidden in a clump of timber behind Hupp's Hill till daylight of the 22d, when, under cover of the intervening woods and ravines, he was marched beyond the right of the Sixth Corps and again concealed not far from the Back road. After Crook had got into this last position, Ricketts's division was pushed out until it confronted the left of the enemy's infantry, the rest of the Sixth Corps extending from Ricketts's left to the Manassas Gap railroad, while the Nineteenth Corps filled in the space between the left of the Sixth and the North Fork of the Shenandoah.

When Ricketts moved out on this new line, in conjunction with Averell's cavalry on his right, the enemy surmising, from information secured from his signal-station, no doubt, that my attack was to be made from Ricketts's front, prepared for it there, but no such intention ever existed. Ricketts was pushed forward only that he might readily join Crook's turning-column as it swung into the enemy's rear. To ensure success, all that I needed now was enough daylight to complete my arrangements, the secrecy of movement imposed by the situation consuming many valuable hours.

While Ricketts was occupying the enemy's attention, Crook, again moving unobserved into the dense timber on the eastern face of Little North Mountain, conducted his command south in two parallel columns until he gained the rear of the enemy's works, when, marching his divisions by the left flank, he led them in an easterly direction down the mountain-side. As he emerged from the timber near the base of the mountain, the Confederates discovered him, of course, and opened with their batteries, but it was too late - they having few troops at hand to confront the turning-column. Loudly cheering, Crook's men quickly crossed the broken stretch in rear of the enemy's left, producing confusion and consternation at every step.

About a mile from the mountain's base Crook's left was joined by Ricketts, who in proper time had begun to swing his division into the action, and the two commands moved along in rear of the works so rapidly that, with but slight resistance, the Confederates abandoned the guns massed near the centre. The swinging movement of Ricketts was taken up successively from right to left throughout my line, and in a few minutes the enemy was thoroughly routed, the action, though brief, being none the less decisive. Lomax's dismounted cavalry gave way first, but was shortly followed by all the Confederate infantry in an indescribable panic precipitated doubtless by fears of being caught and captured in the pocket formed by Tumbling Run and the North Fork of the Shenandoah River. The stampede was complete, the enemy leaving the field without semblance of organization, abandoning

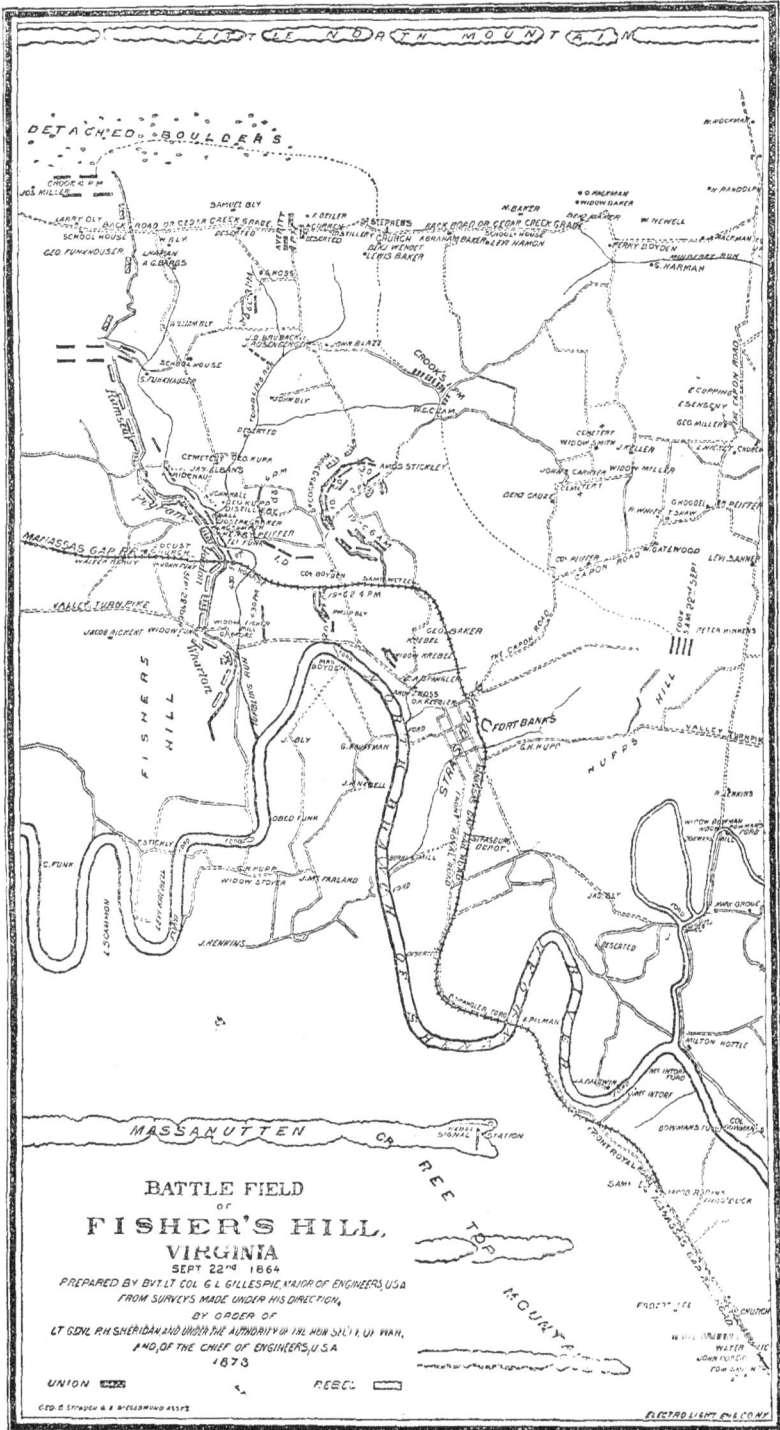

BATTLE FIELD
of
FISHER'S HILL,
VIRGINIA
SEPT 22nd 1864

PREPARED BY BVT.LT COL G.L.GILLESPIE, MAJOR OF ENGINEERS,U.S.A.
FROM SURVEYS MADE UNDER HIS DIRECTION,
BY ORDER OF
LT. GENL. P.H.SHERIDAN AND UNDER THE AUTHORITY OF THE HON. SECT'Y OF WAR,
AND OF THE CHIEF OF ENGINEERS, U.S.A.
1873

UNION ▬▬   REBEL ▭▭

nearly all his artillery and such other property as was in the works, and the rout extending through the fields and over the roads toward Woodstock, Wright and Emory in hot pursuit.

Midway between Fisher's Hill and Woodstock there is some high ground, where at night-fall a small squad endeavored to stay us with two pieces of artillery, but this attempt at resistance proved fruitless, and, notwithstanding the darkness, the guns were soon captured. The chase was then taken up by Devin's brigade as soon as it could be passed to the front, and continued till after daylight the next morning, but the delays incident to a night pursuit made it impossible for Devin to do more than pick up stragglers.

Our success was very great, yet I had anticipated results still more pregnant. Indeed, I had high hopes of capturing almost the whole of Early's army before it reached New Market, and with this object in view, during the manœuvres of the 21st I had sent Torbert up the Luray Valley with Wilson's division and two of Merritt's brigades, in the expectation that he would drive Wickham out of the Luray Pass by Early's right, and by crossing the Massanutten Mountain near New Market, gain his rear, Torbert started in good season, and after some slight skirmishing at Gooney Run, got as far as Milford, but failed to dislodge Wickham. In fact, he made little or no attempt to force Wickham from his position, and with only a feeble effort withdrew. I heard nothing at all from Torbert during the 22d, and supposing that everything was progressing favorably, I was astonished and chagrined on the morning of the 23d, at Woodstock, to receive the intelligence that he had fallen back to Front Royal and Buckton ford. My disappointment was extreme, but there was now no help for the situation save to renew and emphasize Torbert's orders, and this was done at once, notwithstanding that I thought the delay had so much diminished the chances of his getting in the rear of Early as to make such a result a very remote possibility, unless, indeed, far greater zeal was displayed than had been in the first attempt to penetrate the Luray Valley.

The battle of Fisher's Hill was, in a measure, a part of the battle of the Opequon; that is to say, it was an incident of the pursuit resulting from that action. In many ways, however, it was much more satisfactory, and particularly so because the plan arranged on the evening of the 20th was carried out to the very letter by Generals Wright, Crook, and Emory, not only in all their preliminary manœuvres, but also during the fight itself. The only drawback was with the cavalry, and to this day I have been unable to account satisfactorily for Torbert's failure. No doubt, Wickham's position near Milford was a strong one, but Torbert ought to have made a fight. Had he been defeated in this, his withdrawal then to await the result at Fisher's Hill would have been justified, but it does not appear that he made any serious effort at all to dislodge the Confederate cavalry: his impotent attempt not only chagrined me very much, but occasioned much unfavorable comment throughout the army.

We reached, Woodstock early on the morning of the 23d, and halted there some little time to let the troops recover their organization, which had been broken in the night march they had just made. When the commands had closed up we pushed on toward Edinburg, in the hope of making more captures at Narrow Passage Creek; but the Confederates, too fleet for us, got away; so General Wright halted the infantry not far from Edinburg, till rations could be brought the men. Meanwhile I, having remained at Woodstock, sent Devin's brigade to press the enemy under every favorable opportunity, and if possible prevent him from halting long enough to reorganize. Notwithstanding Devin's efforts the Confederates managed to assemble a considerable force to resist him, and being too weak for the rear-guard, he awaited the arrival of Averell, who, I had informed him, would be hurried to the front with all possible despatch, for I thought that Averell must be close at hand. It turned out, however, that he was not near by at all, and, moreover, that without good reason he had refrained from taking any part whatever in pursuing the enemy in the flight from Fisher's Hill, and in fact had gone into camp and left to the infantry the work of pursuit.

It was nearly noon when Averell came up, and a great deal of precious time had been lost. We had some hot words, but hoping that he would retrieve the mistake of the night before, I directed him to proceed to the front at once, and in conjunction with Devin close with the enemy. He reached Devin's command about 3 o'clock in the afternoon, just as this officer was pushing the Confederates so energetically that they were abandoning Mount Jackson, yet Averell utterly failed to accomplish anything. Indeed, his indifferent attack was not at all worthy the excellent soldiers he commanded, and when I learned that it was his intention to withdraw from the enemy's front, and this, too, on the indefinite report of a signal-officer that a "brigade or division" of Confederates was turning his right flank, and that he had not seriously attempted to verify the information, I sent him this order:

> " HEADQUARTERS   MIDDLE MILITARY DIVISION,
> "Woodstock, Va., Sept. 23, 1864.
>
> "BREVET MAJOR-GENERAL AVERELL:
>
> "Your report and report of signal-officer received. I do not want you to let the enemy bluff you or your command, and I want you to distinctly understand this note. I do not advise rashness, but I do desire resolution and actual fighting, with necessary casualties, before you retire. There must now be no backing or filling by you without a superior force of the enemy actually engaging you.
>
> "P. H. SHERIDAN,
> "Major-General   Commanding."

Some little time after this note went to Averell, word was brought me that he had already carried out the programme indicated when forwarding the report of the expected turning of his right, and that he had actually withdrawn and gone into camp near Hawkinsburg. I then decided to relieve him from the command of his division, which I did, ordering him to Wheeling, Colonel William H. Powell being assigned to succeed him.

The removal of Averell was but the culmination of a series of events extending back to the time I assumed command of the Middle Military Division. At the outset, General Grant, fearing discord on account of Averell's ranking Torbert, authorized me to relieve the former officer, but I hoped that if any trouble of this sort arose, it could be allayed, or at least repressed, during the campaign against Early, since the different commands would often have to act separately. After that, the dispersion of my army by the return of the Sixth Corps and Torbert's cavalry to the Army of the Potomac would take place, I thought, and this would restore matters to their normal condition; but Averell's dissatisfaction began to show itself immediately after his arrival at Martinsburg, on the 14th of August, and, except when he was conducting some independent expedition, had been manifested on all occasions since. I therefore thought that the interest of the service would be subserved by removing one whose growing indifference might render the best-laid plans inoperative.*

The failure of Averell to press the enemy the evening of the 23d gave Early time to collect his scattered forces and take up a position on the east side of the North Fork of the Shenandoah, his left resting on the west side of that stream at Rude's Hill, a commanding point about two miles

---

*"HEADQUARTERS MIDDLE MILITARY DIVISION.
"HARRISONBURG, VA., SEPT. 25, 1864 - 11:30 P. M.
"LIEUT-GENERAL GRANT, Comd'g, &c., City Point, Va.:

" * * * I have relieved Averell from his command. Instead of following the enemy when he was broken at Fisher's Hill (so there was not a cavalry organization left), he went into camp and let me pursue the enemy for a distance of fifteen miles, with infantry, during the night.* * *

" P. H. SHERIDAN, Major-General."

south of Mt. Jackson. Along this line he had
constructed some slight works during the night,
and at daylight on the 24th I moved the Sixth
and Nineteenth corps through Mt. Jackson to attack him, sending Powell's division to pass around
his left flank, toward Timberville, and Devin's
brigade across the North Fork, to move along the
base of Peaked Ridge and attack his right. The
country was entirely open, and none of these
manœuvres could be executed without being observed, so as soon as my advance began, the enemy
rapidly retreated in line of battle up the valley
through New Market, closely followed by Wright
and Emory, their artillery on the pike and their
columns on its right and left. Both sides moved
with celerity, the Confederates stimulated by the
desire to escape, and our men animated by the
prospect of wholly destroying Early's army. The
stern-chase continued for about thirteen miles,
our infantry often coming within range, yet whenever we began to deploy, the Confederates increased the distance between us by resorting to a
double quick, evading battle with admirable tact.
While all this was going on, the open country
permitted us a rare and brilliant sight, the bright
sun gleaming from the arms and trappings of the
thousands of pursuers and pursued.

Near New Market, as a last effort to hold the

enemy, I pushed Devin's cavalry - comprising about five hundred men - with two guns right up on Early's lines, in the hope that the tempting opportunity given him to capture the guns would stay his retreat long enough to let my infantry deploy within range, but he refused the bait, and after momentarily checking Devin he continued on with little loss and in pretty good order.

All hope of Torbert's appearing in rear of the Confederates vanished as they passed beyond New Market. Some six miles south of this place Early left the Valley Pike and took the road to Keezletown, a move due in a measure to Powell's march by way of Timberville toward Lacy's Springs, but mainly caused by the fact that the Keezletown road ran immediately along the base of Peaked Mountain - a rugged ridge affording protection to Early's right flank - and led in a direction facilitating his junction with Kershaw, who had been ordered back to him from Culpeper the day after the battle of the Opequon. The chase was kept up on the Keezeltown road till darkness overtook us, when my weary troops were permitted to go into camp; and as soon as the enemy discovered by our fires that the pursuit had stopped, he also bivouacked some five miles farther south toward Port Republic.

The next morning Early was joined by Lomax's

cavalry from Harrisonburg, Wickham's and Payne's brigades of cavalry also uniting with him from the Luray Valley. His whole army then fell back to the mouth of Brown's Gap to await Kershaw's division and Cutshaw's artillery, now on their return.

By the morning of the 25th the main body of the enemy had disappeared entirely from my front, and the capture of some small squads of Confederates in the neighboring hills furnished us the only incidents of the day. Among the prisoners was a tall and fine looking officer, much worn with hunger and fatigue. The moment I saw him I recognized him as a former comrade, George W. Carr, with whom I had served in Washington Territory. He was in those days a lieutenant in the Ninth Infantry, and was one of the officers who superintended the execution of the nine Indians at the Cascades of the Columbia in 1856. Carr was very much emaciated, and greatly discouraged by the turn events had recently taken. For old acquaintance sake I gave him plenty to eat, and kept him in comfort at my headquarters until the next batch of prisoners was sent to the rear, when he went with them. He had resigned from the regular army at the commencement of hostilities, and, full of high anticipation, cast his lot with the Confederacy,

but when he fell into our hands, his bright dreams
having been dispelled by the harsh realities of
war, he appeared to think that for him there was
no future.

Picking up prisoners here and there, my troops
resumed their march directly south on the Valley
pike, and when the Sixth and Nineteenth corps
reached Harrisonburg they went into camp, Powell in the meanwhile pushing on to Mt. Crawford,
and Crook taking up a position in our rear at the
junction of the Keezletown road and the Valley
pike. Late in the afternoon Torbert's cavalry
came in from New Market arriving at that place
many hours later than it had been expected.

The succeeding day I sent Merritt to Port Republic to occupy the enemy's attention, while
Torbert, with Wilson's division and the regular
brigade, was ordered to Staunton, whence he was
to proceed to Waynesboro' and blow up the railroad bridge. Having done this, Torbert, as he returned, was to drive off whatever cattle he could
find, destroy all forage and breadstuffs, and burn
the mills. He took possession of Waynesboro' in
due time, but had succeeded in only partially
demolishing the railroad bridge when, attacked
by Pegram's division of infantry and Wickham's
cavalry, he was compelled to fall back to Staunton. From the latter place he retired to Bridge-

water and Spring Hill, on the way, however, fully executing his instructions regarding the destruction of supplies.

While Torbert was on this expedition, Merritt had occupied Port Republic, but he happened to get there the very day that Kershaw's division was marching from Swift Run Gap to join Early. By accident Kershaw ran into Merritt shortly after the latter had gained the village. Kershaw's four infantry brigades attacked at once, and Merrit, forced out of Port Republic, fell back toward Cross Keys; and in anticipation that the Confederates could be coaxed to that point, I ordered the infantry there, but Torbert's attack at Waynesboro' had alarmed Early, and in consequence he drew all his forces in toward Rock-fish Gap. This enabled me to re-establish Merritt at Port Republic, send the Sixth and Nineteenth corps to the neighborhood of Mt. Crawford to await the return of Torbert, and to post Crook at Harrisonburg; these dispositions practically obtained till the 6th of October, I holding a line across the valley from Port Republic along North River by Mt. Crawford to the Back road near the mouth of Briery Branch Gap.

It was during this period, about dusk on the evening of October 3, that between Harrisonburg and Dayton my engineer officer, Lieutenant John

R. Meigs, was murdered within my lines. He had gone out with two topographical assistants to plot the country, and late in the evening, while riding along the public road on his return to camp, he overtook three men dressed in our uniform. From their dress, and also because the party was immediately behind our lines and with-. in a mile and a half of my headquarters, Meigs and his assistants naturally thought that they were joining friends, and wholly unsuspicious of anything to the contrary, rode on with the three men some little distance; but their perfidy was abruptly discovered by their suddenly turning upon Meigs with a call for his surrender. It has been claimed that, refusing to submit, he fired on the treacherous party, but the statement is not true, for one of the topographers escaped - the other was captured - and reported a few minutes later at my headquarters that Meigs was killed without resistance of any kind whatever, and without even the chance to give himself up. This man was so cool, and related all the circumstances of the occurrence with such exactness as to prove the truthfulness of his statement. The fact that the murder had been committed inside our lines was evidence that the perpetrators of the crime, having their homes in the vicinity, had been clandestinely visiting them, and been secretly harbored by some of the neighboring residents.   Determining to teach a lesson to these abettors of the foul deed - a lesson they would never forget - I ordered all the houses within an area of five miles to be burned. General Custer, who had succeeded to the command of the Third Cavalry division (General Wilson having been detailed as chief of cavalry to Sherman's army), was charged with this duty, and the next morning proceeded to put the order into execution. The prescribed area included the little village of Dayton, but when a few houses in the immediate neighborhood of the scene of the murder had been burned, Custer was directed to cease his desolating work, but to fetch away all the able-bodied males as prisoners.

CHAPTER III.

WHILE we lay in camp at Harrisonburg it
became necessary to decide whether or not
I would advance to Brown's Gap, and, after driving the enemy from there, follow him through
the Blue Ridge into eastern Virginia. Indeed,
this question began to cause me solicitude as soon
as I knew Early had escaped me at New Market,
for I felt certain that I should be urged to pursue
the Confederates toward Charlottesville and Gordonsville, and be expected to operate on that line
against Richmond. For many reasons I was
much opposed to such a plan, but mainly because
its execution would involve the opening of the

Orange and Alexandria railroad. To protect
this road against the raids of the numerous guerrilla bands that infested the region through which
it passed, and to keep it in operation, would require a large force of infantry, and would also
greatly reduce my cavalry; besides, I should be
obliged to leave a force in the valley strong
enough to give security to the line of the upper
Potomac and the Baltimore and Ohio railroad,
and this alone would probably take the whole of
Crook's command, leaving me a wholly inade-
quate number of fighting men to prosecute a campaign against the city of Richmond. Then, too,
I was in doubt whether the besiegers could hold
the entire army at Petersburg; and in case they
could not, a number of troops sufficient to crush me
might be detached by Lee, moved rapidly by rail,
and, after overwhelming me, be quickly returned
to confront General Meade. I was satisfied, moreover, that my transportation could not supply me
further than Harrisonburg, and if in penetrating
the Blue Ridge I met with protracted resistance,
a lack of supplies might compel me to abandon
the attempt at a most inopportune time.

I therefore advised that the Valley campaign
be terminated north of Staunton, and I be permitted to return, carrying out on the way my original
instructions for desolating the Shenandoah coun-

try so as to make it untenable for permanent
occupation by the Confederates. I proposed to
detach the bulk of my army when this work of
destruction was completed, and send it by way
of the Baltimore and Ohio railroad through
Washington to the Petersburg line, believing that
I could move it more rapidly by that route than
by any other. I was confident that if a movement of this character could be made with celerity it would culminate in the capture of Richmond,
and possibly of General Lee's army, and I was in
hopes that General Grant would take the same
view of the matter; but just at this time he was
so pressed by the Government and by public
opinion at the North, that he advocated the wholly
different conception of driving Early into eastern
Virginia, and adhered to this plan with some
tenacity. Considerable correspondence regarding
the subject took place between us, throughout
which I stoutly maintained that we should not
risk, by what I held to be a false move, all that
my army had gained. I being on the ground,
General Grant left to me the final decision of the
question, and I solved the first step by determining to withdraw down the valley at least as
far as Strasburg, which movement was begun on
the 6th of October.

The cavalry as it retired was stretched across

the country from the Blue Ridge to the eastern slope of the Alleghanies, with orders to drive off all stock and destroy all supplies as it moved northward. The infantry preceded the cavalry, passing down the Valley pike, and as we marched along the many columns of smoke from burning stacks, and mills filled with grain, indicated that the adjacent country was fast losing the features which hitherto had made it a great magazine of stores for the Confederate armies.

During the 6th and 7th of October, the enemy's horse followed us up, though at a respectful distance. This cavalry was now under command of General T. W. Rosser, who on October 5 had joined Early with an additional brigade from Richmond. As we proceeded the Confederates gained confidence, probably on account of the reputation with which its new commander had been heralded, and on the third day's march had the temerity to annoy my rear guard considerably. Tired of these annoyances, I concluded to open the enemy's eyes in earnest, so that night I told Torbert I expected him either to give Rosser a drubbing next morning or get whipped himself, and that the infantry would be halted until the affair was over; I also informed him that I proposed to ride out to Round Top Mountain to see the fight. When I decided to have Rosser chas-

tised, Merritt was encamped at the foot of Round
Top, an elevation just north of Tom's Brook, and
Custer some six miles farther north and west,
near Tumbling Run. In the night Custer was
ordered to retrace his steps before daylight
by the Back road, which is parallel to and
about three miles from the Valley pike, and
attack the enemy at Tom's Brook crossing, while
Merritt's instructions were to assail him on the
Valley pike in concert with Custer. About 7
in the morning, Custer's division encountered
Rosser himself with three brigades, and while
the stirring sounds of the resulting artillery duel
were reverberating through the valley Merritt
moved briskly to the front and fell upon Generals Lomax and Johnson on the Valley pike.
Merritt, by extending his right, quickly established connection with Custer, and the two divisions
moved forward together under Torbert's direction, with a determination to inflict on the enemy
the sharp and summary punishment his rashness
had invited.

The engagement soon became general across
the valley, both sides fighting mainly mounted.
For about two hours the contending lines struggled with each other along Tom's Brook, the
charges and counter charges at many points
being plainly visible from the summit of Round

Top, where I had my headquarters for the time.

The open country permitting a sabre fight, both sides seemed bent on using that arm. In the centre the Confederates maintained their position with much stubbornness, and for a time seemed to have recovered their former spirit, but at last they began to give way on both flanks, and as these receded, Merritt and Custer went at the wavering ranks in a charge along the whole front. The result was a general smash-up of the entire Confederate line, the retreat quickly degenerating into a rout the like of which was never before seen. For twenty-six miles this wild stampede kept up, with our troopers close at the enemy's heels; and the ludicrous incidents of the chase never ceased to be amusing topics around the camp-fires of Merritt and Custer. In the fight and pursuit Torbert took eleven pieces of artillery, with their caissons, all the wagons and ambulances the enemy had on the ground, and three hundred prisoners. Some of Rosser's troopers fled to the mountains by way of Columbia Furnace, and some up the Valley pike and into the Massanutten Range, apparently not discovering that the chase had been discontinued till south of Mount Jackson they rallied on Early's infantry.

After this catastrophe, Early reported to General Lee that his cavalry was so badly demoralized that it should be dismounted; and the citizens of the valley, intensely disgusted with the boasting and swaggering that had characterized the arrival of the "Laurel Brigade"* in that section, baptized the action (known to us as Toms Brook) the "Woodstock Races," and never tired of poking fun at General Rosser about his precipitate and inglorious flight.

On the 10th my army, resuming its retrograde movement, crossed to the north side of Cedar Creek. The work of repairing the Manassas Gap branch of the Orange and Alexandria railroad had been begun some days before, out from Washington, and, anticipating that it would be in readiness to transport troops by the time they could reach Piedmont, I directed the Sixth Corps to continue its march toward Front Royal, expecting to return to the Army of the Potomac by that line. By the 12th, however, my views regarding the reconstruction of this railroad began to prevail, and the work on it was discontinued. The Sixth Corps, therefore, abandoned that route, and moved toward Ashbys Gap with the purpose of marching direct to Washington, but on the 13th

---

*When Rosser arrived from Richmond with his brigade he was proclaimed as the savior of the Valley, and his men came all bedecked with laurel branches.

I recalled it to Cedar Creek, in consequence of the arrival of the enemy's infantry at Fisher's Hill, and the receipt, the night before, of the following despatch, which again opened the question of an advance on Gordonsville and Charlottesville:

(Cipher.)   "WASHINGTON, October 12, 1864, 12 M.
"MAJOR-GENERAL SHERIDAN:

"Lieutenant-General Grant wishes a position taken far enough south to serve as a base for further operations upon Gordonsville and Charlottesville. It must be strongly fortified and provisioned. Some point in the vicinity of Manassas Gap would seem best suited for all purposes. Colonel Alexander, of the Engineers, will be sent to consult with you as soon as you connect with General Augur.
                    "H. W. HALLECK,   Major-General."

As it was well known in Washington that the views expressed in the above despatch were counter to my convictions, I was the next day required by the following telegram from Secretary Stanton to repair to that city:

                    "WASHINGTON, October 13, 1864.
"MAJOR-GENERAL SHERIDAN
       (through General Augur) :
"If you can come here, a consultation on several points is extremely desirable. I propose to visit General Grant, and would like to see you first.
                    "EDWIN M. STANTON,
                        "Secretary of War."

I got all ready to comply with the terms of Secretary Stanton's despatch, but in the mean-

time the enemy appeared in my front in force,
with infantry and cavalry, and attacked Colonel
Thoburn, who had been pushed out toward Strasburg from Crooks command, and also Custers
division of cavalry on the Back road. As afterward appeared, this attack was made in the belief
that all of my troops but Crooks had gone to
Petersburg. From this demonstration there ensued near Hupps Hill a bitter skirmish between
Kershaw and Thoburn, and the latter was finally
compelled to withdraw to the north bank of
Cedar Creek. Custer gained better results, however, on the Back road, with his usual dash
driving the enemys cavalry away from his front,
Merritts division then joining him and remaining
on the right.

The days events pointing to a probability that
the enemy intended to resume the offensive, to
anticipate such a contingency I ordered the Sixth
Corps to return from its march toward Ashbys
Gap. It reached me by noon of the 14th, and
went into position to the right and rear of the
Nineteenth Corps, which held a line along the
north bank of Cedar Creek, west of the Valley pike. Crook was posted on the left of the
Nineteenth Corps and east of the Valley pike,
with Thoburns division advanced to a round
hill, which commanded the junction of Cedar

Creek and the Shenandoah River, while Torbert retained both Merritt and Custer on the right of the Sixth Corps, and at the same time covered with Powell the roads toward Front Royal. My headquarters were at the Belle Grove House, which was to the west of the pike and in rear of the Nineteenth Corps. It was my intention to attack the enemy as soon as the Sixth Corps reached me, but General Early having learned from his demonstration that I had not detached as largely as his previous information had led him to believe, on the night of the 13th withdrew to Fisher's Hill; so, concluding that he could not do us serious hurt from there, I changed my mind. as to attacking, deciding to defer such action till I could get to Washington, and come to some definite understanding about my future operations.

To carry out this idea, on the evening of the 15th I ordered all of the cavalry under General Torbert to accompany me to Front Royal, again intending to push it thence through Chester Gap to the Virginia Central railroad at Charlottesville, to destroy the bridge over the Rivanna River, while I passed through Manassas Gap to Rectortown, and thence by rail to Washington. On my arrival with the cavalry near Front Royal on the 16th, I halted at the house of Mrs. Richards, on the north bank of the river, and there received the following despatch and inclosure from General Wright, who had been left in command at Cedar Creek:

"HEADQUARTERS MIDDLE MILITARY DIVISION,
"October 16, 1864.
"GENERAL:

"I enclose you despatch which explains itself. If the enemy should be strongly re-enforced in cavalry, he might, by turning our right, give us a great deal of trouble. I shall hold on here until the enemy's movements are developed, and shall only fear an attack on my right, which I shall make every preparation for guarding against and resisting.

"Very respectfully, your obedient servant,

"H. G. WRIGHT, Major-General Commanding.

"MAJOR-GENERAL P. H. SHERIDAN,
"Commanding Middle Military Division."

[INCLOSURE.]

"To LIEUTENANT-GENERAL EARLY:

"Be ready to move as soon as my forces join you, and we will crush Sheridan.

"LONGSTREET, Lieutenant-General."

The message from Longstreet had been taken down as it was being flagged from the Confederate signal-station on Three Top Mountain, and afterward translated by our signal officers, who knew the Confederate signal code. I first thought it a ruse, and hardly worth attention, but on reflection deemed it best to be on the safe side, so I abandoned the cavalry raid toward Charlottesville, in order to give. General Wright the entire strength of the army, for it did not seem wise to reduce his numbers while reinforcement for the enemy might be near, and especially when such pregnant messages were reaching Early from one of the ablest of the Confederate generals. Therefore I sent the following note to General Wright:

" HEADQUARTERS M IDDLE M ILITARY D IVISION,
"Front Royal, October 16, 1864.

"GENERAL: The cavalry is all ordered back to you; make your position strong.   If Longstreet's despatch is true, he is under the impression that we have largely detached.   I will go over to Augur, and may get additional news.   Close in Colonel Powell, who will be at this point.   If the enemy should make an advance, I know you will defeat him.   Look well to your ground and be well prepared.   Get up everything that can be spared. I will bring up all I can, and will be up on Tuesday, if not sooner.

"P. H. SHERIDAN, Major-General.

"M AJOR-GENERAL H. G. WRIGHT,
" Commanding Sixth Army Corps."

At 5 o'clock on the evening of the 16th I telegraphed General Halleck from Rectortown, giving him the information which had come to me from Wright, asking if anything corroborative of it had been received from General Grant, and also saying that I would like to see Halleck; the telegram ending with the question: "Is it best for me to go to see you?" Next morning I sent back to Wright all the cavalry except one regiment, which escorted me through Manassas Gap to the terminus of the railroad from Washington. I had with me Lieutenant-Colonel James W. Forsyth, chief-of-staff, and three of my aides, Major George A. Forsyth, Captain Joseph O'Keefe, and Captain Michael V. Sheridan. I rode my black horse, Rienzi, and the others their own respective mounts.

Before leaving Cedar Creek I had fixed the route of my return to be by rail from Washington to Martinsburg, and thence by horseback to Winchester and Cedar Creek, and had ordered three hundred cavalry to Martinsburg to escort me from that point to the front. At Rectortown I met General Augur, who had brought a force out from Washington to reconstruct and protect the line of railroad, and through him received the following reply from General Halleck:

"HEADQUARTERS ARMIES OF THE UNITED STATES,
"WASHINGTON, D. C., October 16, 1864.
"To MAJOR-GENERAL SHERIDAN,
"Rectortown, Va.

"General Grant says that Longstreet brought with him no troops from Richmond, but I have very little confidence in the information collected at his headquarters. If you can leave your command with safety, come to Washington, as I wish to give you the views of the authorities here.

"H. W. HALLECK, Major-General, Chief-of-Staff."

In consequence of the Longstreet despatch, I felt a concern about my absence which I could hardly repress, but after duly considering what Halleck said, and believing that Longstreet could not unite with Early before I got back, and that even if he did Wright would be able to cope with them both, I and my staff, with our horses, took the cars for Washington, where we arrived on the morning of the 17th at about 8 o'clock. I proceeded at an early hour to the War Department, and as soon as I met Secretary Stanton, asked him for a special train to be ready at 12 o'clock to take me to Martinsburg, saying that in view of existing conditions I must get back to my army as quickly as possible. He at once gave the order for the train, and then the Secretary, Halleck, and I proceeded to hold a consultation in regard to my operating east of the Blue Ridge. The upshot was that my views against such a plan were practically agreed to, and two engineer officers were designated to return with me for the purpose of reporting on a defensive line in the valley that could be held while the bulk of my troops were being detached to Petersburg. Colonel Alexander and Colonel Thorn, both of the Engineer Corps, reported to accompany me, and at 12 o'clock we took the train.

We arrived about dark at Martinsburg, and there found the escort of three hundred men which I had ordered before leaving Cedar Creek. We spent that night at Martinsburg, and early next morning mounted and started up the Valley pike for Winchester, leaving Captain Sheridan behind to conduct to the army the Commissioners whom the State of New York had sent down to receive the vote of her troops in the coming Presidential election. Colonel Alexander was a man of enormous weight, and Colonel Thorn correspondingly light, and as both were unaccustomed to riding we had to go slowly, losing so much time, in fact, that we did not reach Winchester till between 3 and 4 o'clock in the afternoon, though the distance is but twenty-eight miles. As soon as we arrived at Colonel Edwards's headquarters in the town, where I intended stopping for the night, I sent a courier to the front to bring me a report of the condition of affairs, and then took Colonel Alexander out on the heights about Winchester, in order that he might overlook the country, and make up his mind as to the utility of fortifying there. By the time we had completed our survey it was dark, and just as we reached Colonel Edwards's house on our return a courier came in from Cedar Creek bringing word that everything was all right, that the enemy was quiet at Fisher's Hill, and that a brigade of Grover's division was to make a reconnoissance in the morning, the 19th, so about 10 o'clock I went to bed greatly relieved, and expecting to rejoin my headquarters at my leisure next day."

Toward 6 o'clock the morning of the 19th, the officer on picket duty at Winchester came to my room, I being yet in bed, and reported artillery firing from the direction of Cedar Creek. I asked him if the firing was continuous or only desultory, to which he replied that it was not a sus-

---

*ORGANIZATION OF THE UNION FORCES COMMANDED BY MAJOR-GENERAL PHILIP H. SHERIDAN AT THE BATTLE OF CEDAR CREEK, VA., OCTOBER 19, 1864.

ARMY OF THE SHENANDOAH.

Major-General Horatio G. Wright. †

ESCORT.

Seventeenth Pennsylvania Cavalry (detachment), Major Weidner H. Spera.
Sixth United States Cavalry, Captain Ira W. Claflin.

SIXTH ARMY CORPS.

(1) Brigadier-General James B. Ricketts.
(2) Brigadier-General George W. Getty.
(3) Major-General Horatio G. Wright.

ESCORT.

First Michigan Cavalry, Company G, Lieutenant William H. Wheeler.

FIRST DIVISION.

Brigadier-General Frank Wheaton.

FIRST BRIGADE:

(1) Colonel William H. Penrose.
(2) Lieutenant-Colonel Edward L. Campbell.
(3) Captain Baldwin Hufty.

Fourth New Jersey, Captain Baldwin Hufty.
Tenth New Jersey (1), Major Lambert Boeman.
      (2), Captain Charles D. Claypool.
Fifteenth New Jersey (1), Lieutenant-Colonel Edward L. Campbell.
      (2), Captain Jas. W. Penrose.

† Commanded during General Sheridan's temporary absence in the early part of the battle.

tained fire, but rather irregular and fitful. I re-marked: "It's all right; Grover has gone out this morning to make a reconnoissance, and he is merely feeling the enemy." I tried to go to sleep again, but grew so restless that I could not, and soon got up and dressed myself. A little later the picket officer came back and reported that the firing, which could be distinctly heard from his

SECOND BRIGADE:
(1) Colonel Joseph E. Hamblin.
(2) Colonel Ranald S. Mackenzie.
(3) Lieutenant-Colonel Egbert Olcott.
Second Connecticut Heavy Artillery (1), Colonel Ranald S. Mackenzie.
(2), Major Edward W. Jones.
Sixty-fifth New York (1), Lieutenant-Colonel Thomas H. Higinbotham.
(2), Captain Henry C. Fisk.
One Hundred and Twenty-first New York (1),Lieutenant-Colonel Egbert Olcott.
(2), Captain Daniel D/Jackson.
Ninety-fifth and Ninety-sixth Pennsylvania, Captain John Harper.
THIRD BRIGADE:*
Colonel Oliver Edwards.
Thirty-seventh Massachusetts, Lieutenant-Colonel George L. Montague.
Forty-ninth Pennsylvania, Lieutenant-Colonel Baynton J. Hickman.
Eighty-second Pennsylvania, Colonel Isaac C. Bassett.
One Hundred and Nineteenth Pennsylvania, Lieutenant-Colonel Gideon Clark.
Second Rhode Island (battalion), Captain Elisha H. Rhodes.
Fifth Wisconsin (battalion), Major Charles W. Kempf.
Seventeenth Pennsylvania Cavalry, Major Coe Durland.
SECOND DIVISION.
(1) Brigadier-General George W. Getty.
(2) Brigadier-General Lewis A. Grant.
(3) Brigadier-General George W. Getty.
FIRST BRIGADE:
Colonel James M. Warner.
Sixty-second New York, Lieutenant-Colonel Theodore B. Hamilton.
Ninety-third Pennsylvania, Captain David C. Keller.

* At Winchester, Va., and not engaged in the battle.

line on the heights outside of Winchester, was still going on. I asked him if it sounded like a battle, and as he again said that it did not, I still inferred that the cannonading was caused by Grover's division banging away at the enemy simply to find out what he was up to. However, I went down-stairs and requested that breakfast be hurried up, and at the same time ordered the

Ninety-eighth Pennsylvania (1), Lieutenant-Colonel John B. Kohler.
(2), Captain Gottfried Bauer.
One Hundred and Second Pennsylvania (1), Major James H. Coleman.
(2), Captain James Patchell.
One Hundred and Thirty-ninth Pennsylvania, Lieutenant-Colonel John G. Parr.

SECOND BRIGADE:

(1) Brigadier-General Lewis A. Grant.
(2) Lieutenant-Colonel Amass S. Tracy.
(3) Brigadier-General Lewis A. Grant.

Second Vermont (1), Lieutenant-Colonel Amasa S. Tracy.
(2), Captain Elijah Wales.
(3), Lieutenant-Colonel Amasa S. Tracy.
Third Vermont (battalion), Major Horace W. Floyd.
Fourth Vermont (1), Major Horace W. Floyd.
(2), Colonel George P. Foster.*
Fifth Vermont, Major Enoch E. Johnson.
Sixth Vermont (battalion) (1), Captain Edwin R. Kinney.
(2), Captain Wm. J. Sperry.
Eleventh Vermont (First Heavy Artillery), Lieutenant - Colonel Charles Hunsdon.

THIRD BRIGADE:

(1) Brigadier-General Daniel D. Bidwell.
(2) Lieutenant-Colonel Winsor B. French.

First Maine (Veteran), Major Stephen C. Fletcher.
Forty-third New York (battalion), Major Charles A. Milliken.
Forty-ninth New York (battalion), Lieutenant-Colonel Erastus D. Holt.
Seventy-seventh New York, Lieutenant-Colonel Winsor B. French.

*Corps officer of the day at the beginning of the battle; later, rejoined brigade and commanded the left of its line.

horses to be saddled and in readiness, for I concluded to go to the front before any further ex-
aminations were made in regard to the defensive
line.

We mounted our horses between half-past 8
and 9, and as we were proceeding up the street
which leads directly through Winchester, from
the Logan residence, where Edwards was quar-

One Hundred and Twenty-second New York (1), Lieutenant-Colonel Augustus
W. Dwight.
(2), Major Jabez M. Brewer.
Sixty-first Pennsylvania (battalion), Captain David J. Taylor.

THIRD DIVISION.
Colonel J. Warren Keifer.

FIRST BRIGADE:
Colonel William Emerson.

Fourteenth New Jersey, Captain Jacob J. Janeway.
One Hundred and Sixth New York (1), Captain Alvah W. Briggs.
(2), Captain Peter Robertson.
One Hundred and Fifty-first New York (1), Captain Browning N. Wiles.
(2), Captain Hiram A. Kimball.
One Hundred and Eighty-fourth New York (battalion), Major William D.
Ferguson.
Eighty-seventh Pennsylvania (battalion) (1), Captain Edgar M. Ruhl.
(2), Captain John A. Salsbury
Tenth Vermont (1), Colonel William W. Henry.
(2), Captain Henry H. Dewey.

SECOND BRIGADE:
Colonel William H. Ball.

Sixth Maryland, Major Joseph C., Hill.
Ninth New York Heavy Artillery, Major James W. Snyder.
One Hundred and Tenth Ohio, Lieutenant-Colonel Otho H. Binkley.
One Hundred and Twenty-second Ohio, Lieutenant-Colonel Moses M. Granger.
One Hundred and Twenty-sixth Ohio (1), Major George W. Voorhes.
(2), Captain George W. Hoge.
Sixty-seventh Pennsylvania, Lieutenant John F. Young.
One Hundred and Thirty-eighth Pennsylvania, Major Lewis A. May.

tered, to the Valley pike, I noticed that there were many women at the windows and doors of the houses, who kept shaking their skirts at us and who were otherwise markedly insolent in their demeanor, but supposing this conduct to be instigated by their well-known and perhaps natural prejudices, I ascribed to it no unusual significance. On reaching the edge of the town I halted a

ARTILLERY BRIGADE:

Colonel Charles H. Tompkins.

Maine Light, 5th Battery (E), Captain Greenleaf T. Stevens.
New York Light, 1st Battery, Lieutenant Orsamus R. Van Etten.
First Rhode Island Light, Battery C, Lieutenant Jacob H. Lamb.
First Rhode Island Light, Battery G, Captain George W. Adams.
Fifth United States, Battery M, Captain James McKnight.

NINETEENTH ARMY CORPS.

Brigadier-General William H. Emory.

FIRST DIVISION.

(1) Brigadier-General James W. McMillan.
(2) Brigadier-General William Dwight.

FIRST BRIGADE:

Colonel Edwin P. Davis.

Twenty-ninth Maine (1), Major George H. Nye.
(2), Captain Alfred L. Turner.
Thirtieth Massachusetts, Captain Samuel D. Shipley.
Ninetieth New York (1), Lieutenant-Colonel Nelson Shaurman.
(2), Captain Henry de La Paturelle.
One Hundred and Fourteenth New York, Lieutenant-Colonel Henry B. Morse.
One Hundred and Sixteenth New York, Colonel George M. Love.
One Hundred and Fifty-third New York (1), Lieutenant- Colonel Alexander Strain.
(2), Captain George H. McLaughlin.

SECOND BRIGADE:

(1) Colonel Stephen Thomas.
(2) Brigadier-General James W. McMillan.

Twelfth Connecticut, Lieutenant-Colonel George N. Lewis.
One Hundred and Sixtieth New York, Captain Henry P. Underhill.

moment, and there heard quite distinctly the sound of artillery firing in an unceasing roar. Concluding from this that a battle was in progress, I now felt confident that the women along the street had received intelligence from the battle-field by the "grape-vine telegraph," and were in raptures over some good news, while I as yet was utterly ignorant of the actual situation. Moving

Forty-seventh Pennsylvania, Major J. P. Shindel Gobin.
Eighth Vermont (1), Major John B. Mead.
    (2), Captain Moses McFarland.
    (3), Colonel Stephen Thomas.
    THIRD BRIGADE:*
    Colonel Leonard D. H. Currie.
Thirtieth Maine, Colonel Thomas H. Hubbard.
One Hundred and Thirty-third New York, Major Anthony J. Allaire.
One Hundred and Sixty-second New York, Colonel Justus W. Blanchard.
One Hundred and Sixty-fifth New York (six companies), Lieutenant-Colonel Gouverneur Carr.
One Hundred and Seventy-third New York, Major George W. Rogers.
    ARTILLERY:
New York Light, Fifth Battery, Captain Elijah. D. Taft.
    SECOND DIVISION.
    (1) Brigadier-General Cuvier Grover.
    (2) Brigadier-General Henry W. Birge.
    FIRST BRIGADE:
    (1) Brigadier-General Henry W. Birge.
    (2) Colonel Thomas W. Porter.
Ninth Connecticut (battalion), Captain John G. Healy.
Twelfth Maine, Lieutenant-Colonel Edwin Ilsley.
Fourteenth Maine (1), Colonel Thomas W. Porter.
    (2), Captain John K. Laing.
Twenty-sixth Massachusetts (battalion), Lieutenant John S. Cooke.
Fourteenth New Hampshire (1), Captain Theodore A. Ripley.
    (2), Captain Oliver H. Marston.
Seventy-fifth New York, Major Benjamin F. Thurber.

* Guarding wagon-trains, and not engaged in the battle.

on, I put my head down toward the pommel of my saddle and listened intently, trying to locate and interpret the sound, continuing in this position till we had crossed Mill Creek, about half a mile from Winchester.   The result of my efforts in the interval was the conviction that the travel of the sound was increasing too rapidly to be accounted for by my own rate of

SECOND BRIGADE:

Colonel Edward L. Molineux.

Thirteenth Connecticut, Colonel Charles D. Blinn.
Eleventh Indiana, Lieutenant-Colonel William W. Darnall.
Twenty-second Iowa, Colonel Harvey Graham.
Third Massachusetts Cavalry (dismounted), Colonel Lorenzo D. Sargent.
One Hundred and Thirty-first New York, Colonel Nicholas W. Day.
One Hundred and Fifty-ninth New York, Lieutenant-Colonel William Walter-
    mire.

THIRD BRIGADE:

(1) Colonel Daniel Macauley.
(2) Lieutenant-Colonel Alfred Neafie.

Thirty-eighth Massachusetts, Major Charles F. Allen.
One Hundred and Twenty-eighth New York, Captain Charles R. Anderson.
One Hundred and Fifty-sixth New York (1), Lieutenant-Colonel Alfred Neafie.
                            (2), Captain Alfred Cooley.
One Hundred and Seventy-fifth New York (battalion), Captain Charles
    McCarthey.
One Hundred and Seventy-sixth New York, Major Charles Lewis.

FOURTH BRIGADE :

Colonel David Shunk.

Eighth Indiana (1), Lieutenant-Colonel Alexander J. Kenny.
            (2), Major John R. Polk.
Eighteenth Indiana, Lieutenant-Colonel William S. Charles.
Twenty-fourth Iowa (1), Lieutenant-Colonel John Q. Wilds.
                (2), Captain Leander Clark.
                (3), Major Edward Wright.
Twenty-eighth Iowa (1), Lieutenant-Colonel Bartholomew W. Wilson.
                (2), Major John Meyer.

motion, and that therefore my army must be falling back.

At Mill Creek my escort fell in behind, and we were going ahead at a regular pace, when, just as we made the crest of the rise beyond the stream, there burst upon our view the appalling spectacle of a panic-stricken army - hundreds of slightly wounded men, throngs of others unhurt but ut-

ARTILLERY:

Maine Light, First Battery (A) (1), Lieutenent Eben D. Haley.
(2), Lieutenant John S. Snow.

RESERVE ARTILLERY:

Major Albert W. Bradbury.
Indiana Light, Seventeenth Battery, Lieutenant Hezekiah Hinkson.
First Rhode Island Light, Battery D, Lieutenant Frederick Chase.

ARMY OF WEST VIRGINIA.

Brigadier-General George Crook.

FIRST DIVISION

(1) Colonel Joseph Thoburn.
(2) Colonel Thomas M. Harris.

FIRST BRIGADE:

Lieutenant-Colonel Thomas F. Wildes.

Thirty-fourth Massachusetts, Captain Andrew Potter.
Fifth New York Heavy Artillery, Second Battalion, Captain Frederick C. Wilkie.
One Hundred and Sixteenth Ohio, Captain Wilbert B. Teters.
One Hundred and Twenty-third Ohio, Major Horace Kellogg.

SECOND BRIGADE:*

Colonel William B. Curtis.

First West Virginia, Lieutenant-Colonel Jacob Weddle.
Fourth West Virginia, Captain Benjamin D. Boswell.
Twelfth West Virginia, Lieutenant-Colonel Robert S. Northcott.

* At Winchester. Va., and not engaged in the battle.

terly demoralized, and baggage-wagons by the score, all pressing to the rear in hopeless confusion, telling only too plainly that a disaster had occurred at the front. On accosting some of the fugitives, they assured me that the army was broken up, in full retreat, and that all was lost; all this with a manner true to that peculiar indifference that takes possession of panic-stricken

THIRD BRIGADE:

(1) Colonel Thomas M. Harris.
(2) Colonel Milton Wells.
Twenty-third Illinois (battalion),* Captain Samuel A. Simison.
Fifty-fourth Pennsylvania, Captain John Suter.
Tenth West Virginia (1), Lieutenant-Colonel Moses S. Hall.
(2), Major Henry H. Withers.
Eleventh West Virginia, Lieutenant-Colonel Van H. Bukey.
Fifteenth West Virginia (1), Colonel Milton Wells.
(2), Major John W. Holliday.

SECOND DIVISION.
Colonel Rutherford B. Hayes.

FIRST BRIGADE:
Colonel Hiram F. Duval.

Twenty-third Ohio, Lieutenant-Colonel James M. Comly,
Thirty-sixth Ohio, Lieutenant-Colonel William H. G. Adney.
Fifth West Virginia (battalion), Lieutenant-Colonel William H. Enochs.
Thirteenth West Virginia (1), Colonel William R. Brown.†
(2), Lieutenant-Colonel James R. Hall.

SECOND BRIGADE:
Lieutenant-Colonel Benjamin F. Coates.

Thirty-fourth Ohio (battalion), Lieutenant-Colonel Luther Furney.
Ninety-first Ohio, Major Lemuel Z. Cadot.
Ninth West Virginia, Captain John S. P. Carroll.
Fourteenth West Virginia, Major Shriver Moore.

* At Winchester, Va., and not engaged in the battle.
† Corps officer of the day.

men. I was greatly disturbed by the sight, but
at once sent word to Colonel Edwards, commanding the brigade in Winchester, to stretch his
troops across the valley, near Mill Creek, and stop
all fugitives, directing also that the transportation
be passed through and parked on the north side
of the town.

As I continued at a walk a few hundred yards

ARTILLERY BRIGADE.

Captain Henry A. Du Pont.

First Ohio Light, Battery L, Captain Frank C. Gibbs.
First Pennsylvania Light, Battery D, Lieutenant William Munk.
Fifth United States, Battery B (1), Lieutenant Henry F. Brewerton.
"(2), Lieutenant Charles Holinan.

PROVISIONAL DIVISION.*

Colonel J. Howard Kitching.

CAVALRY.

Brigadier-General Alfred T. A. Torbert.

ESCORT.

First Rhode Island, Major William H. Turner, Jr.

FIRST DIVISION.

Brigadier-General Wesley Merritt.

FIRST BRIGADE:

Colonel James H. Kidd.

First Michigan, Captain Andrew W. Duggan.
Fifth Michigan, Major Smith H. Hastings.
Sixth Michigan, Major Charles W. Deane.
Seventh Michigan, Major Daniel H. Darling.
New York Light Artillery, Sixth Battery, Captain Joseph W. Martin.

*Only a small detachment from the First Brigade, and the Sixth New York Heavy Artillery,
from the Second Brigade, engaged in the battle.

farther, thinking all the time of Longstreet's telegram to Early, "Be ready when I join you, and we will crush Sheridan," I was fixing in my mind what I should do. My first thought was to stop the army in the suburbs of Winchester as it came back, form a new line, and fight there; but as the situation was more maturely considered a better conception prevailed. I was sure the troops,

SECOND BRIGADE:

Colonel Thomas C. Devin.

Fourth New York,* Major Edward Schwartz.
Sixth New Work, Captain George E. Farmer.
Ninth New York, Colonel George S. Nichols.
Nineteenth New York (First Dragoons), Colonel Alfred Gibbs.
First United States Artillery, Batteries K and L, Lieutenant Franck E. Taylor.

RESERVE BRIGADE:

(1) Colonel Charles R. Lowell, Jr.
(2) Lieutenant-Colonel Casper Crowninshield.

Second Massachusetts (1). Lieutenant-Colonel Casper Crowninshield.
(2), Captain Archibald McKendry.
First United States, Captain Eugene M. Baker.
Second United States, Captain Robert S. Smith.
Fifth United States, Lieutenant Gustavus Urban.

SECOND DIVISION. †

Colonel William H. Powell.

FIRST BRIGADE:

Colonel Alpheus S. Moore.

Eighth Ohio (detachment),--.
Fourteenth Pennsylvania, Major Thomas Gibson.
Twenty-second Pennsylvania, Lieutenant-Colonel Andrew J. Greenfield.

SECOND BRIGADE:

Colonel Henry Capehart.

First New York, Major Timothy Quinn.
First West Virginia, Major Harvey Farabee.

* Detailed for duty at General Sheridan's headquarters.
† From Department of West Virginia.

had confidence in me, for heretofore we had been successful; and as at other times they had seen me present at the slightest sign of trouble or distress, I felt that I ought to try now to restore their broken ranks, or, failing in that, to share their fate because of what they had done hitherto.

About this time Colonel Wood, my chief commissary, arrived from the front and gave me

Second West Virginia, Lieutenant-Colonel John J. Hoffman.
Third West Virginia, Lieutenant-Colonel John L. McGee.

ARTILLERY:

Fifth United States, Battery L, Lieutenant Gulian V. Weir.

THIRD DIVISION.

Brigadier-General George A. Custer.

FIRST BRIGADE.

Colonel Alexander C. M. Pennington, Jr.

First Connecticut, Captain Edwin W. French.
Third New Jersey, Lieutenant-Colonel Charles C. Suydam.
Second New York, Captain Andrew S. Glover.
Fifth New York, Major Theodore A. Boice.
Second Ohio, Lieutenant-Colonel George A. Purington.
Eighteenth Pennsylvania, Major John W. Phillips.

SECOND BRIGADE:

Colonel William Wells.

Third Indiana (two companies), Lieutenant Benjamin F. Gilbert.
First New Hampshire (battalion), Colonel John L. Thompson.
Eighth New York, Lieutenant-Colonel William H. Benjamin.
Twenty-second New York, Major Charles C. Brown.
First Vermont, Lieutenant-Colonel John W. Bennett.

HORSE-ARTILLERY:

Second United States, Batteries B and L, Captain Charles H. Peirce.
Third United States, Batteries C, F, and K, Captain Dunbar R. Ransom.

fuller intelligence, reporting that everything was gone, my headquarters captured, and the troops dispersed. When I heard this I took two of my aides-de-camp, Major George A. Forsyth and Captain Joseph O'Keefe, and with twenty men from the escort started for the front, at the same time directing Colonel James W. Forsyth and Colonels Alexander and Thom to remain behind and do what they could to stop the runaways.

For a short distance I traveled on the road, but soon found it so blocked with wagons and wounded men that my progress was impeded, and I was forced to take to the adjoining fields to make haste. When most of the wagons and wounded were past I returned to the road, which was thickly lined with unhurt men, who, having got far enough to the rear to be out of danger, had halted, without any organization, and begun cooking coffee, but when they saw me they abandoned their coffee, threw up their hats, shouldered their muskets, and as I passed along turned to follow with enthusiasm and cheers. To acknowledge this exhibition of feeling I took off my hat, and with Forsyth and O'Keefe rode some distance in advance of my escort, while every mounted officer who saw me galloped out on either side of the pike to tell the men at a distance that I had come back. In this way the news was spread to the stragglers off the road, when they, too, turned their faces to the front and marched toward the enemy, changing in a moment from the depths of depression to the extreme of enthusiasm. I already knew that even in the ordinary condition of mind enthusiasm is a potent element with soldiers, but what I saw that day convinced me that if it can be excited from a state of despondency its power is almost irresistible. I said nothing except to remark, as I rode among those on the road: "If I had been with you this morning this disaster would not have happened. We must face the other way; we will go back and recover our camp."

My first halt was made just north of Newtown, where I met a chaplain digging his heels into the sides of his jaded horse, and making for the rear with all possible speed. I drew up for an instant, and inquired of him how matters were going at the front. He replied, "Everything is lost; but all will be right when you get there"; yet notwithstanding this expression of confidence in me, the parson at once resumed his breathless pace to the rear. At Newtown I was obliged to make a circuit to the left, to get round the village. I could not pass through it, the streets were so crowded, but meeting on this detour Major McKinley, of

Crooks staff, he spread the news of my return through the motley throng there.

When nearing the Valley pike, just south of Newtown I saw about three-fourths of a mile west of the pike a body of troops, which proved to be Rickettss and Wheatons divisions of the Sixth Corps, and then learned that the Nineteenth Corps had halted a little to the right and rear of these; but I did not stop, desiring to get to the extreme front. Continuing on parallel with the pike, about midway between Newtown and Middletown I crossed to the west of it, and a little later came up in rear of Gettys division of the Sixth Corps. When I arrived, this division and the cavalry were the only troops in the presence of and resisting the enemy; they were apparently acting as a rear guard at a point about three miles north of the line we held at Cedar Creek when the battle began. General Torbert was the first officer to meet me, saying as he rode up, "My God! I am glad youve come." Gettys division, when I found it, was about a mile north of Middletown, posted on the reverse slope of some slightly rising ground, holding a barricade made with fence-rails, and skirmishing slightly with the enemys pickets. Jumping my horse over the line of rails, I rode to the crest of the elevation, and there taking off my hat, the men rose up from behind their barricade with cheers of recognition. An officer of the Vermont brigade, Colonel A. S. Tracy, rode out to the front, and joining me, informed me that General Louis A. Grant was in command there, the regular division commander, General Getty, having taken charge of the Sixth Corps in place of Ricketts, wounded early in the action, while temporarily commanding the corps. I then turned back to the rear of Getty's division, and as I came behind it, a line of regimental flags rose up out of the ground, as it seemed, to welcome me. They were mostly the colors of Crook's troops, who had been stampeded and scattered in the surprise of the morning. The color-bearers, having withstood the panic, had formed behind the troops of Getty. The line with the colors was largely composed of officers, among whom I recognized Colonel R. B. Hayes, since president of the United States, one of the brigade commanders. At the close of this incident I crossed the little narrow valley, or depression, in rear of Getty's line, and dismounting on the opposite crest, established that point as my headquarters. In a few minutes some of my staff joined me, and the first directions I gave were to have the Nineteenth Corps and the two divisions of Wright's corps brought to the front, so they could be formed on Getty's division, prolonged to the right; for I had already decided to attack the enemy from that line as soon as I could get matters in shape to take the offensive. Crook met me at this time, and strongly favored my idea of attacking, but said, however, that most of his troops were gone. General Wright came up a little later, when I saw that he was wounded, a ball having grazed the point of his chin so as to draw the blood plentifully.

Wright gave me a hurried account of the day's events, and when told that we would fight the enemy on the line which Getty and the cavalry were holding, and that he must go himself and send all his staff to bring up the troops, he zealously fell in with the scheme; and it was *then* that the Nineteenth Corps and two divisions of the Sixth were ordered to the front from where they had been halted to the right and rear of Getty.

After this conversation I rode to the east of the Valley pike and to the left of Getty's division, to a point from which I could obtain a good view of the front, in the mean time sending Major Forsyth to communicate with Colonel Lowell (who occupied a position close in toward the suburbs of Middletown and directly in front of Getty's left) to learn whether he could hold on there. Lowell replied that he could. I then ordered Custer's

division back to the right flank, and returning to
the place where my headquarters had been established I met near them Ricketts's division under
General Keifer and General Frank Wheaton's
division, both marching to the front. When the
men of these divisions saw me they began cheering and took up the double quick to the front,
while I turned back toward Getty's line to point
out where these returning troops should be placed.
Having done this, I ordered General Wright to
resume command of the Sixth Corps, and Getty,
who was temporarily in charge of it, to take command of his own division. A little later the Nineteenth Corps came up and was posted between
the right of the Sixth Corps and Middle Marsh
Brook.

All this had consumed a great deal of time, and
I concluded to visit again the point to the east of
the Valley pike, from where I had first observed the
enemy, to see what he was doing. Arrived there,
I could plainly see him getting ready for attack,
and Major Forsyth now suggested that it would
be well to ride along the line of battle before the
enemy assailed us, for although the troops had
learned of my return, but few of them had seen
me. Following his suggestion I started in behind
the men, but when a few paces had been taken I
crossed to the front and, hat in hand, passed along

the entire length of the infantry line; and it is from this circumstance that many of the officers and men who then received me with such heartiness have since supposed that that was my first appearance on the field. But at least two hours had elapsed since I reached the ground, for it was after mid-day when this incident of riding down the front took place, and I arrived not later, certainly, than half-past 10 o'clock.

After re-arranging the line and preparing to attack I returned again to observe the Confederates, who shortly began to advance on us. The attacking columns did not cover my entire front, and it appeared that their onset would be mainly directed against the Nineteenth Corps, so, fearing that they might be too strong for Emory on account of his depleted condition (many of his men not having had time to get up from the rear), and Getty's division being free from assault, I transferred a part of it from the extreme left to the support of the Nineteenth Corps. The assault was quickly repulsed by Emory, however, and as the enemy fell back Getty's troops were returned to their original place. This repulse of the Confederates made me feel pretty safe from further offensive operations on their part, and I now decided to suspend the fighting till my thin ranks were further strengthened by the men who were continually coming up from the rear, and particularly till Crooks troops could be assembled on the extreme left.

In consequence of the despatch already mentioned, "Be ready when I join you, and we will crush Sheridan," since learned to have been fictitious, I had been supposing all day that Longstreets troops were present, but as no definite intelligence on this point had been gathered, I concluded, in the lull that now occurred, to ascertain something positive regarding Longstreet; and Merritt having been transferred to our left in the morning, I directed him to attack an exposed battery then at the edge of Middletown, and capture some prisoners. Merritt soon did this work effectually, concealing his intention till his troops got close in to the enemy, and then by a quick dash gobbling up a number of Confederates. When the prisoners were brought in, I learned from them that the only troops of Longstreets in the fight were of Kershaw's division, which had rejoined Early at Brown's Gap in the latter part of September, and that the rest of Longstreets corps was not on the field. The receipt of this information entirely cleared the way for me to take the offensive, but on the heels of it came information that Longstreet was marching by the Front Royal pike to strike my rear at Winchester, driving Powell's cavalry in as he advanced. This renewed my uneasiness, and caused me to delay the general attack till after assurances came from Powell denying utterly the reports as to Longstreet, and confirming the statements of the prisoners.

Between half-past 3 and 4 o'clock, I was ready to assail, and decided to do so by advancing my infantry line in a swinging movement, so as to gain the Valley pike with my right between Middletown and the Belle Grove House; and when the order was passed along, the men pushed steadily forward with enthusiasm and confidence. General Early's troops extended some little distance beyond our right, and when my flank neared the overlapping enemy, he turned on it, with the effect of causing a momentary confusion, but General McMillan quickly realizing the danger, broke the Confederates at the reentering angle by a counter charge with his brigade, doing his work so well that the enemy's flanking troops were cut off from their main body and left to shift for themselves. Custer, who was just then moving in from the west side of Middle Marsh Brook, followed McMillan's timely blow with a charge of cavalry, but before starting out on it, and while his men were forming, riding at full speed himself; to throw his arms around my neck. By the time he had disengaged himself from this embrace, the troops broken by McMillan had gained some little distance to their rear, but Custer's troopers sweeping across the Middletown meadows and down toward Cedar Creek, took many of them prisoners before they could reach the stream - so I forgave his delay.

My whole line as far as the eye could see was now driving everything before it, from behind trees, stone walls, and all such sheltering obstacles, so I rode toward the left to ascertain how matters were getting on there. As I passed along behind the advancing troops, first General Grover, and then Colonel Mackenzie, rode up to welcome me. Both were severely wounded, and I told them to leave the field, but they implored permission to remain till success was certain. When I reached the Valley pike Crook had reorganized his men, and as I desired that they should take part in the fight, for they were the very same troops that had turned Early's flank at the Opequon and at Fisher's Hill, I ordered them to be pushed forward; and the alacrity and celerity with which they moved on Middletown demonstrated that their ill-fortune of the morning had not sprung from lack of valor.

Meanwhile Lowell's brigade of cavalry, which, it will be remembered, had been holding on, dismounted, just north of Middletown ever since the time I arrived from Winchester, fell to the rear for the purpose of getting their led horses. A momentary panic was created in the nearest brigade of infantry by this withdrawal of Lowell, but as soon as his men were mounted they charged the enemy clear up to the stone walls in the edge of Middletown; at sight of this the infantry brigade renewed its attack, and the enemy's right gave way. The accomplished Lowell received his death-wound in this courageous charge.

All our troops were now moving on the retreating Confederates, and as I rode to the front Colonel Gibbs, who succeeded Lowell, made ready for another mounted charge, but I checked him from pressing the enemy's right, in the hope that the swinging attack from my right would throw most of the Confederates to the east of the Valley pike, and hence off their line of retreat through Strasburg to Fisher's Hill. The eagerness of the men soon frustrated this anticipation, however, the left insisting on keeping pace with the centre and right, and all pushing ahead till we regained our old camps at Cedar Creek. Beyond Cedar Creek, at Strasburg, the pike makes a sharp turn to the west toward Fisher's Hill, and here Merritt uniting with Custer, they together fell on the flank of the retreating columns, taking many prisoners,

Executive Mansion
Washington, Oct. 22, 1864

Major General Sheridan.

With great pleasure I ten-
der to you and your brave army, the thanks
of the Nation, and my own personal admiration and gratitude, for the months of operation in the Shenandoah Valley; and
especially, for the splendid work of October 19, 1864.

Your Obt. Servt.
Abraham Lincoln.

wagons, and guns, among the prisoners being Major-General Ramseur, who, mortally wounded, died the next day.

When the news of the victory was received, General Grant directed a salute of one hundred shotted guns to be fired into Petersburg, and the President at once thanked the army in an autograph letter. A few weeks after, he promoted me, and I received notice of this in a special letter from the-secretary of War, saying, "that for the personal gallantry, military skill, and just confidence in the courage and patriotism of your troops, displayed by you on the 19th day of October at Cedar Run, whereby, under the blessing of Providence, your routed army was reorganized, a great National disaster averted, and a brilliant victory achieved over the rebels for the third time in pitched battle within thirty days, Philip H. Sheridan is appointed a major-general in the United States Army."

The direct result of the battle was the recapture of all the artillery, transportation, and camp equipage we had lost, and in addition twenty-four pieces of the enemy's artillery, twelve hundred prisoners, and a number of battle-flags. But more still flowed from this victory, succeeding as it did the disaster of the morning, for the re-occupation of our old camps at once re-established a *morale* which for some hours had been greatly endangered by ill-fortune.

It was not till after the battle that I learned fully what had taken place before my arrival, and then found that the enemy, having gathered all the strength he could through the return of convalescents and other absentees, had moved quietly from Fisher's Hill, in the night of the 18th and early on the morning of the 19th, to surprise my army, which, it should be remembered, was posted on the north bank of Cedar Creek, Crook holding on the left of the Valley pike, with Thoburn's division advanced toward the creek, and Duval's (under Colonel Rutherford B. Hayes) and Kitching's provisional divisions to the north and rear of Thoburn. The Nineteenth Corps was on the right of Crook, extending in a semi-circular line from the pike nearly to Meadow Brook, while the Sixth Corps lay to the west of the brook in readiness to be used as a movable column. Merritt's division was to the right and rear of the Sixth Corps, and about a mile and a half west of Merritt was Custer covering the fords of Cedar Creek as far west as the Middle road.

General Early's plan was for one column under General Gordon, consisting of three divisions of infantry (Gordon's, Ramseur's, and Pegram's), and Payne's brigade of cavalry, to cross the Shenandoah

River directly east of the Confederate works at Fisher's Hill, march around the northerly face of the Massanutten Mountain, and again cross the Shenandoah at Bowman's and McInturff's fords. Payne's task was to capture me at the Belle Grove House. General Early himself, with Kershaw's and Wharton's divisions, was to move through Strasburg, Kershaw, accompanied by Early, to cross Cedar Creek at Roberts's ford and connect with Gordon, while Wharton was to continue on the Valley pike to Hupp's Hill and join the left of Kershaw, when the crossing of the Valley pike over Cedar Creek became free.

Lomax's cavalry, then in the Luray Valley, was ordered to join the right of Gordon on the field of battle, while Rosser was to carry the crossing of Cedar Creek on the Back road and attack Custer. Early's conceptions were carried through in the darkness with little accident or delay, Kershaw opening the fight by a furious attack on Thoburn's division, while at dawn and in a dense fog Gordon struck Crook's extreme left, surprising his pickets, and bursting into his camp with such suddenness as to stampede Crook's men. Gordon directing his march on my headquarters (the Belle Grove House), successfully turned our position as he gained the Valley pike, and General Wright was thus forced to order the withdrawal of the

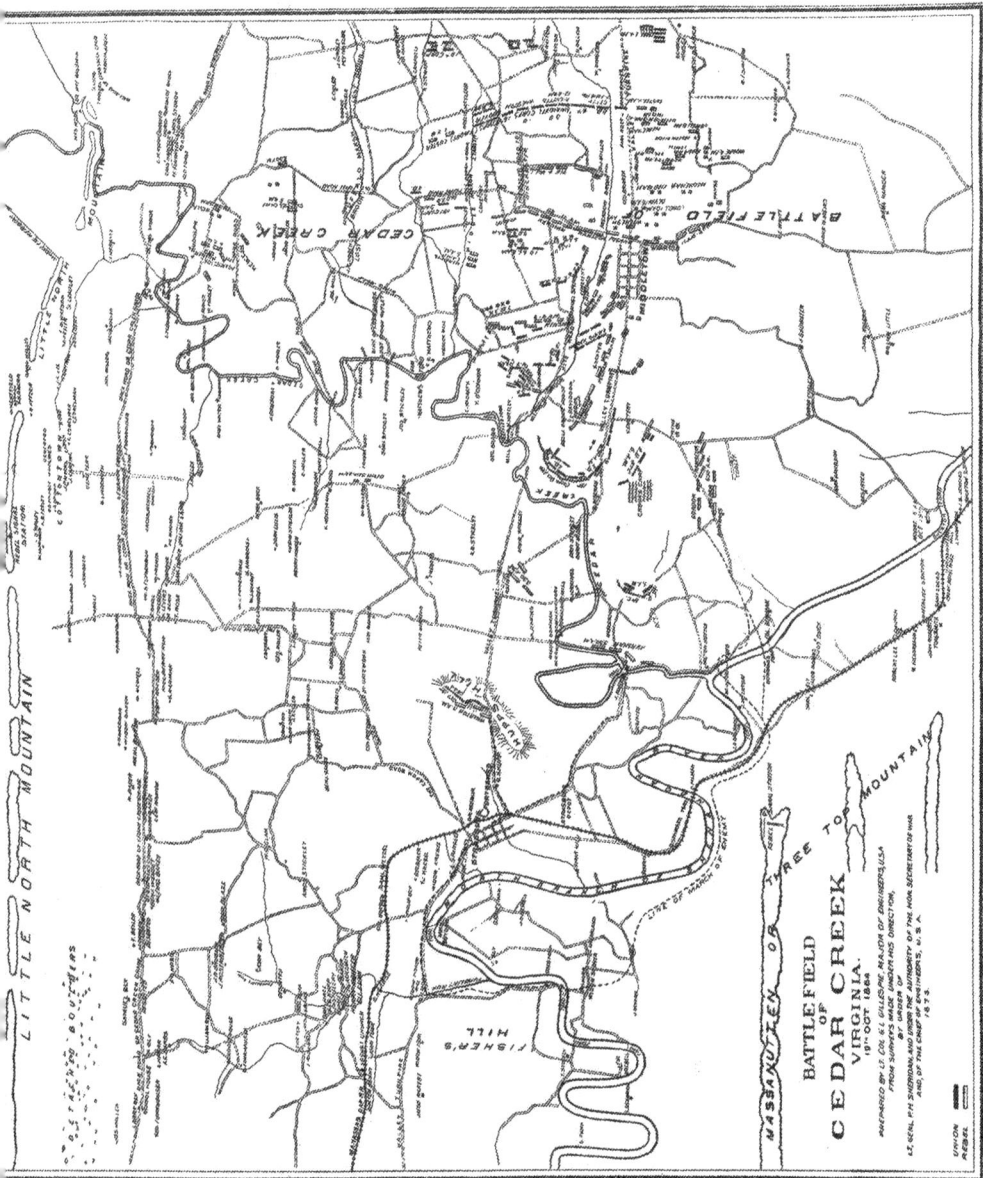

BATTLE FIELD
OF
CEDAR CREEK
VIRGINIA.
19th OCT 1864.

PREPARED BY LT. COL. G.L. GILLESPIE, MAJOR OF ENGINEERS, U.S.A.
FROM SURVEYS MADE UNDER HIS DIRECTION,
BY ORDER OF
LT. GEN. P.H. SHERIDAN, AND UNDER THE AUTHORITY OF THE HON. SECRETARY OF WAR
AND, OF THE CHIEF OF ENGINEERS, U.S.A.
1873.

Nineteenth Corps from its post at the Cedar Creek crossing and this enabled Wharton to get over the stream there unmolested and join Kershaw early in the action.

After Crook's troops had been driven from their camps, General Wright endeavored to form a line with the Sixth Corps to hold the Valley pike to the left of the Nineteenth, but failing in this he ordered the withdrawal of the latter corps, Ricketts, temporarily commanding the Sixth Corps, checking Gordon till Emory had retired. As already stated, Wharton was thus permitted to cross Cedar Creek on the pike, and now that Early had a continuous line, he pressed his advantage so vigorously that the whole Union army was soon driven from its camps in more or less disorder; and though much disjointed resistance was displayed, it may be said that no systematic stand was made until Getty's division, aided by Torbert's cavalry, which Wright had ordered to the left early in the action, took up the ground where, on arriving from Winchester, I found them.

When I left my command on the 16th, little did I anticipate that anything like this would happen. Indeed, I felt satisfied that Early was, of himself, too weak to take the offensive, and although I doubted the Longstreet despatch, yet I was confident that, even should it prove true, I could get back before the junction could be made, and at the worst I felt certain that my army was equal to confronting the forces of Longstreet and Early combined. Still, the surprise of the morning might have befallen me as well as the general on whom it did descend, and though it is possible that this could have been precluded had Powell's cavalry been closed in, as suggested in my despatch from Front Royal, yet the enemy's desperation might have prompted some other clever and ingenious scheme for relieving his fallen fortunes in the Shenandoah Valley.

CHAPTER IV.

GENERAL EARLY REORGANIZES HIS FORCES - MOSBY THE GUERRILLA - GENERAL MERRITT SENT TO OPERATE AGAINST MOSBY - ROSSER AGAIN ACTIVE - GENERAL CUSTER SURPRISED - COLONEL YOUNG SENT TO CAPTURE GILMORE THE GUERRILLA - COLONEL YOUNG'S SUCCESS - CAPTURE OF GENERAL KELLY AND GENERAL CROOK - SPIES - WAS WILKES BOOTH A SPY? - DRIVING THE CONFEDERATES OUT OF THE VALLEY - THE BATTLE OF WAYNESBORO' - MARCHING TO JOIN THE ARMY OF THE POTOMAC.

EARLY'S broken army practically made no halt in its retreat after the battle of Cedar Creek until it reached New Market, though at Fisher's Hill was left a small rear-guard of cavalry, which hastily decamped, however, when charged by Gibbs's brigade on the morning of the 20th. Between the date of his signal defeat and the 11th of November, the enemy's scattered forces had sufficiently reorganized to permit his again making a reconnoissance in the valley as far north as Cedar Creek, my army having meanwhile withdrawn to Kernstown, where it had been finally decided that a defensive line should be held to enable me to detach troops to General Grant.

and where, by reconstructing the Winchester and Potomac railroad from Stephenson's depot to Harper's Ferry, my command might be more readily supplied. Early's reconnoissance north of Cedar Creek ended in a rapid withdrawal of his infantry after feeling my front, and with the usual ill-fortune to his cavalry; Merritt and Custer driving Rosser and Lomax with ease across Cedar Creek on the Middle and Back roads, while Powell's cavalry struck McCausland near Stony Point, and after capturing two pieces of artillery and about three hundred officers and men. chased him into the Luray Valley.

Early got back to New Market on the 14th of November, and, from lack of subsistence, being unable to continue demonstrations to prevent my reinforcement of General Grant, began himself to detach to General Lee by returning Mershaw's division to Petersburg, as was definitely ascertained by Torbert in a reconnoissance to Mount Jackson. At this time General Grant wished me to send him the Sixth Corps, and it was got ready for the purpose, but when I informed him that Torbert's reconnoissance had developed the fact that Early still retained four divisions of infantry and one of cavalry, it was decided, on my suggestion, to let the Sixth Corps remain till the season should be a little further advanced, when the inclemency of the weather would preclude infantry campaigning. These conditions came about early in December, and by the middle of the month the whole of the Sixth Corps was at Petersburg; simultaneously with its transfer to that line Early sending his Second Corps to Lee.

During the entire campaign I had been annoyed by guerrilla bands under such partisan chiefs as Mosby, White, Gilmore, McNeil, and others, and this had considerably depleted my line-of-battle strength, necessitating as it did large escorts for my supply-trains. The most redoubtable of these leaders was Mosby, whose force was made up from the country around Upperville, east of the Blue Ridge, to which section he always fled for a hiding-place when he scented danger. I had not directed any special operations against these partisans while the campaign was active, but as Mosby's men had lately killed, within my lines, my chief quartermaster, Colonel Tolles, and Medical Inspector Ohlenchlager, I concluded to devote particular attention to these "irregulars" during the lull that now occurred; so on the 28th of November, I directed General Merritt to march to the Loudoun Valley and operate against Mosby, taking care to clear the country of forage and subsistence, so as to prevent the guerrillas from being harbored there in the future, their destruction or capture being wellnigh impossible, on account of their intimate knowledge of the mountain region. Merritt carried out his instructions with his usual sagacity and thoroughness, sweeping widely over each side of his general line of march with flankers, who burned the grain and brought in large herds of cattle, hogs and sheep, which were issued to the troops.

While Merritt was engaged in this service the Baltimore and Ohio railroad once more received the attention of the enemy; Rosser, with two brigades of cavalry, crossing the Great North Mountain, capturing the post of New Creek, with about five hundred prisoners and seven guns, destroying all the supplies of the garrison, and breaking up the railroad track. This slight success of the Confederates in West Virginia, and the intelligence that they were contemplating further raids in that section, led me to send Crook there with one division, his other troops going to City Point; and I hoped that all the threatened places would thus be sufficiently protected, but negligence at Beverly resulted in the capture of that station by Rosser on the 11th of January.

In the meanwhile, Early established himself with Wharton's division at Staunton in winter quarters, posting his cavalry in that neighborhood

Maj. Gen'l P. H. SHERIDAN'S
CAMPAIGNS
FOURTH EXPEDITION-CEN'.
MERRITT'S RAID TO LOUDOUN.

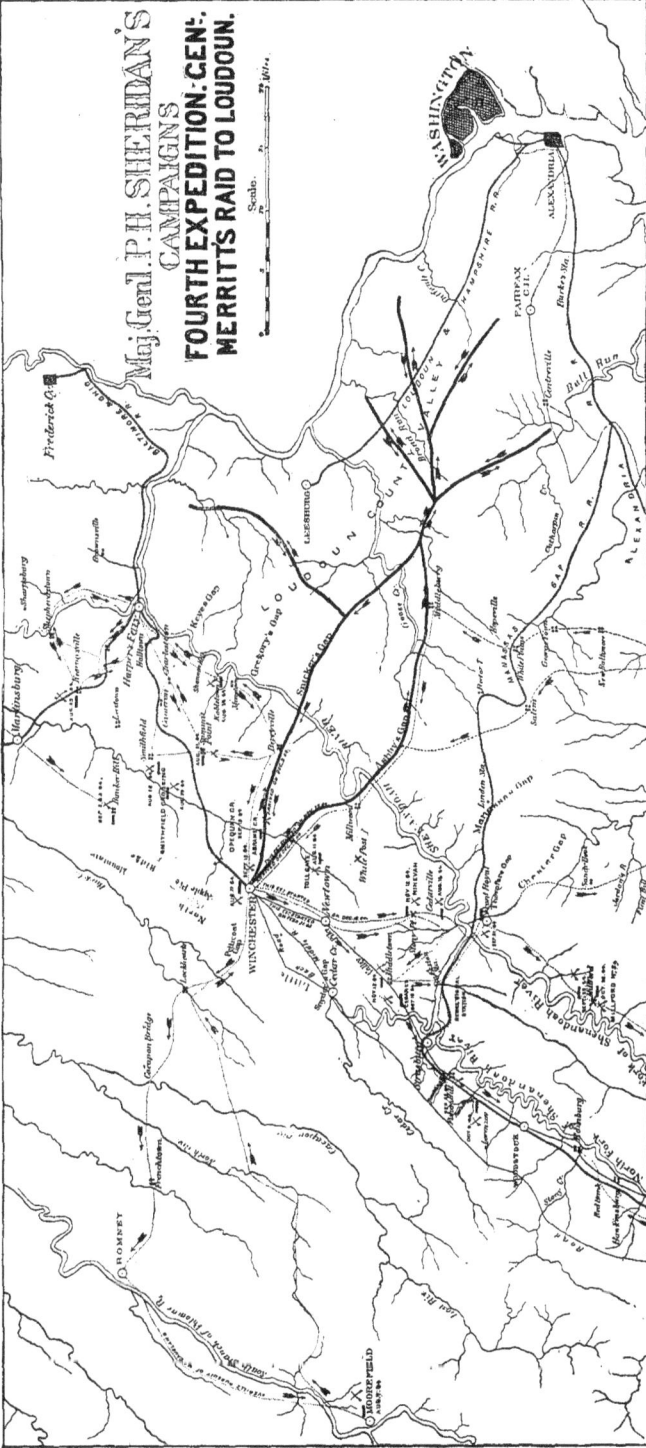

Scale.

also, except a detachment at New Market, and another small one at the signal-station on Three Top Mountain. The winter was a most severe one, snow falling frequently to the depth of several inches, and the mercury often sinking below zero. The rigor of the season was very much against the success of any mounted operations, but General Grant being very desirous to have the railroads broken up about Gordonsville and Charlottesville, on the 19th of December I started the cavalry out for that purpose, Torbert, with Merritt and Powell, marching through Chester Gap, while Custer moved toward Staunton to make a demonstration in Torbert's favor, hoping to hold the enemy's troops in the valley. Unfortunately, Custer did not accomplish all that was expected of him, and being surprised by Rosser and Payne near Lacy's Springs before reveille, had to abandon his bivouac and retreat down the valley, with the loss of a number of prisoners, a few horses, and a good many horse equipments, for, because of the suddenness of Rosser's attack, many of the men had no time to saddle up. As soon as Custer's retreat was assured, Wharton's division of infantry was sent to Charlottesville to check Torbert, but this had already been done by Lomax, with the assistance of infantry sent up from Richmond. Indeed,

Maj.Genl. P.H.SHERIDAN'S
CAMPAIGNS

FIFTH EXPEDITION. GENL.
TORBERT'S RAID TO CORDONSVILLE.

Scale

from the very beginning of the movement the Confederates had been closely observing the columns of Torbert and Custer, and in consequence of the knowledge thus derived, Early had marched Lomax to Gordonsville in anticipation of an attack there, at the same time sending Rosser down the valley to meet Custer. Torbert in the performance of his task captured two pieces of artillery from Johnson's and McCausland's brigades, at Liberty Mills on the Rapidan River, but in the main the purpose of the raid utterly failed, so by the 27th of December he returned, many of his men badly frost-bitten from the extreme cold which had prevailed.

This expedition practically closed all operations for the season, and the cavalry was put into winter cantonment near Winchester. The distribution of my infantry to Petersburg and West Virginia left with me in the beginning of the new year, as already stated, but the one small division of the Nineteenth Corps. On account of this diminution of force, it became necessary for me to keep thoroughly posted in regard to the enemy, and I now realized more than I had done hitherto how efficient my scouts had become since under the control of Colonel Young; for not only did they bring me almost every day intelligence from within Early's lines, but they also operated efficiently against the guerrillas infesting West Virginia.

Harry Gilmore, of Maryland, was the most noted of these since the death of McNeil, and as the scouts had reported him in Harrisonburg the latter part of January, I directed two of the most trustworthy to be sent to watch his movements and ascertain his purposes. In a few days these spies returned with the intelligence that Gilmore was on his way to Moorefield, the centre of a very disloyal section in West Virginia, about ninety miles southwest of Winchester, where, under the guise of a camp-meeting, a gathering was to take place, at which he expected to enlist a number of men, be joined by a party of about twenty recruits coming from Maryland, and then begin depredations along the Baltimore and Ohio railroad. Believing that Giimore might be captured, I directed Young to undertake the task, and as a preliminary step he sent to Moorefield two of his men who early in the war had "refugeed" from that section and enlisted in one of the Union regiments from West Virginia. In about a week these men came back and reported that Gilmore was living at a house between three and four miles from Moorefield, and gave full particulars as to his coming and going, the number of men he had about there and where they rendezvoused.

With this knowledge at hand I directed Young to take twenty of his best men and leave that night for Moorefield, dressed in Confederate uniforms, telling him that I would have about three hundred cavalry follow in his wake when he had got about fifteen miles start, and instructing him to pass his party off as a body of recruits for Gilmore coming from Maryland and pursued by the Yankee cavalry. I knew this would allay suspicion and provide him help on the road; and, indeed, as Colonel Whittaker, who alone knew the secret, followed after the fleeing "Marylanders," he found that their advent had caused so little remark that the trail would have been lost had he not already known their destination. Young met with a hearty welcome wherever he halted on the way, and as he passed through the town of Moorefield learned with satisfaction that Gilmore still made his headquarters at the house where the report of the two scouts had located him a few days before. Reaching the designated place about 12 o'clock on the night of the 5th of February, Young, under the representation that he had come directly from Maryland and was being pursued by the Union cavalry, gained immediate access to Gilmore's room. He found the bold guerrilla snugly tucked in bed, with two pistols lying on a chair near by. He was sleeping so soundly that to arouse him Young had to give him a violent shake. As he awoke and asked who was disturbing his slumbers, Young, pointing at him a cocked six-shooter, ordered him to dress without delay, and in answer to his inquiry, informed him that he was a prisoner to one of Sheridan's staff. Meanwhile Gilmore's men had learned of his trouble, but the early appearance of Colonel Whittaker caused them to disperse; thus the last link between Maryland and the Confederacy was carried a prisoner to Winchester, whence he was sent to Fort Warren.

The capture of Gilmore caused the disbandment of the party he had organized at the "camp-meeting," most of the men he had recruited returning to their homes discouraged, though some few joined the bands of Woodson and young Jesse McNeil, which, led by the latter, dashed into Cumberland, Maryland, at 3 o'clock on the morning of the 21st of February and made a reprisal by carrying off General Crook and General Kelly, and doing their work so silently and quickly that they escaped without being noticed, and were some distance on their way before the colored watchman at the hotel where Crook was quartered could compose himself enough to give the alarm. A troop of cavalry gave hot chase from Cumberland, striving to intercept the party at Moorefield and other points, but all efforts were fruitless, the prisoners soon being beyond reach.

Although I had adopted the general rule of employing only soldiers as scouts, there was an occasional exception to it. I cannot say that these exceptions proved wholly that an iron-clad observance of the rule would have been best, but I am sure of it in one instance. A man named Lomas, who claimed to be a Marylander, offered me his services as a spy, and coming highly recommended from Mr. Stanton, who had made use of him in that capacity, I employed him. He made many pretensions, often appearing over anxious to impart information seemingly intended to impress me with his importance, and yet was more than ordinarily intelligent, but in spite of that my confidence in him was by no means unlimited. I often found what he reported to me as taking place within the Confederate lines corroborated by Youngs men, but generally there were discrepancies in his tales, which led me to suspect that he was employed by the enemy as well as by me. I felt, however, that with good watching he could do me little harm, and if my suspicions were incorrect he might be very useful, so I held on to him.

Early in February Lomas was very solicitous for me to employ a man who, he said, had been

with Mosby, but on account of some quarrel in
the irregular camp had abandoned that leader.
Thinking that with two of them I might destroy
the railroad bridges east of Lynchburg, I concluded, after the Mosby man had been brought
to my headquarters by Lomas about 12 o'clock
one night, to give him employment, at the same
time informing Colonel Young that I suspected
their fidelity, however, and that he must test
it by shadowing their every movement. When
Lomas's companion entered my room he was
completely disguised, but on discarding the various contrivances by which his identity was concealed he proved to be a rather slender, dark-
complexioned, handsome young man, of easy
address and captivating manners. He gave his
name as Renfrew, answered all my questions satisfactorily, and went into details about Mosby
and his men which showed an intimacy with
them at some time. I explained to the two men
the work I had laid out for them, and stated the
sum of money I would give to have it done, but
stipulated that in case of failure there would be
no compensation whatever beyond the few dollars
necessary for their expenses. They readily as-
sented, and it was arranged that they should
start the following night. Meanwhile Young had
selected his men to shadow them, and in two

days reported my spies as being concealed at Strasburg, where they remained, without making the slightest effort to continue on their mission, and were busy, no doubt, communicating with the enemy, though I was not able to fasten this on them.   On the 16th of February they returned to Winchester, and reported their failure, telling so many lies about their hazardous adventure as to remove all remaining doubt as to their double-dealing.   Unquestionably they were spies from the enemy, and hence liable to the usual penalties of such service; but it struck me that through them I might deceive Early as to the time of opening the spring campaign, I having already received from General Grant an intimation of what was expected of me. I therefore retained the men without even a suggestion of my knowledge of their true character, Young meanwhile keeping close watch over all their doings.

Toward the last of February General Early had at Staunton two brigades of infantry under Wharton. All the rest of the infantry except Echols brigade, which was in southwestern Virginia, had been sent to Petersburg during the winter, and Fitz. Lees two brigades of cavalry also. Rossers men were mostly at their homes, where, on account of a lack of subsistence and forage in the valley, they had been permitted to go, subject to call. Lomax's cavalry was at Mill-boro', west of Staunton where supplies were obtainable. It was my aim to get well on the road before Early could collect these scattered forces, and as many of the officers had been in the habit of amusing themselves fox-hunting during the Patter part of the winter, I decided to use the hunt as an expedient for stealing a march on the enemy, and had it given out offcially that a grand fox-chase would take place on the 29th of February. Knowing that Lomas and Renfrew would spread the announcement South, they were permitted to see several red foxes that had been secured, as well as a large pack of hounds which Colonel Young had collected for the sport, and were then started on a second expedition to burn the bridges. Of course, they were shadowed as usual, and two days later, after they had communicated with friends from their hiding-place in Newtown, they were arrested. On the way north to Fort Warren they escaped from their guards when passing through Baltimore, and I never heard of them again, though I learned that, after the assassination of Mr. Lincoln, Secretary Stanton strongly suspected his friend Lomas of being associated with the conspirators, and it then occurred to me that the good-looking Renfrew may have been Wilkes Booth, for he certainly bore a strong resemblance to Booth's pictures.

On the 27th of February my cavalry entered upon the campaign which cleared the Shenandoah Valley of every remnant of organized Confederates. General Torbert being absent on leave at this time, I did not recall him, but appointed General Merritt Chief of Cavalry for Torbert had disappointed me on two important occasions - in the Luray Valley during the battle of Fisher's Hill, and on the recent Gordonsville expedition - and I mistrusted his ability to conduct any operations requiring much self-reliance. The column was composed of Custer's and Devin's divisions of cavalry, and two sections of artillery, comprising in all about 10,000 officers and men. On wheels we had, to accompany this column, eight ambulances, sixteen ammunition wagons, a pontoon train for eight canvas boats, and a small supply-train, with. fifteen days' rations of coffee, sugar, and salt, it being intended to depend on the country for the meat and bread ration, the men carrying in their haversacks nearly enough to subsist them till out of the exhausted valley.

Grant's orders were for me to destroy the Virginia Central railroad and the James River canal, capture Lynchburg if practicable, and then join General Sherman in North Carolina wherever he might be found, or return to Winchester, but as to joining Sherman I was to be governed by the state of affairs after the projected capture of Lynchburg. The weather was cold, the valley and surrounding mountains being still covered with snow; but this was fast disappearing, however, under the heavy rain that was coming down as the column moved along up the Valley pike at a steady gait that took us to Woodstock the first day. The second day we crossed the North Fork of the Shenandoah on our pontoon-bridge, and by night-fall reached Lacy's Springs, having seen nothing of the enemy as yet but a few partisans who hung on our flanks in the afternoon.

March 1 we encountered General Rosser at Mt. Crawford, he having been able to call together only some five or six hundred of his troops, our unsuspected march becoming known to Early only the day before. Rosser attempted to delay us here, trying to burn the bridges over the Middle Fork of the Shenandoah, but two regiments from Colonel Capehart's brigade swam the stream and drove Rosser to Kline's Mills, taking thirty prisoners and twenty ambulances and wagons.

Meanwhile General Early was busy at Staunton, but not knowing my objective point, he had ordered the return of Echol's brigade from southwestern Virginia for the protection of Lynchburg, directed Lomax's cavalry to concentrate at Pond Gap for the purpose of harassing me if I moved toward Lynchburg, and at the same time marched Wharton's two brigades of infantry, Nelson's artillery, and Rosser's cavalry to Waynesboro', whither he went also to remain till the object of my movement was ascertained.

I entered Staunton the morning of March 2, and finding that Early had gone to Waynesboro' with his infantry and Rosser, the question at once arose whether I should continue my march to Lynchburg direct, leaving my adversary in my rear, or turn east and open the way through Rock-fish Gap to the Virginia Central railroad and James River canal. I felt confident of the success of the latter plan, for I knew that Early numbered there not more than two thousand men; so, influenced by this, and somewhat also by the fact that Early had left word in Staunton that he would fight at Waynesboro', I directed Merritt to move toward that place with Custer, to be closely followed by Devin, who was to detach one brigade to destroy supplies at Swoope's depot. The by-roads were miry beyond description, rain having fallen almost incessantly since we left Winchester, but notwithstanding the down-pour the column pushed on, men and horses growing almost unrecognizable from the mud covering them from head to foot.

General Early was true to the promise made his friends in Staunton, for when Custer neared Waynesboro' he found, occupying a line of breast-works on a ridge west of the town, two brigades of infantry, with eleven pieces of artillery and Rosser's cavalry. Custer, when developing the position of the Confederates, discovered that their left was somewhat exposed instead of resting on South River; he therefore made his dispositions for attack, sending around that flank the dismounted regiments from Pennington's brigade, while he himself, with two brigades, partly mounted and partly dismounted, assaulted along the whole line of breastworks. Pennington's flanking movement stampeded the enemy in short order, thus enabling Custer to carry the front with little resistance, and as he did so the Eighth New York and First Connecticut, in a charge in column, broke through the opening made by Custer, and continued on through the town of Waynesboro', never stopping till they crossed South River. There, finding themselves immediately in the enemy's rear, they promptly formed as foragers and held the east bank of the stream till all the Confederates surrendered except Rosser, who succeeded in making his way back to the valley, and Generals Early, Wharton, Long, and Lilley, who, with fifteen or twenty men, escaped across the Blue Ridge. I followed up the victory immediately by despatching Capehart through Rock-fish Gap, with orders to encamp on the east side of the Blue Ridge. By reason of this move all the enemy's stores and transportation fell into our hands, while we captured on the field seventeen battle flags, sixteen hundred officers and men, and eleven pieces of artillery. This decisive victory closed hostilities in the Shenandoah Valley. The prisoners and artillery were sent back to Winchester next morning, under a guard of 1,500 men, commanded by Colonel J. H. Thompson, of the First New Hampshire.

The night of March 2 Custer camped at Brookfield, Devin remaining at Waynesboro.' The former started for Charlottesville the next morning early, followed by Devin with but two brigades, Gibbs having been left behind to blow up the iron railroad bridge across South River. Because of the incessant rains and spring thaws the roads were very soft, and the columns cut them up terribly, the mud being thrown by the sets of fours across the road in ridges as much as two feet high, making it most difficult to get our wagons along, and distressingly wearing on the animals toward the middle and rear of the columns. Conse-

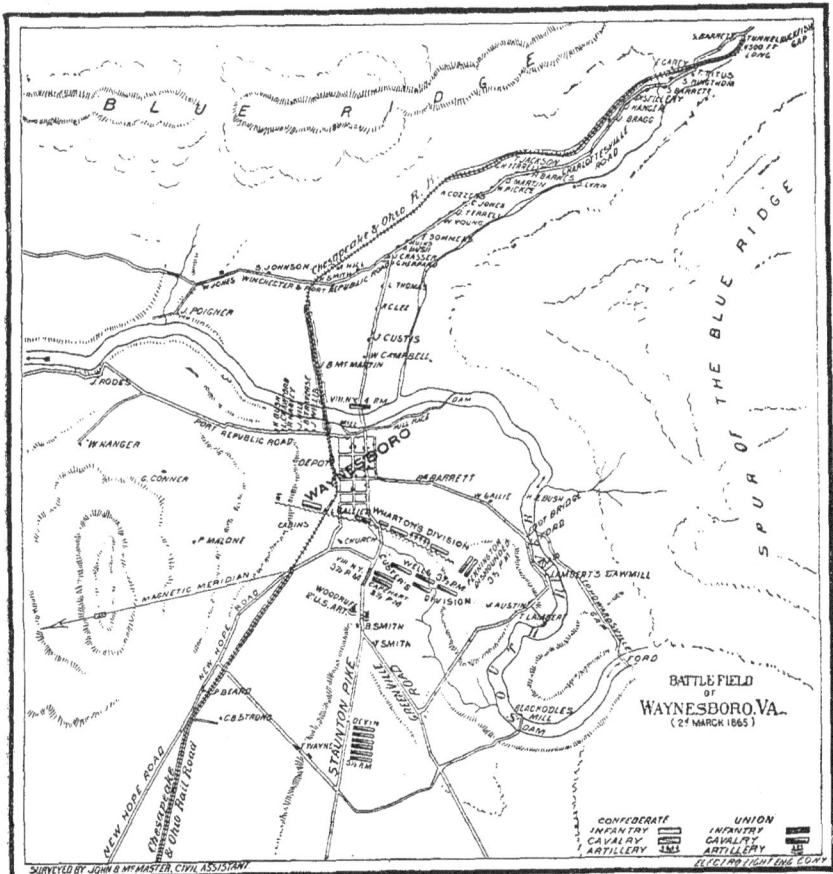

BATTLE FIELD
OF
WAYNESBORO, VA.
(2d MARCH 1865)

SURVEYED BY JOHN B. McMASTER, CIVIL ASSISTANT

quently I concluded to rest at Charlottesville for a couple of days and recuperate a little, intending at the same time to destroy, with small parties, the railroad from that point toward Lynchburg. Custer reached Charlottesville the 3d, in the afternoon, and was met at the outskirts by adeputation of its citizens, headed by the mayor, who surrendered the town with mediæval ceremony, formally handing over the keys of the public buildings and of the University of Virginia. But this little scene did not delay Custer long enough to prevent his capturing, just beyond the village, a small body of cavalry and three pieces of artillery. Gibbs's brigade, which was bringing up my mud-impeded train, did not arrive until the 5th of March. In the mean time Young's scouts had brought word that the garrison of Lynchburg was being increased and the fortifications strengthened, so that its capture would be improbable. I decided, however, to move toward the place as far as Amherst Court House, which is sixteen miles short of the town, so Devin, under Merritt's supervision, marched along the James River, destroying the canal, while Custer pushed ahead on the railroad and broke it up. The two columns were to join at New Market, whence I intended to cross the James River at some point east of Lynchburg, if practicable, so as to make

my way to Appomattox Court House, and destroy
the Southside railroad as far east as Farmville.
Owing to its swollen condition the river was un-
fordable, but knowing that there was a covered
bridge at Duguidsville, I hoped to secure it by a
dash, and cross there, but the enemy, anticipating this, had filled the bridge with inflammable
material, and just as our troops got within striking distance it burst into flames. The bridge at
Hardwicksville also having been burned by the
enemy, there was now no means of crossing except by pontoons, but, unfortunately, I had only
eight of these, and they could not be made to
span the swollen river.

Being thus unable to cross until the river should
fall, and knowing that it was impracticable to join
General Sherman, and useless to adhere to my
alternative instructions to return to Winchester,
I now decided to destroy still more thoroughly
the James River canal and the Virginia Central
railroad and then join General Grant in front of
Petersburg. I was master of, the whole country
north of the James as far down as Goochland;
hence the destruction of these arteries of supply
could be easily compassed, and feeling that the
war was nearing its end, I desired my cavalry to
be in at the death.

On March 9 the main column started eastward

down the James River, destroying locks, dams, and boats, having been preceded by Colonel Fitzhugh's brigade of Devin's division in a forced march to Goochland and Beaver Dam Creek, with orders to destroy everything below Columbia. I made Columbia on the 10th, and from there sent a communication to General Grant reporting what had occurred, informing him of my condition and intention, asking him to send forage and rations to meet me at the White House, and also a pontoon-bridge to carry me over the Pamunkey, for in view of the fact that hitherto it had been impracticable to hold Lee in the trenches around Petersburg, I regarded as too hazardous a march down the south bank of the Pamunkey, where the enemy, by sending troops out from Richmond, might fall upon my flank and rear. It was of the utmost importance that General Grant should receive these despatches without chance of failure, in order that I might depend absolutely on securing supplies at the White House; therefore I sent the message in duplicate, one copy overland direct to City Point by two scouts, Campbell and Rowan, and the other by Fannin and Moore, who were to go down the James River in a small boat to Richmond, join the troops in the trenches in front of Petersburg, and, deserting to the Union lines, deliver their tidings into General Grant's hands.   Each set of messengers got through, but the copy confided to Campbell and Rowan was first at Grant's headquarters.

I halted for one day at Columbia to let my trains catch up, for it was still raining and the mud greatly delayed the teams, fatiguing and wearying the mules so much that I believe we should have been forced to abandon most of the wagons except for the invaluable help given by some two thousand negroes who had attached themselves to the column: they literally lifted the wagons out of the mud. From Columbia Merritt, with Devin's division, marched to Louisa Court House and destroyed the Virginia Central to Frederick's Hall. Meanwhile Custer was performing similar work from Frederick's Hall to Beaver Dam Station, and also pursued for a time General Early, who, it was learned from despatches captured in the telegraph office at Frederick's Hall, was in the neighborhood with a couple of hundred men. Custer captured some of these men and two of Early's staff-officers, but the commander of the Valley District, accompanied by a single orderly, escaped across the South Anna and next day made his way to Richmond, the last man of the Confederate army that had so long contended with us in the Shenandoah Valley.

At Frederick's Hall, Young's scouts brought me

word from Richmond that General Longstreet was assembling a force there to prevent my junction with Grant, and that Pickett's division, which had been sent toward Lynchburg to oppose my march, and Fitzhugh Lee's cavalry, were moving east on the Southside railroad, with the object of circumventing me. Reasoning that Longstreet could interpose effectually only by getting to the White House ahead of me, I pushed one column under Custer across the South Anna, by way of Ground Squirrel bridge, to Ashland, where it united with Merritt, who had meanwhile marched through Hanover Junction. Our appearance at Ashland drew the Confederates out in that direction, as was hoped, so, leaving Colonel Pennington's brigade there to amuse them, the united command retraced its route to Mount Carmel church to cross the North Anna. After dark Pennington came away, and all the troops reached the church by midnight of the 15th.

Resuming the march at an early hour next morning, we took the road by way of King William Court House to the White House, where, arriving on the 18th, we found, greatly to our relief, the supplies which I had requested to be sent there. In the meanwhile the enemy had marched to Hanover Court House, but being unable either to cross the Pamunkey there or fore-

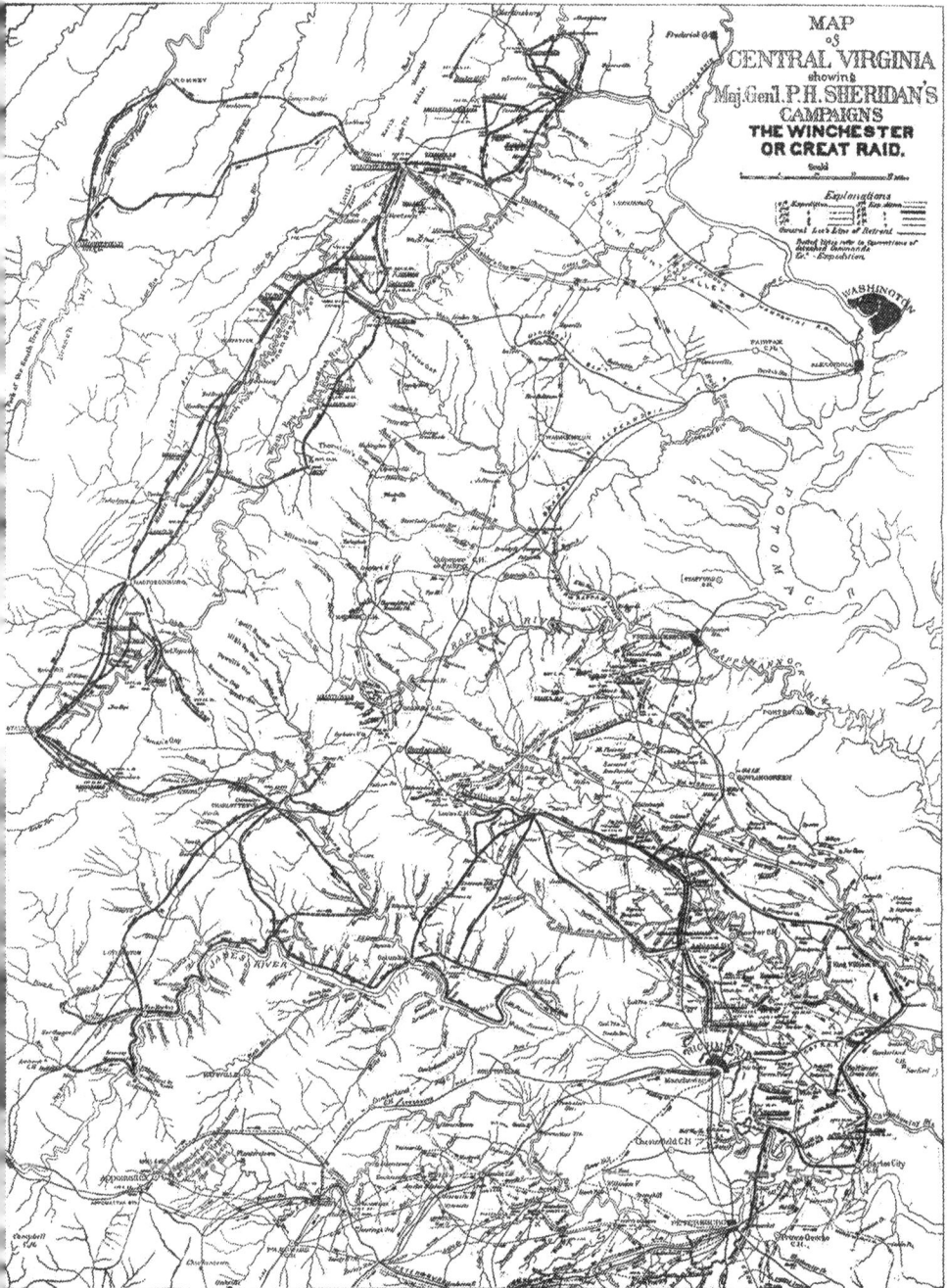

MAP
of
CENTRAL VIRGINIA
showing
Maj. Genl. P. H. SHERIDAN'S
CAMPAIGNS
THE WINCHESTER
OR GREAT RAID.

stall me at the White House on the south side of the river, he withdrew to Richmond without further effort to impede my column.

The hardships of this march far exceeded those of any previous campaigns by the cavalry. Almost incessant rains had drenched us for sixteen days and nights, and the swollen streams and wellnigh bottomless roads east of Staunton presented grave difficulties on every hand, but surmounting them all, we destroyed the enemy's means of subsistence, in quantities beyond computation, and permanently crippled the Virginia Central railroad, as well as the James River canal, and as each day brought us nearer the Army of the Potomac, all were filled with the comforting reflection that our work in the Shenandoah Valley had been thoroughly done, and every one was buoyed up by the cheering thought that we should soon take part in the final struggle of the war.

CHAPTER V.

THE transfer of my command from the Shenandoah Valley to the field of operations in
front of Petersburg was not anticipated by General Grant; indeed, the despatch brought from
Columbia by my scouts, asking that supplies be
sent me at the White House, was the first word
that reached him concerning the move. In view
of my message the general-in-chief decided to
wait my arrival before beginning spring operations with the investing troops south of the James
River, for he felt the importance of having my
cavalry at hand in a campaign which he was convinced would wind up the war. We remained a
few days at the White House resting and refitting
the cavalry, a large amount of shoeing being
necessary; but nothing like enough horses were at

hand to replace those that had died or been disabled on the mud march from Staunton to the Pamunkey River, so a good many of the men were still without mounts, and all such were sent by boat to the dismounted camp near City Point. When all was ready the column set out for Hancock Station, a point on the military railroad in front of Petersburg, and arriving there on the 27th of March, was in orders reunited with its comrades of the Second Division, who had been serving with the Army of the Potomac since we parted from them the previous August. General Crook, who had been exchanged within a few days, was now in command of this Second Division. The reunited corps was to enter upon the campaign as a separate army, I reporting directly to General Grant; the intention being thus to reward me for foregoing, of my own choice, my position as a department, commander by joining the armies at Petersburg.

Taking the road across the Peninsula, I started from the White House with Merritt's column on the 25th of March, and encamped that night at Harrison's Landing. Very early next morning, in conformity with a request from General Grant, I left by boat for City Point, Merritt meanwhile conducting the column across the James River to the point of rendezvous. The trip to City Point did not take long, and on arrival at army head-quarters the first person I met was General John A. Rawlins, General Grant's chief-of-staff. Raw-lins was a man of strong likes and dislikes, and positive always both in speech and action, ex-hibiting marked feelings when greeting any one, and on this occasion met me with much warmth. His demonstrations of welcome over, we held a few minutes' conversation about the coming cam-paign, he taking strong ground against a part of the plan of operations adopted, namely, that which contemplated my joining General Sher-man's army. His language was unequivocal and vehement, and when he was through talking, he conducted me to General Grant's quarters, but he himself did not enter.

General Grant was never impulsive, and always met his officers in an unceremonious way, with a quiet "How are you?" soon putting one at his ease, since the pleasant tone in which he spoke gave assurance of welcome, although his manner was otherwise impassive. When the ordinary greeting was over, he usually waited for his visitor to open the conversation, so on this occasion I began by giving him the details of my march from Winchester, my reasons for not joining Sher-man, as contemplated in my instructions, and the motives which had influenced me to march to

the White House. The other provision of my orders on setting out from Winchester - the alternative return to that place - was not touched
upon, for the wisdom of having ignored that
was fully apparent. Commenting on this recital
of my doings, the General referred only to the
tortuous course of my march from Waynesboro'
down, our sore trials, and the valuable services of
the scouts who had brought him tidings of me,
closing with the remark that it was rare a department commander voluntarily deprived himself of
independence, and added that I should not suffer
for it. Then turning to the business for which he
had called me to City Point, he outlined what he
expected me to do; saying that I was to cut loose
from the Army of the Potomac by passing its
left flank to the southward along the line of the
Danville railroad, and after crossing the Roanoke
River, join General Sherman. While speaking, he
handed me a copy of a general letter of instructions that had been drawn up for the army on the
24th. The letter contained these words concerning the movements of my command:

"The cavalry under General Sheridan, joined by the division
now under General Davies, will move at the same time (29th
inst.) by the Weldon road and the Jerusalem plank-road, turning west from the latter before crossing the Nottoway, and west
with the whole column before reaching Stony Creek. General
Sheridan will then move independently under other instructions

which will be given him. All dismounted cavalry belonging to the Army of the Potomac, and the dismounted cavalry from the Middle Military Division not required for guarding property belonging to their arm of the service, will report to Brigadier-General Benham to be added to the defenses of City Point."

When I had gone over the entire letter I showed plainly that I was dissatisfied with it, for, coupled with what the General had outlined orally, which I supposed was the "other instructions," I believed it foreshadowed my junction with General Sherman. Rawlins thought so too, as his vigorous language had left no room to doubt, so I immediately began to offer my objections to the programme. These were, that it would be bad policy to send me down to the Carolinas with a part of the Army of the Potomac, to come back to crush Lee after the destruction of General Johnston's army; such a course would give rise to the charge that his own forces around Petersburg were not equal to the task, and would seriously affect public opinion in the North; that in fact my cavalry belonged to the Army of the Potomac, which army was able unaided to destroy Lee, and I could not but oppose any dispersion of its strength.

All this was said in a somewhat emphatic manner, and when I had finished he quietly told me that the portion of my instructions from which I so strongly dissented was intended as a "blind" to cover any check the army in its general move

to the left might meet with, and prevent that
element in the North which held that the war
could be ended only through negotiation, from
charging defeat. The fact that my cavalry was
not to ultimately join Sherman was a great relief
to me, and after expressing the utmost confidence
in the plans unfolded for closing the war by directing every effort to the annihilation of Lee's
army, I left him to go to General Ingalls's quarters.
On the way I again met Rawlins, who, when I
told him that General Grant had intimated his
intention to modify the written plan of operations
so far as regarded the cavalry, manifested the
greatest satisfaction, and I judged from this that
the new view of the matter had not previously
been communicated to the chief-of-staff, though
he must have been acquainted of course with the
programme made out on the 24th of March.

Toward noon General Grant sent for me to accompany him up the river. When I joined the
General he informed me that the President was
on board the boat - the steamer *Mary Martin.*
For some days Mr. Lincoln had been at City
Point, established on the steamer *River Queen,*
having come down from Washington to be nearer
his generals, no doubt, and also to be conveniently
situated for the reception of tidings from the
front when operations began, for he could not

endure the delays in getting news to Washington. This trip up the James had been projected by General Meade, but on account of demands at the front he could not go, so the President, General Grant, and I composed the party. We steamed up to where my cavalry was crossing on the pontoon-bridge below the mouth of the Dutch Gap canal, and for a little while watched the column as it was passing over the river, the bright sunshine presaging good weather, but only to delude, as was proved by the torrents of rain brought by the succeeding days of March. On the trip the President was not very cheerful. In fact, he was dejected, giving no indication of his usual means of diversion, by which (his quaint stories) I had often heard he could find relief from his cares. He spoke to me of the impending operations and asked many questions, laying stress upon the one, "What would be the result when the army moved out to the left, if the enemy should come down and capture City Point?" the question being prompted, doubtless, by the bold assault on our lines and capture of Fort Steadman two days before by General Gordon. I answered that I did not think it at all probable that General Lee would undertake such a desperate measure to relieve the strait he was in; that General Hartranft's successful check to Gordon had ended, I thought, attacks of such a character; and in any event General Grant would give Lee all he could attend to on the left. Mr. Lincoln said nothing about my proposed route of march, and I doubt if he knew of my instructions, or was in possession at most of more than a very general outline of the plan of campaign. It was late when the *Mary Martin* returned to City Point, and I spent the night there with General Ingalls.

The morning of the 27th I went out to Hancock Station to look after my troops and prepare for moving two days later. In the afternoon I received a telegram from General Grant, saying: "General Sherman will be here this evening to spend a few hours. I should like to have you come down." Sherman's coming was a surprise - at least to me it was-this despatch being my first intimation of his expected arrival. Well knowing the zeal and emphasis with which General Sherman would present his views, there again came into my mind many misgivings with reference to the movement of the cavalry, and I made haste to start for Grant's headquarters. I got off a little after 7 o'clock, taking the rickety military railroad, the rails of which were laid on the natural surface of the ground, with grading only here and there at points of absolute necessity, and had not gone far when the locomotive jumped the track. This delayed my arrival at City Point till near midnight, but on repairing to the little cabin that sheltered the general-in-chief, I found him and Sherman still up talking over the problem whose solution was near at hand. As already stated, thoughts as to the tenor of my instructions became uppermost the moment I received the telegram in the afternoon, and they continued to engross and disturb me all the way down the railroad, for I feared that the telegram foreshadowed, under the propositions Sherman would present, a more specific compliance with the written instructions than General Grant had orally assured me would be exacted.

My entrance into the shanty suspended the conversation for a moment only, and then General Sherman, without prelude, rehearsed his plans for moving his army, pointing out with every detail how he would come up through the Carolinas to join the troops besieging Petersburg and Richmond, and intimating that my cavalry, after striking the Southside and Danville railroads, could join him with ease. I made no comments on the projects for moving his own troops, but as soon as opportunity offered, dissented emphatically from the proposition to have me join the Army of the Tennessee, repeating in substance what I had previously expressed to General Grant.

My uneasiness made me somewhat too earnest, I fear, but General Grant soon mollified me, and smoothed matters over by practically repeating what he had told me in regard to this point at the close of our interview the day before, so I pursued the subject no further. In a little while the conference ended, and I again sought lodging at the hospitable quarters of Ingalls.

Very early the next morning, while I was still in bed, General Sherman came to me and renewed the subject of my joining him, but when he saw that I was unalterably opposed to it the conversation turned into other channels, and after we had chatted awhile: he withdrew, and later in the day went up the river with the President, General Grant, and Admiral Porter, I returning to my command at Hancock Station, where my presence was needed to put my troops in march next day.

During the entire winter General Grant's lines fronting Petersburg had extended south of the Appomattox River, practically from that stream around to where the Vaughn road crosses Hatcher's Run, and this was nearly the situation when the cavalry concentrated at Hancock Station, General Weitzel holding the line north of the Appomattox, fronting Richmond and Bermuda Hundred.

The instructions of the 24th of March contemplated that the campaign should begin with the movement of Warren's corps (the Fifth) at 3 o'clock on the morning of the 29th, and Humphreys's (the Second) at 6; the rest of the infantry holding on in the trenches. The cavalry was to move in conjunction with Warren and Humphreys, and make its way out beyond our left as these corps opened the road.

The night of the 28th I received the following additional instructions, the general tenor of which again disturbed me, for although I had been assured that I was not to join General Sherman, it will be seen that the supplemental directions distinctly present that alternative, and I therefore feared that during the trip up the James River on the morning of the 28th General Grant had returned to his original views:

"HEADQUARTERS ARMIES OF THE UNITED STATES,
"City Point, Va., March 28, 1865.
" MAJOR-GENERAL P. H. SHERIDAN:
"The Fifth Army Corps will move by the Vaughn road at 3 A. M. to-morrow morning. The Second moves at about 9 A. M., having but about three miles to march to reach the point designated for it to take on the right of the Fifth Corps, after the latter reaches Dinwiddie Court House.

"Move your cavalry at as early an hour as you can, and without being confined to any particular road or roads. You may go out by the nearest roads in rear of the Fifth Corps, pass by its left, and passing near to or through Dinwiddie, reach the right and rear of the enemy as soon as you can. It is not the intention to attack the enemy in his intrenched position, but to force him out if possible. Should he come out and attack us, or get himself where he can be attacked, move in with your entire force in your own way, and with the full reliance that the army will engage or follow the enemy, as circumstances will dictate. I shall be on the field, and will probably be able to communicate with you; should I not do so, and you find that the enemy keeps within his main intrenched line, you may cut loose and push for the Danville road. If you find it practicable I would like you to cross the Southside road, between Petersburg and Burkeville, and destroy it to some extent. I would not advise much detention, however, until you reach the Danville road, which I would like you to strike as near to the Appomattox as possible; make your destruction of that road as complete as possible; you can then pass on to the Southside road, west of Burkeville, and destroy that in like manner.

"After having accomplished the destruction of the two railroads, which are now the only avenues of supply to Lee's army, you may return to this army, selecting your road farther south, or you may go on into North Carolina and join General Sherman. Should you select the latter course, get the information to me as early as possible, so that I may send orders to meet you at Goldsboro'.   U. S. GRANT, Lieut.-General."

These instructions did not alter my line of march for the morrow, and I trusted matters would so come about as. not to require compliance with those portions relative to the railroads and to joining Sherman; so early on the 29th I moved my cavalry out toward Ream's Station on the Weldon road, Devin commanding the First Division, with Colonels Gibbs, Stagg, and Fitzhugh in charge of the brigades; the Third Division under Custer, Colonels Wells, Capehart, and Pennington being the brigade commanders.

These two divisions united were commanded by
Merritt, as they had been since leaving Winchester. Crook headed the Second Division, his
brigades being under General Davies and Colonels John I. Gregg and Smith.*

Our general direction was westward, over such
routes as could be found, provided they did not
embarrass the march of the infantry.   The roads,

*THE APPOMATTOX CAMPAIGN.

ORGANIZATION OF THE CAVALRY COMMAND ON THE MORNING OF MARCH
31, 1865.

MAJOR-GENERAL PHILIP H. SHERIDAN.
Captain Thomas W. C. Moore, Aide-de-camp.
Captain Michael V. Sheridan, Aide-de-camp.

PRINCIPAL STAFF-OFFICERS:
Lieutenant-Colonel James W. Forsyth, Chief-of-Staff.
Lieutenant-Colonel Frederick C. Newhall, Adjutant-General.
Colonel Frank T. Sherman, Inspector-General.
Captain Andrew J. McGonnigle, Chief Quartermaster.
Lieutenant-Colonel John Kellogg, Chief Commissary of Subsistence.
Surgeon James T. Ghiselin, Medical Director.
Captain George L. Gillespie, Chief Engineer.
Captain Ocran H. Howard, Chief Signal Officer.

ARMY OF THE SHENANDOAH.
Brigadier-General Wesley Merritt.

FIRST DIVISION.
Brigadier-General Thomas C. Devin.

FIRST BRIGADE:
Colonel Peter Stagg.

First Michigan, Lieutenant-Colonel George R. Maxwell.
Fifth Michigan, Lieutenant-Colonel Smith H. Hastings.
Sixth Michigan, Lieutenant-Colonel Harvey H. Vinton.
Seventh Michigan, Lieutenant-Colonel George G. Briggs.

SECOND BRIGADE:
Colonel Charles L. Fitzhugh.

Sixth New York, Major Harrison White.
Ninth New York, Major James R. Dinnin.

from the winter's frosts and rains, were in a
frightful state, and when it was sought to avoid
a spot which the head of the column had proved
almost bottomless, the bogs and quicksands of
the adjoining fields demonstrated that to make a
detour was to go from bad to worse.   In the face
of these discouragements we floundered on, however, crossing on the way a series of small streams

Nineteenth New York (First N. Y. Dragoons), Major Howard M. Smith.
Seventeenth Pennsylvania, Lieutenant-Colonel Coe Durland.
Twentieth Pennsylvania, Lieutenant-Colonel Gabriel Middleton.
THIRD (RESERVE) BRIGADE:
Brigadier-General Alfred Gibbs.
Second Massachusetts, Colonel Caspar Crowninshield.
Sixth Pennsylvania, Colonel Charles L. Leiper.
First United States, Captain Richard S. C. Lord.
Fifth United States, Captain Thomas Drummond.
Sixth United States, Major Robert M. Morris.
ARTILLERY:
Fourth United States, Batteries C and E, Captain Marcus P. Miller.
THIRD DIVISION.
Brigadier-General George A. Custer.
FIRST BRIGADE:
Colonel Alexander C. M. Pennington.
First Connecticut, Colonel Brayton Ives.
Third New Jersey, Lieutenant-Colonel William P. Robeson.
Second New York, Colonel Alanson M. Randol.
Second Ohio, Lieutenant-Colonel A. Bayard Nettleton.
SECOND BRIGADE:
Colonel William Wells.
Eighth New York, Major James Bliss.
Fifteenth New York, Colonel John J. Coppinger.
First Vermont, Lieutenant-Colonel Josiah Hall.
THIRD BRIGADE:
Colonel Henry Capehart.
First New York, Captain John J. OBrien.
First West Virginia, Captain S. Bentley Howe.

swollen to their banks. Crook and Devin reached
the county-seat of Dinwiddie about 5 o'clock in
the evening, having encountered only a small
picket, that at once gave way to our advance.
Merritt left Custer at Malon's crossing of Row-
anty Creek to care for the trains containing our
subsistence and the reserve ammunition, these
being stuck in the mire at intervals all the way

Second West Virginia, Lieutenant-Colonel James Allen.
Third West Virginia, Major John S. Witcher.

SECOND DIVISION.
(Army of the Potomac.)
Major-General George Crook.

FIRST BRIGADE:
Brigadier-General Henry F. Davies.

First New Jersey, Colonel Hugh H. Janeway.
Tenth New York, Colonel M. Henry Avery.
Twenty-fourth New York, Colonel Walter C. Newberry.
First Pennsylvania, Major Hampton S. Thomas.
Second United States Artillery, Battery A, Lieutenant James H. Lord.

SECOND BRIGADE:
Colonel J. Irvin Gregg.

Fourth Pennsylvania, Lieutenant-Colonel Alexander P. Duncan.
Eighth Pennsylvania, Lieutenant-Colonel William A. Carrie.
Sixteenth Pennsylvania, Lieutenant-Colonel John K. Robison.
Twenty-first Pennsylvania, Colonel Oliver B. Knowles.
* First U. S. Artillery, Batteries H and I, Lieut. Chandler P. Eakin.

THIRD BRIGADE:
Colonel Charles H. Smith.

First Maine, Lieutenant-Colonel Jonathan P. Cilley.
Second New York Mounted Rifles, Major Paul Chadbourne.
Sixth Ohio, Major John H. Cryer.
Thirteenth Ohio, Lieutenant-Colonel Stephen R. Clark.

*Detached with Artillery Brigade, Ninth Army Corps.

back to the Jerusalem plank-road; and to make any headway at all with the trains, Custer's men often had to unload the wagons and lift them out of the boggy places.

Crook and Devin camped near Dinwiddie Court House in such manner as to cover the Vaughn, Flatfoot, Boydton, and Five Forks roads; for, as these all intersected at Dinwiddie, they offered a chance for the enemy's approach toward the rear of the Fifth Corps, as Warren extended to the left across the Boydton road. Any of these routes leading to the south or west might also be the one on which, in conformity with one part of my instructions, I was expected to get out toward the Danville and Southside railroads, and the Five Forks road would lead directly to General Lee's right flank, in case opportunity was found to comply with the other part. The place was, therefore, of great strategic value, and getting it without cost repaid us for floundering through the mud.

Dinwiddie Court House, though a most important point in the campaign, was far from attractive in feature, being made up of a half-dozen unsightly houses, a ramshackle tavern propped up on two sides with pine poles, and the weather-beaten building that gave official name to the cross-roads. We had no tents - there were none in the command - so I took possession of the tavern for shelter for myself and staff, and just as we had finished looking over its primitive interior a rain-storm set in.

The wagon containing my mess equipment was back somewhere on the road, hopelessly stuck in the mud, and hence we had nothing to eat except some coffee which two young women living at the tavern kindly made for us; a small quantity of the berry being furnished from the haversacks of my escort. By the time we got the coffee, rain was falling in sheets, and the evening bade fair to be a most dismal one; but songs and choruses set up by some of my staff - the two young women playing accompaniments on a battered piano-relieved the situation and enlivened us a little. However, the dreary night brought me one great comfort; for General Grant, who that day had moved out to Gravelly Run, sent me instructions to abandon all idea of the contemplated raid, and directed me to act in concert with the infantry under his immediate command, to turn, if possible, the right flank of Lee's army. The despatch made my mind easy with respect to the objectionable feature of my original instructions, and of course relieved me also from the anxiety growing out of the letter received at Hancock Station the night of the 28th; so, notwithstanding

the suspicions excited by some of my staff concerning the Virginia feather-bed that had been
assigned me, I turned in at a late hour and slept
most soundly.

The night of the 29th the left of General Grant's
infantry - Warren's corps - rested on the Boydton road, not far from its intersection with the
Quaker road. Humphreys's corps was next to
Warren; then came Ord, next Wright, and then
Parke, with his right resting on the Appomattox.
The moving of Warren and Humphreys to the left
during the day was early discovered by General
Lee. He met it by extending the right of his
infantry on the White Oak road, while drawing
in the cavalry of W. H. F. Lee and Rosser along
the south bank of Stony Creek to cover a crossroads called Five Forks, to anticipate me there; for
assuming that my command was moving in conjunction with the infantry, with the ultimate purpose of striking the Southside railroad, Lee made
no effort to hold Dinwiddie, which he might have
done with his cavalry, and in this he made a fatal
mistake. The cavalry of Fitz. Lee was ordered at
this same time from Sunderland depot to Five
Forks, and its chief placed in command of all the
mounted troops of General Lee's army.

At daylight on the 30th I proceeded to make
dispositions under the new conditions imposed by

my modified instructions, and directed Merritt to push Devin out as far as the White Oak road to make a reconnoissance to Five Forks, Crook being instructed to send Davies's brigade to support Devin. Crook was to hold, with Gregg's brigade, the Stony Creek crossing of the Boydton plank-road, retaining Smith's near Dinwiddie, for use in any direction required. On the 29th W. H. F. Lee conformed the march of his cavalry with that of ours, but my holding Stony Creek in this way forced him to make a détour west of Chamberlin's Run, in order to get in communication with his friends at Five Forks.

The rain that had been falling all night gave no sign of stopping, but kept pouring down all day long, and the swamps and quicksands mired the horses, whether they marched in the roads or across the adjacent fields. Undismayed, nevertheless, each column set out for its appointed duty, but shortly after the troops began to move I received from General Grant this despatch, which put a new phase on matters:

" HEADQUARTERS   ARMIES OF THE UNITED STATES,
"GRAVELLY RUN, March 30, 1865.
"MAJOR-GENERAL SHERIDAN:
"The heavy rain of to-day will make it impossible for us to do much until it dries up a little, or we get roads around our rear repaired. You may, therefore, leave what cavalry you deem necessary to protect the left, and hold such positions as

you deem necessary for that purpose, and send the remainder back to Humphreys Station* where they can get hay and grain. Fifty wagons loaded with forage will be sent to you in the morning. Send an officer back to direct the wagons back to where you want them. Report to me the cavalry you will leave back, and the position you will occupy. Could not your cavalry go back by the way of Stony Creek depot and destroy or capture the store of supplies there?

"U. S. GRANT, Lieut.-General."

When I had read and pondered this, I determined to ride over to General Grants headquarters on Gravelly Run, and get a clear idea of what it was proposed to do, for it seemed to me that a suspension of operations would be a serious mistake. Mounting a powerful gray pacing horse called Breckenridge (from its capture from one of Breckenridges staff-officers at Missionary Ridge), and that I knew would carry me through the mud, I set out accompanied by my Assistant Adjutant-General, Colonel Frederick C. Newhall, and an escort of about ten or fifteen men. At first we rode north up the Boydton plank-road, and coming upon our infantry pickets from a direction where the enemy was expected to appear, they began to fire upon us, but seeing from our actions that we were friends, they ceased, and permitted us to pass the outposts. We then struggled on in a northeasterly direction across-country, till we

*Humphreys Station was back on the military railroad.

struck the Vaughn road.   This carried us to
army headquarters, which were established south
of Gravelly Run in an old corn-field. I rode to
within a few yards of the front of General Grant's
tent, my horse plunging at every step almost to
his knees in the mud, and dismounted near a
camp-fire, apparently a general one, for all the
staff-officers were standing around it on boards
and rails placed here and there to keep them
from sinking into the mire.

Going directly to General Grant's tent, I found
him and Rawlins talking over the question of suspending operations till the weather should im-
prove. No orders about the matter had been
issued yet, except the despatch to me; and Rawlins, being strongly opposed to the proposition,
was frankly expostulating with General Grant,
who, after greeting me, remarked, in his quiet way:
"Well, Rawlins, I think you had better take command." Seeing that there was a difference up
between Rawlins and his chief, I made the excuse
of being wet and cold, and went outside to the
fire.   Here General Ingalls met me and took me
to his tent, where I was much more comfortable
than when standing outside, and where a few
minutes later we were joined by General Grant.
Ingalls then retired, and General Grant began
talking of our fearful plight, resulting from the

rains and mud, and saying that because of this it seemed necessary to suspend operations. I at once begged him not to do so, telling him that my cavalry was already on the move in spite of the difficulties, and that although a suspension of operations would not be fatal, yet it would give rise to the very charge of disaster to which he had referred at City Point, and, moreover, that we would surely be ridiculed, just as General Burnside's army was after the mud march of 1863. His better judgment was against suspending operations, but the proposition had been suggested by all sorts of complaints as to the impossibility of moving the trains and the like, so it needed little argument to convince him, and without further discussion he said, in that manner which with him meant a firmness of purpose that could not be changed by further complainings, "We will go on." I then told him that I believed I could break in the enemy's right if he would let me have the Sixth Corps; but saying that the condition of the roads would prevent the movement of infantry, he replied that I would have to seize Five Forks with the cavalry alone.

On my way back to Dinwiddie I stopped at the headquarters of General Warren, but the General being asleep, I went to the tent of one of his staff-officers. Colonel William T. Gentry, an old personal friend with whom I had served in Oregon. In a few minutes Warren came in and we had a short conversation, he speaking rather despondently of the outlook, being influenced no doubt by the depressing weather.

From Warren's headquarters I returned by the Boydton road to Dinwiddie Court House, fording Gravelly Run with ease. When I got as far as the Dabney road I sent Colonel Newhall out on it toward Five Forks, with orders for Merritt to develop the enemy's position and strength, and then rode on to Dinwiddie to endeavor to get all my other troops up. Merritt was halted at the intersection of the Five Forks and Gravelly Church roads when Newhall delivered the orders, and in compliance moving out Gibbs's brigade promptly, sharp skirmishing was brought on, Gibbs driving the Confederates to Five Forks, where he found them behind a line of breastworks running along the White Oak road. The reconnoissance demonstrating the intention of the enemy to hold this point, Gibbs was withdrawn.

That evening, at 7 o'clock, I reported the position of the Confederate cavalry, and stated that it had been reinforced by Pickett's division of infantry. On receipt of this despatch, General Grant offered me the Fifth Corps, but I declined to take it, and again asked for the Sixth, saying that with it I believed I could turn the enemy's (Pickett's) left, or break through his lines. The morning of the 31st General Grant replied that the Sixth Corps could not be taken from its position in the line, and offered me the Second; but in the mean time circumstances had changed, and no corps was ordered.

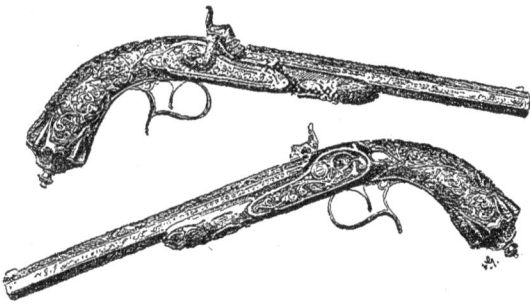

CHAPTER VI.

T HE night of March 30 Merritt, with Devins
division and Daviess brigade, was camped
on the Five Forks road about two miles in front
of Dinwiddie, near J. Boisseaus. Crook, with
Smith and Greggs brigades, continued to cover
Stony Creek, and Custer was still back at Ro-
wanty Creek, trying to get the trains up. This
force had been counted while crossing the creek
on the 29th, the three divisions numbering 9,000
enlisted men, Crook having 3,300, and Custer and
Devin 5,700.

During the 30th, the enemy had been concentrating his cavalry, and by evening General W.
H. F. Lee and General Rosser had joined Fitzhugh Lee near Five Forks. To this force was
added, about dark, five brigades of infantry - three
from Picketts division, and two from Johnsons-

148

all under command of Pickett. The infantry came by the White Oak road from the right of General Lee's intrenchments, and their arrival became positively known to me about dark, the confirmatory intelligence being brought in then by some of Young's scouts who had been inside the Confederate lines.

On the 31st, the rain having ceased, directions were given at an early hour to both Merritt and Crook to make reconnoissances preparatory to securing Five Forks, and about 9 o'clock Merritt started for the crossroads, Davies's brigade supporting him. His march was necessarily slow because of the mud, and the enemy's pickets resisted with obstinacy also, but the coveted crossroads fell to Merritt without much trouble, as the bulk of the enemy was just then bent on other things. At the same hour that Merritt started, Crook moved Smith's brigade out northwest from Dinwiddie to Fitzgerald's crossing of Chamberlain's Creek, to cover Merritt's left, supporting Smith by placing Gregg to his right and rear. The occupation of this ford was timely, for Pickett, now in command of both the cavalry and infantry, was already marching to get in Merritt's rear by crossing Chamberlain's Creek.

To hold on to Fitzgerald's ford Smith had to make a sharp fight, but Mumford's cavalry attacking Devin, the enemy's infantry succeeded in getting over Chamberlain's Creek at a point higher up than Fitzgerald's ford, and assailing Davies, forced him back in a northeasterly direction toward the Dinwiddie and Five Forks road in company with Devin. The retreat of Davies permitted Pickett to pass between Crook and Merritt, which he promptly did, effectually separating them and cutting off both Davies and Devin from the road to Dinwiddie, so that to get to that point they had to retreat across the country to B. Boisseau's and then down the Boydton road.

Gibbs's brigade had been in reserve near the intersection of the Five Forks and Dabney roads, and directing Merritt to hold on there, I ordered Gregg's brigade to be mounted and brought to Merritt's aid, for if Pickett continued in pursuit north of the Five Forks road he would expose his right and rear, and I determined to attack him, in such case, from Gibbs's position. Gregg arrived in good season, and as soon as his men were dismounted on Gibbs's left, Merritt assailed fiercely, compelling Pickett to halt and face a new foe, thus interrupting an advance that would finally have carried Pickett into the rear of Warren's corps.

It was now about 4 o'clock in the afternoon and we were in a critical situation, but having ordered

Merritt to bring Devin and Davies to Dinwiddie by the Boydton road, staff-officers were sent to hurry Custer to the same point, for with its several diverging roads the Court House was of vital importance, and I determined to stay there at all hazards. At the same time orders were sent to Smith's brigade, which, by the advance of Pickett past its right flank and the pressure of W. H. F. Lee on its front, had been compelled to give up Fitzgerald's crossing, to fall back toward Dinwiddie but to contest every inch of ground so as to gain time.

When halted by the attack of Gregg and Gibbs, Pickett, desisting from his pursuit of Devin, as already stated, turned his undivided attention to this unexpected force, and with his preponderating infantry pressed it back on the Five Forks road toward Dinwiddie, though our men, fighting dismounted behind barricades at different points, displayed such obstinacy as to make Pickett's progress slow, and thus give me time to look out a line for defending the Court House. I selected a place about three-fourths of a mile northwest of the crossroads, and Custer coming up quickly with Capehart's brigade, took position on the left of the road to Five Forks in some open ground along the crest of a gentle ridge. Custer got Capehart into place just in time to lend a hand to

Smith, who, severely pressed, came back on us here from his retreat along Chamberlain's "bed" -the vernacular for a woody swamp such as that through which Smith retired. A little later the brigades of Gregg and Gibbs, falling to the rear slowly and steadily, took up in the woods a line which covered the Boydton Road some distance to the right of Capehart, the intervening gap to be filled with Pennington's brigade.   By this time our horse-artillery, which for two days had been stuck in the mud, was all up, and every gun was posted in this line.

It was now near sunset, and the enemy's cavalry thinking the day was theirs, made a dash at Smith, but just as the assailants appeared in the open fields, Capehart's men opened so suddenly on their left flank as to cause it to recoil in astonishment, which permitted Smith to connect his brigade with Custer unmolested. We were now in good shape behind the familiar barricades, and having a continuous line, excepting only the gap to be filled with Pennington, that covered Dinwiddie and the Boydton Road. My left rested in the woods about half a mile west of the Court House, and the barricades extended from this flank in a semicircle through the open fields in a northeasterly direction, to a piece of thick timber on the right, near the Boydton Road.

A little before the sun went down the Confederate infantry was formed for the attack, and, fortunately for us, Pennington's brigade came up
and filled the space to which it was assigned
between Capehart and Gibbs, just as Pickett
moved out across the cleared fields in front of
Custer, in deep lines that plainly told how greatly
we were outnumbered.

Accompanied by Generals Merritt and Custer
and my staff, I now rode along the barricades to
encourage the men. Our enthusiastic reception
showed that they were determined to stay. The
cavalcade drew the enemy's fire, which emptied
several of the saddles - among others Mr. Theodore Wilson, correspondent of the New York
Herald, being wounded. In reply our horse-
artillery opened on the advancing Confederates,
but the men behind the barricades lay still till
Pickett's troops were within short range. Then
they opened, Custer's repeating rifles pouring out
such a shower of lead that nothing could stand
up against it. The repulse was very quick, and
as the gray lines retired to the woods from which
but a few minutes before they had so confidently
advanced, all danger of their taking Dinwiddie
or marching to the left and rear of our infantry
line was over, at least for the night. The enemy
being thus checked, I sent a staff-officer - Captain

Sheridan - to General Grant to report what had taken place during the afternoon, and to say that I proposed to stay at Dinwiddie, but if ultimately compelled to abandon the place, I would do so by retiring on the Vaughn road toward Hatcher's Run, for I then thought the attack might be renewed next morning. Devin and Davies joined me about dark, and my troops being now well in hand, I sent a second staff-officer - Colonel John Kellogg-to explain my situation more fully, and to assure General Grant that I would hold on at Dinwiddie till forced to let go.

By following me to Dinwiddie the enemy's infantry had completely isolated itself, and hence there was now offered the Union troops a rare opportunity. Lee was outside of his works, just as we desired, and the general-in-chief realized this the moment he received the first report of my situation; General Meade appreciated it too from the information he got from Captain Sheridan, *en route* to army headquarters with the first tidings, and sent this telegram to General Grant:

"HEADQUARTERS OF THE ARMY OF THE POTOMAC,
"March 31, 1865. 9:45 P. M.
"LIEUTENANT - GENERAL GRANT:

"Would it not be well for Warren to go down with his whole corps and smash up the force in front of Sheridan? Humphreys can hold the line to the Boydton plank-road, and the refusal along with it. Bartlett's brigade is now on the road from G.

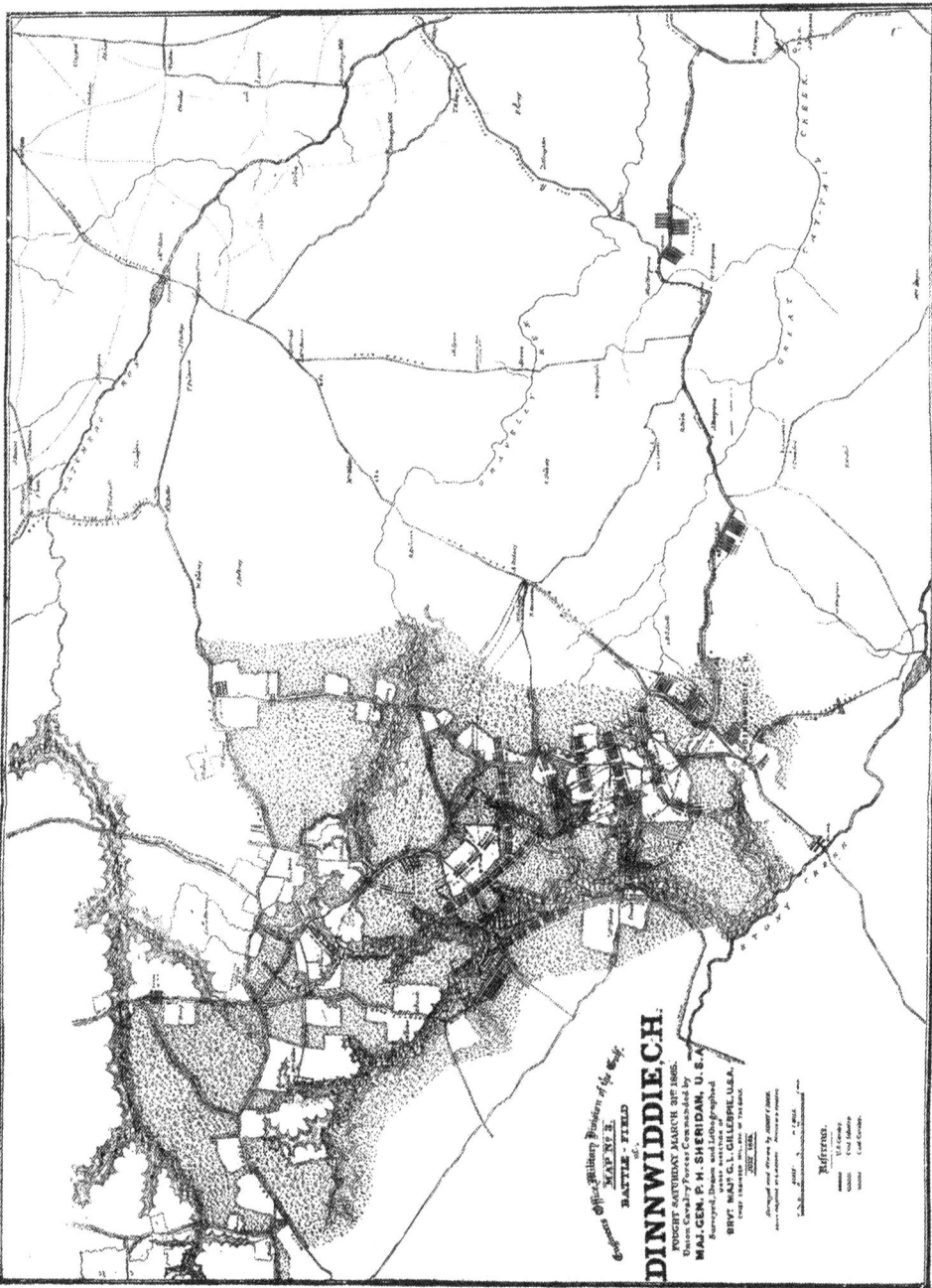

Engineer Office Military Division of the Miss.

MAP N° 3

BATTLE FIELD

of

DINNWIDDIE.C.H.

FOUGHT SATURDAY MARCH 31ST 1865

Union Cavalry Forces Commanded by

MAJ. GEN. P. H. SHERIDAN, U. S. A.

Surveyed, Drawn and Lithographed

BRV. MAJ. G. L. GILLESPIE, U.S.A.

Reference.

Boisseau's, running north, where it crosses Gravelly Run, he having gone down the White Oak road. Warren could go at once that way, and take the force threatening Sheridan in rear at Dinwiddie, and move on the enemy's rear with the other two.

"G. G. Meade, Major-General."

An hour later General Grant replied in these words :

"Headquarters Armies of the United States,
"Dabneys Mills, March 31, 1865. 10:15 p. m.
"Major General Meade,
"Commanding Army of the Potomac.
"Let Warren move in the way you propose, and urge him not to stop for anything. Let Griffin go on as he was first directed.*
"U. S. Grant, Lieutenant-General."

These two despatches were the initiatory steps in sending the Fifth Corps, under Major-General G. K. Warren, to report to me, and when I received word of its coming and also that General Mackenzie's cavalry from the Army of the James was likewise to be added to my command, and that discretionary authority was given me to use all my forces against Pickett, I resolved to destroy him, if it was within the bounds of possibility, before he could rejoin Lee.

In a despatch, dated 10:05 p. m., telling me of the coming of Warren and Mackenzie, General Grant also said that the Fifth Corps should reach me by 12 o'clock that night, but at that hour

*Griffin had been ordered by Warren to the Boydton road to protect his rear.

not only had none of the corps arrived, but no report from it, so believing that if it came all the way down to Dinwiddie the next morning, our opportunity would be gone, I concluded that it would be best to order Warren to move in on the enemy's rear while the cavalry attacked in front, and, therefore, at 3 o'clock in the morning of April 1 sent this despatch to General Warren:

"CAVALRY HEADQUARTERS, DINWIDDIE C. H.,
"April 1, 1865. 3. A. M.
" MAJOR-GENERAL WARREN,
"Commanding Fifth Army Corps.

"I am holding in front of Dinwiddie Court House, on the road leading to Five Forks, for three-quarters of a mile with General Custer's division. The enemy are in his immediate front, lying so as to cover the road just this side of A. Adams's house, which leads across Chamberlain's bed, or run. I understand you have a division at J. Boisseau's;* if so, you are in rear of the enemy's line and almost on his flank. I will hold on here. Possibly they may attack Custer at daylight ; if so, attack instantly and in full force. Attack at daylight anyhow, and I will make an effort to get the road this side of Adams's house, and if I do, you can capture the whole of them. Any force moving down the road I am holding, or on the White Oak road, will be in the enemy's rear, and in all probability get any force that may escape you by a flank movement. Do not fear my leaving here. If the enemy remains, I shall fight at daylight.

"P. H. SHERIDAN, Major-General."

With daylight came a slight fog, but it lifted almost immediately, and Merritt moved Custer

*This "J." was an error; it should have been "G." J. Boisseau's house was in possession of the enemy. The division in question was near G. or Dr. Boisseau's, on the Crump road, north of Gravelly Run.

and Devin forward. As these divisions advanced the enemy's infantry fell back on the Five Forks road, Devin pressing him along the road, while Custer extended on the left over toward Chamberlain's Run, Crook being held in watch along Stony Creek, meanwhile, to be utilized as circumstances might require when Warren attacked.

The order of General Meade to Warren the night of March 31 - a copy being sent me also- was positive in its directions, but as midnight came without a sign of or word from the Fifth Corps, notwithstanding that was the hour fixed for its arrival, I nevertheless assumed that there were good reasons for its non-appearance, but never once doubted that measures would be taken to comply with my despatch of 3 A. M., and therefore hoped that, as Pickett was falling back slowly toward Five Forks, Griffin's and Crawford's divisions would come in on the Confederate left and rear by the Crump road near J. Boisseau's house.

But they did not reach there till after the enemy had got by. As a matter of fact, when Pickett was passing the all-important point Warren's men were just breaking from the bivouac in which their chief had placed them the night before, and the head of Griffin's division did not get to Boisseau's till after my cavalry, which meanwhile had been joined by Ayres's division of the Fifth Corps

by way of the Boydton and Dabney roads. By
reason of the delay in moving Griffin and Crawford, the enemy having escaped, I massed the
Fifth Corps at J. Boisseau's so that the men could
be rested, and directed it to remain there;
General Warren himself had not then come up.
General Mackenzie, who had reported just after
daybreak, was ordered at first to stay at Dinwiddie Court House, but later was brought along
the Five Forks road to Dr. Smith's, and Crook's
division was directed to continue watching the
crossings of Stony Creek and Chamberlain's Run.

That we had accomplished nothing but to oblige
our foe to retreat was to me bitterly disappointing,
but still feeling sure that he would not give up
the Five Forks crossroads without a fight, I pressed
him back there with Merritt's cavalry, Custer advancing on the Scott road, while Devin drove the
rear-guard along that leading from J. Boisseau's
to Five Forks.

By 2 o'clock in the afternoon Merritt had forced
the enemy inside his intrenchments, which began
with a short return about three-quarters of a mile
east of the Forks and ran along the south side of
the White Oak road to a point about a mile west
of the Forks. From the left of the return over
toward Hatcher's Run was posted Mumford's cavalry, dismounted. In the return itself was Wallace's

brigade, and next on its right came Ransom's, then Stewart's, then Terry's, then Corse's. On the right of Corse was W. H. F. Lee's division of cavalry. Ten pieces of artillery also were in this line, three on the right of the works, three near the centre at the crossroads, and four on the left, in the return. Rosser's cavalry was guarding the Confederate trains north of Hatcher's Run beyond the crossing of the Ford road.

I felt certain the enemy would fight at Five Forks - he had to - so, while we were getting up to his intrenchments, I decided on my plan of battle. This was to attack his whole front with Merritt's two cavalry divisions, make a feint of turning his right flank, and with the Fifth Corps assail his left. As the Fifth Corps moved into action, its right flank was to be covered by Mackenzie's cavalry, thus entirely cutting off Pickett's troops from communication with Lee's right flank, which rested near the Butler house at the junction of the Claiborne and White Oaks roads. In execution of this plan, Merritt worked his men close in toward the intrenchments, and while he was thus engaged, I ordered Warren to bring up the Fifth Corps, sending the order by my engineer officer, Captain Gillespie, who had reconnoitred the ground in the neighborhood of Gravelly Run Church, where the infantry was to form for attack.

Gillespie delivered the order about 1 o'clock, and when the corps was put in motion, General Warren joined me at the front. Before he came, I had received, through Colonel Babcock, authority from General Grant to relieve him, but I did not wish to do it, particularly on the eve of battle; so, saying nothing at all about the message brought me, I entered at once on the plan for defeating Pickett, telling Warren how the enemy was posted, explaining with considerable detail, and concluding by stating that I wished his troops to be formed on the Gravelly Church road, near its junction with the White Oak road, with two divisions to the front, aligned obliquely to the White Oak road, and one in reserve, opposite the centre of these two.

General Warren seemed to understand me clearly, and then left to join his command, while I turned my attention to the cavalry, instructing Merritt to begin by making demonstrations as though to turn the enemy's right, and to assault the front of the works with his dismounted cavalry as soon as Warren became engaged. Afterward I rode around to Gravelly Run Church, and found the head of Warren's column just appearing, while he was sitting under a tree making a rough sketch of the ground. I was disappointed that more of the corps was not already up, and as the precious minutes went by without any apparent effort to hurry the troops on to the field, this disappointment grew into disgust. At last I expressed to Warren my fears that the cavalry might expend all their ammunition before the attack could be made, that the sun would go down before the battle could be begun, or that troops from Lee's right, which, be it remembered, was less than three miles away from my right, might, by striking my rear, or even by threatening it, prevent the attack on Pickett.

Warren did not seem to me to be at all solicitous; his manner exhibited decided apathy, and he remarked with indifference that "Bobby Lee was always getting people into trouble." With unconcern such as this, it is no wonder that fully three hours' time was consumed in marching his corps from J. Boisseau's to Gravelly Run Church, though the distance was but two miles. However, when my patience was almost worn out, Warren reported his troops ready, Ayres's division being formed on the west side of the Gravelly Church road, Crawford's on the east side, and Griffin in reserve behind the right of Crawford, a little different from my instructions. The corps had no artillery present, its batteries, on account of the mud, being still north of Gravelly Run. Meanwhile Merritt had been busy working his men close up to the intrenchments from the angle of the return west, along the White Oak road.

About 4 o'clock Warren began the attack. He was to assault the left flank of the Confederate infantry at a point where I knew Pickett's intrenchments were refused, almost at right angles with the White Oak road. I did not know exactly how far toward Hatcher's Run this part of the works extended, for here the videttes of Mumford's cavalry were covering, but I did know where the refusal began. This return, then, was the point I wished to assail, believing that if the assault was made with spirit, the line could be turned. I therefore intended that Ayres and Crawford should attack the refused trenches squarely, and when these two divisions and Merritt's cavalry became hotly engaged, Griffin's division was to pass around the left of the Confederate line; and I personally instructed Griffin how I wished him to go in, telling him also that as he advanced, his right flank would be taken care of by Mackenzie, who was to be pushed over toward the Ford road and Hatcher's Run.

The front of the corps was oblique to the White Oak road; and on getting there, it was to swing round to the left till perpendicular to the road, keeping closed to the left. Ayres did his part well, and to the letter, bringing his division square up to the front of the return near the angle; but

Crawford did not wheel to the left, as was intended. On the contrary, on receiving fire from Mumford's cavalry, Crawford swerved to the right and moved north from the return, thus isolating his division from Ayres; and Griffin, uncertain of the enemy's position, naturally followed Crawford.

The deflection of this division on a line of march which finally brought it out on the Ford road near C. Young's house, frustrated the purpose I had in mind when ordering the attack, and caused a gap between Ayres and Crawford, of which the enemy quickly took advantage, and succeeded in throwing a part of Ayres's division into confusion. At this juncture I sent word to General Warren to have Crawford recalled; for the direction he was following was not only a mistaken one, but, in case the assault at the return failed, he ran great risk of capture. Warren could not be found, so I then sent for Griffin - first by Colonel Newhall, and then by Colonel Sherman - to come to the aid of Ayres, who was now contending alone with that part of the enemy's infantry at the return. By this time Griffin had observed and appreciated Crawford's mistake, however, and when the staff-officers reached him, was already faced to the left; so, marching across Crawford's rear, he quickly joined Ayres, who meanwhile had rallied his troops and carried the return.

When Ayres's division went over the flank of the enemy's works, Devin's division of cavalry, which had been assaulting the front, went over in company with it; and hardly halting to reform, the intermingling infantry and dismounted cavalry swept down inside the intrenchments, pushing to and beyond Five Forks, capturing thousands of prisoners. The only stand the enemy tried to make was when he attempted to form near the Ford road. Griffin pressed him so hard there, however, that he had to give way in short order, and many of his men, with three pieces of artillery, fell into the hands of Crawford while on his circuitous march.

The right of Custer's division gained a foothold on the enemy's works simultaneously with Devin's, but on the extreme left Custer had a very severe combat with W. H. F. Lee's cavalry, as well as with Corse's and Terry's infantry. Attacking Terry and Corse with Pennington's brigade dismounted, he assailed Lee's cavalry with his other two brigades mounted, but Lee held on so obstinately that Custer gained but little ground till our troops, advancing behind the works, drove Corse and Terry out. Then Lee made no further stand except at the west side of the Gillian field, where, assisted by Corse's brigade, he endeavored to cover the retreat, but just before dark Custer,

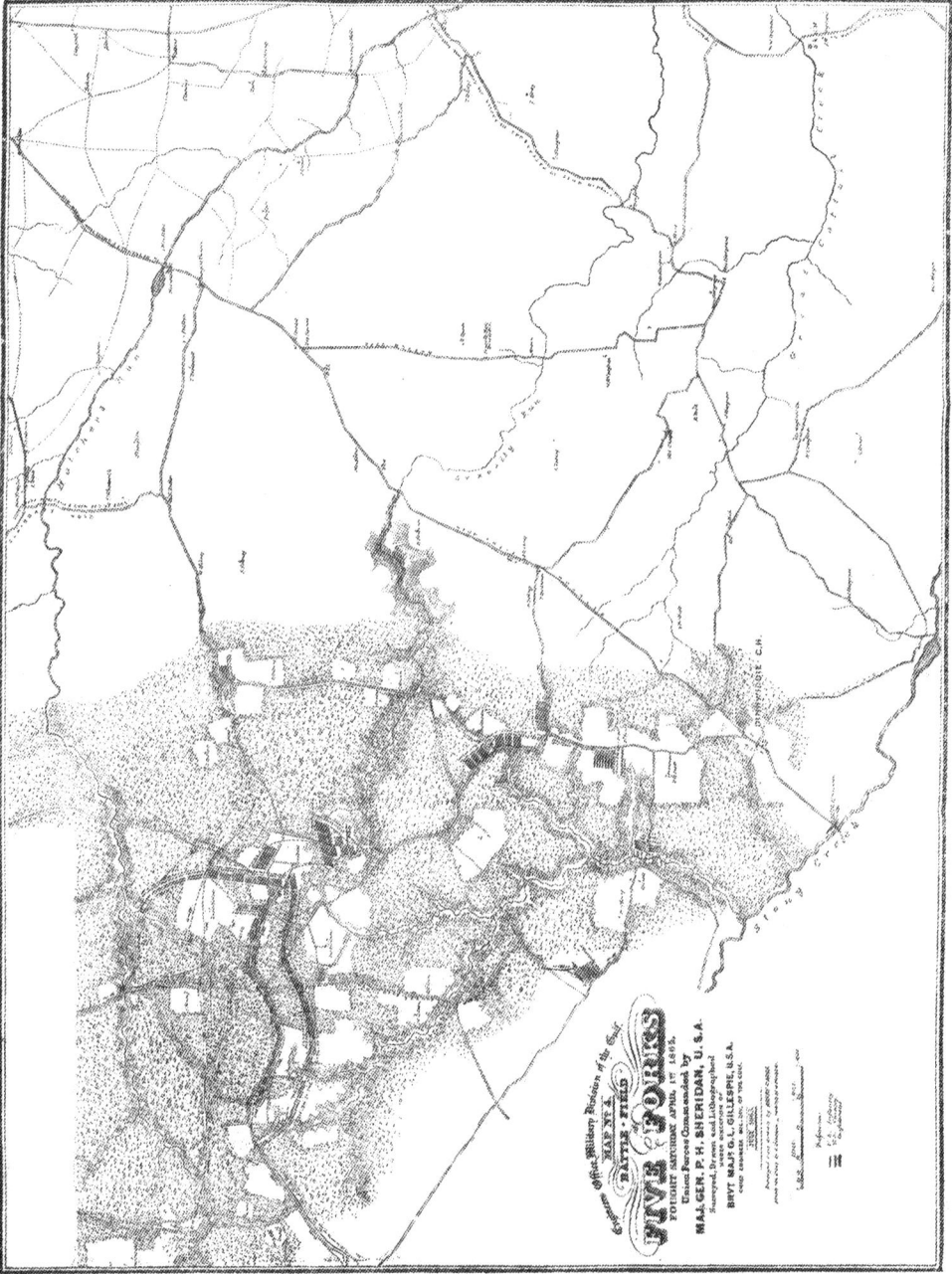

Official Military Division of the East

MAP N.4

BATTLE FIELD

FIVE FORKS

FOUGHT SATURDAY APRIL 1ST 1865.

Union Forces Commanded by

MAJ. GEN. P. H. SHERIDAN, U.S.A.

Surveyed, Drawn and Lithographed
under direction of

BRVT MAJ G. L. GILLESPIE, U.S.A.

1865

in concert with some Fifth Corps regiments under Colonel Richardson, drove the last of the enemy westward on the White Oak road.

Our success was unqualified; we had overthrown Pickett, taken six guns, thirteen battle-flags, and nearly six thousand prisoners. When the battle was practically over, I turned to consider my position with reference to the main Confederate army. My troops, though victorious, were isolated from the Army of the Potomac, for on the 31st of March the extreme left of that army had been thrown back nearly to the Boydton plank-road, and hence there was nothing to prevent the enemy's issuing from his trenches at the intersection of the White Oak and Claiborne roads and marching directly on my rear. I surmised that he might do this that night or early next morning. It was therefore necessary to protect myself in this critical situation, and General Warren having sorely disappointed me, both in the moving of his corps and in its management during the battle, I felt that he was not the man to rely upon under such circumstances, and deeming that it was to the best interest of the service as well as but just to myself, I relieved him, ordering him to report to General Grant.

I then put Griffin in command of the Fifth Corps, and directed him to withdraw from the pursuit as quickly as he could after following the enemy a short distance, and form in line of battle near Gravelly Run Church, at right angles with the White Oak road, with Ayres and Crawford facing toward the enemy at the junction of the White Oak and Claiborne roads, leaving Bartlett, now commanding Griffin's division, near the Ford road. Mackenzie also was left on the Ford road at the crossing of Hatcher's Run, Merritt going into camp on the widow Gillian's plantation. As I had been obliged to keep Crook's division along Stony Creek throughout the day, it had taken no active part in the battle.

Years after the war, in 1879, a Court of Inquiry was given General Warren in relation to his conduct on the day of the battle. He assumed that the delay in not granting his request for an inquiry, which was first made at the close of the war, was due to opposition on my part. In this he was in error; I never opposed the ordering of the Court, but when it was finally decided to convene it I naturally asked to be represented by counsel, for the authorization of the Inquiry was so peculiarly phrased that it made me practically a respondent.*

*"NEW YORK CITY, May 3, 1880.
"MAJOR GENERAL W. S. HANCOCK, U. S. A.
    "President Court of Inquiry, Governor's Island.
    "Sir: Since my arrival in this city, under a subpoena to appear and testify before the Court of which you are president, I have been indirectly and unoffi-

Briefly stated, in my report of the battle of Five Forks there were four imputations concerning General Warren. The first implied that Warren failed to reach me on the 1st of April, when I had reason to expect him; the second, that the tactical handling of his corps was unskillful; the

cially informed that the Court some time ago forwarded an invitation to me (which has not been received) to appear personally or by counsel, in order to aid it in obtaining a knowledge as to the facts concerning the movements terminating in the battle of Five Forks,' with reference to the direct subjects of its inquiry. Any invitation of this character I should always and do consider it incumbent on me to accede to, and do everything in my power in furtherance of the specific purposes for which courts of inquiry are by law instituted.

"The order convening the Court (a copy of which was not received by me at my division headquarters until two days after the time appointed for the Court to assemble) contemplates an inquiry based on the application of Lieutenant-Colonel G. K. Warren, Corps of Engineers, as to his conduct while major-general commanding the Fifth Army Corps, under my command, in reference to accusations or imputations assumed in the order to have been made against him, and I understand through the daily press that my official report of the battle of Five Forks has been submitted by him as a basis of inquiry.

"If it is proposed to inquire, either directly or indirectly, as to any action of mine so far as the commanding general Fifth Army Corps was concerned, or my motives for such action, I desire to be specifically informed wherein such action or transaction is alleged to contain an accusation or imputation to become a subject of inquiry, so that, knowing what issues are raised, I may intelligently aid the Court in arriving at the facts.

"It is a long time since the battle of Five Forks was fought, and during the time that has elapsed the official reports of that battle have been received and acknowledged by the Government; but now, when the memory of events has in many instances grown dim, and three of the principal actors on that field are dead - Generals Griffin, Custer, and Devin, whose testimony would have been valuable - an investigation is ordered which might perhaps do injustice unless the factspertinent to the issues are fully developed.

"My duties are such that it will not be convenient for me to be present continuously during the sessions of the Court. In order, however, that everything may be laid before it in my power pertinent to such specific issues as are legally raised, I beg leave to introduce Major Asa Bird Gardner as my counsel.

"Very respectfully,

"P. H. SHERIDAN, Lieut.-General."

third, that he did not exert himself to get his corps up to Gravelly Run Church; and the fourth, that when portions of his line gave way he did not exert himself to restore confidence to his troops. The Court found against him on the first and second counts, and for him on the third and fourth. This finding was unsatisfactory to General Warren, for he hoped to obtain such an unequivocal recognition of his services as to cast discredit on my motives for relieving him. These were prompted by the conditions alone - by the conduct of General Warren as described, and my consequent lack of confidence in him.

It will be remembered that in my conversation with General Grant on the 30th, relative to the suspension of operations because of the mud, I asked him to let me have the Sixth Corps to help me in breaking in on the enemy's right, but that it could not be sent me; it will be recalled also that the Fifth Corps was afterward tendered and declined. From these facts it has been alleged that I was prejudiced against General Warren, but this is not true. As we had never been thrown much together I knew but little of him. I had no personal objection to him, and certainly could have none to his corps. I was expected to do an extremely dangerous piece of work, and knowing the Sixth Corps well - my cavalry having campaigned with it so successfully in the Shenandoah Valley - I naturally preferred it, and declined the Fifth for no other reason. But the Sixth could not be given, and the turn of events finally brought me the Fifth after my cavalry, under the most trying difficulties, had drawn the enemy from his works, and into such a position as to permit the realization of General Grant's hope to break up with my force Lee's right flank. Pickett's isolation offered an opportunity which we could not afford to neglect, and the destruction of his command would fill the measure of General Grant's expectations as well as meet my own desires. The occasion was not an ordinary one, and as I thought that Warren had not risen to its demand in the battle, I deemed it injudicious and unsafe under the critical conditions existing to retain him longer. That I was justified in this is plain to all who are disposed to be fair-minded, so with the following extract from General Sherman's review of the proceedings of the Warren Court, and with which I am convinced the judgment of history will accord, I leave the subject:

"It would be an unsafe and dangerous rule to hold the commander of an army in battle to a technical adherence to any rule of conduct for managing his command. He is responsible for results, and holds the lives and reputations of every officer and soldier under his orders as subordinate to the great end-victory. The most important events are usually compressed into an hour, a minute, and he cannot stop to analyze his reasons. He must act on the impulse, the conviction, of the instant, and should be sustained in his conclusions, if not manifestly unjust. The power to command men, and give vehement impulse to their joint action, is something which cannot be defined by words, but it is plain and manifest in battles, and whoever commands an army in chief must choose his subordinates by reason of qualities which can alone be tested in actual conflict.

"No one has questioned the patriotism, integrity, and great intelligence of General Warren. These are attested by a long record of most excellent service, but in the clash of arms at and near Five Forks, March 31 and April 1, 1865, his personal activity fell short of the standard fixed by General Sheridan, on whom alone rested the great responsibility for that and succeeding days.

"My conclusion is that General Sheridan was perfectly justified in his action in this case, and he must be fully and entirely sustained if the United States expects great victories by her arms in the future."

CHAPTER VII.

RESULT OF THE BATTLE OF FIVE FORKS - RETREAT
OF LEE - AN INTERCEPTED DESPATCH - AT AMELIA
COURT HOUSE - BATTLE OF SAILORS CREEK-
THE CONFEDERATES' STUBBORN RESISTANCE - A
COMPLETE VICTORY - IMPORTANCE OF THE BATTLE.

W HEN the news of the battle at Five Forks
reached General Grant, he realized that the
decisive character of our victory would necessitate
the immediate abandonment of Richmond and
Petersburg by the enemy; and fearing that Lee
would escape without further injury, he issued
orders, the propriety of which must be settled
by history, to assault next morning the whole
intrenched line. But Lee could not retreat at
once. He had not anticipated disaster at Five
Forks, and hence was unprepared to withdraw on
the moment; and the necessity of getting off his
trains and munitions of war, as well as being
obliged to cover the flight of the Confederate
Government, compelled him to hold on to Richmond and Petersburg till the afternoon of the 2d,
though before that Parke, Ord, and Wright had
carried his outer intrenchments at several points,

thus materially shortening the line of investment.

The night of the 1st of April, General Humphreys's corps - the Second - had extended its left toward the White Oak road, and early next morning, under instructions from General Grant, Miles's division of that corps reported to me, and supporting him with Ayres's and Crawford's divisions of the Fifth Corps, I then directed him to advance toward Petersburg and attack the enemy's works at the intersection of the Claiborne and White Oak roads.

Such of the enemy as were still in the works Miles easily forced across Hatcher's Run, in the direction of Sutherland's depot, but the Confederates promptly took up a position north of the little stream, and Miles being anxious to attack, I gave him leave, but just at this time General Humphreys came up with a request to me from General Meade to return Miles. On this request I relinquished command of the division, when, supported by the Fifth Corps it could have broken in the enemy's right at a vital point; and I have always since regretted that I did so, for the message Humphreys conveyed was without authority from General Grant, by whom Miles had been sent to me, but thinking good feeling a desideratum just then, and wishing to avoid wrangles, I faced the Fifth Corps about and marched it down to Five Forks, and out the Ford road to the crossing of Hatcher's Run. After we had gone, General Grant, intending this quarter of the field to be under my control, ordered Humphreys with his other two divisions to move to the right, in toward Petersburg. This left Miles entirely unsupported, and his gallant attack made soon after was unsuccessful at first, but about 3 o'clock in the afternoon he carried the point which covered the retreat from Petersburg and Richmond.

Merritt had been sent westward, meanwhile, in the direction of Ford's Station, to break the enemy's horse which had been collecting to the north of Hatcher's Run. Meeting with but little opposition, Merritt drove this cavalry force in a northerly direction toward Scott's Corners, while the Fifth Corps was pushed toward Sutherland's depot, in the hope of coming in on the rear of the force that was confronting Miles when I left him. Crawford and Merritt engaged the enemy lightly just before night, but his main column, retreating along the river road south of the Appomattox, had got across Namozine Creek, and the darkness prevented our doing more than to pick up some stragglers. The next morning the pursuit was resumed, the cavalry again in advance, the Fifth Corps keeping up with it all the while, and as we pressed our adversaries hundreds and hundreds of prisoners, armed and unarmed, fell into our hands, together with many wagons and five pieces of artillery. At Deep Creek the rear-guard turned on us, and a severe skirmish took place. Merritt, finding the enemy very strong, was directed to await the arrival of Crook and for the rear division of the Fifth Corps; but by the time they reached the creek, darkness had again come to protect the Confederates, and we had to be content with meagre results at that point.

From the beginning it was apparent that Lee, in his retreat, was making for Amelia Court House, where his columns north and south of the Appomattox River could join, and where, no doubt, he expected to meet supplies, so Crook was ordered to march early on April 4 to strike the Danville railroad, between Jettersville and Burkeville, and then move south along the railroad toward Jettersville, Merritt to move toward Amelia Court House, and the Fifth Corps to Jettersville itself.

The Fifth Corps got to Jettersville about 5 in the afternoon, and I immediately intrenched it across the Burkeville road with the determination to stay there till the main army could come up, for I hoped we could force Lee to surrender at Amelia Court House, since a firm hold on Jettersville would cut him off from his line of retreat toward Burkeville.

Accompanied only by my escort - the First United States Cavalry, about two hundred strong -I reached Jettersville some little time before the Fifth Corps, and having nothing else at hand I at once deployed this handful of men to cover the crossroads till the arrival of the corps. Just as the troopers were deploying, a man on a mule, heading for Burkeville, rode into my pickets. He was arrested, of course, and being searched there was found in his boots this telegram in duplicate, signed by Lee's Commissary-General. "The army is at Amelia Court House, short of provisions. Send 300,000 rations quickly to Burkeville Junction." One copy was addressed to the supply department at Danville, and the other to that at Lynchburg. I surmised that the telegraph lines north of Burkeville had been broken by Crook after the despatches were written, which would account for their being transmitted by messenger. There was thus revealed not only the important fact that Lee was concentrating at Amelia Court House, but also a trustworthy basis for estimating his troops, so I sent word to Crook to strike up the railroad toward me, and to Merritt -who, as I have said, had followed on the heels of the enemy - to leave Mackenzie there and himself close in on Jettersville. Staff-officers were also despatched to hurry up Griffin with the

Fifth Corps, and his tired men redoubled their strides.

My troops too were hard up for rations, for in the pursuit we could not wait for our trains, so I concluded to secure if possible these provisions intended for Lee. To this end I directed Young to send four of his best scouts to Burkeville Junction. There they were to separate, two taking the railroad toward Lynchburg and two toward Danville, and as soon as a telegraph station was reached the telegram was to be transmitted as it had been written and the provisions thus hurried forward.

Although the Fifth Corps arrived at Jettersville the evening of April 4, as did also Crook's and Merritt's cavalry, yet none of the army of the Potomac came up till about 3 o'clock the afternoon of the 5th the Second Corps, followed by the Sixth, joining us then. General Meade arrived at Jettersville an hour earlier, but being ill, requested me to put his troops in position. The Fifth Corps being already intrenched across the Amelia Court House road facing north, I placed the Sixth on its right and the Second on its left as they reached the ground.

As the enemy had been feeling us ever since morning, to learn what he was up to I directed Crook to send Davies' brigade on a reconnoissance to Paine's crossroads. Davies soon found out that Lee was trying to escape by that flank, for at the crossroads he found the Confederate trains and artillery moving rapidly westward. Having driven away the escort, Davies succeeded in burning nearly two hundred wagons, and brought off five pieces of artillery. Among these wagons were some belonging to General Lee's and to General Fitzhugh Lee's headquarters. This work through, Davies withdrew and rejoined Crook, who, with Smith and Gregg, was established near Flat Creek.

It being plain that Lee would attempt to escape as soon as his trains were out of the way, I was most anxious to attack him when the Second Corps began to arrive, for I felt certain that unless we did so he would succeed in passing by our left flank, and would thus again make our pursuit a stern-chase; but General Meade, whose plan of attack was to advance his right flank on Amelia Court House, objected to assailing before all his troops were up.

I then sent despatches to General Grant, explaining what Davies had done, and telling him that the Second Corps was arriving, and that I wished he himself was present. I assured him of my confidence in our capturing Lee if we properly exerted ourselves, and informed him, finally, that I would put all my cavalry, except Mackenzie, on my left, and that, with such a disposition of my forces, I could see no escape for Lee. I also inclosed him this letter, which had just been captured:

"AMELIA C. H., April 5, 1865.
"DEAR MAMMA:

"Our army is ruined, I fear. We are all safe as yet. Shyron left us sick. John Taylor is well-saw him yesterday. We are in line of battle this morning. Genera! Robert Lee is in the field near us. My trust is still in the justice of our cause, and that of God. General Hill is killed. I saw Murray a few minutes since. Bernard, Terry said, was taken prisoner, but may yet get out. I send this by a negro I see passing up the railroad to Mechlenburg. Love to all.

"Your devoted son,
"WM. B. TAYLOR, Colonel."

General Grant, who on the 5th was accompanying General Ord's column toward Burkeville Junction, did not receive this intelligence till nearly nightfall, when within about ten miles of the Junction. He set out for Jettersville immediately, but did not reach us till near midnight, too late of course to do anything that night. Taking me with him, we went over to see Meade, whom he then directed to advance early in the morning on Amelia Court House. In this interview Grant also stated that the orders Meade had already issued would permit Lee's escape, and therefore must be changed, for it was not the aim only to follow the enemy, but to get ahead of him, remarking during the conversation that "he had no doubt Lee was moving right then." On this same occasion Meade expressed a desire to have in the proposed attack all the troops of the Army of the Potomac under his own command, and asked for the return of the Fifth Corps. I made no objections, and it was ordered to report to him.

When, on the morning of the 6th, Meade advanced toward Amelia Court House, he found, as predicted, that Lee was gone. It turned out that the retreat began the evening of the 5th and continued all night. Satisfied that this would be the case, I did not permit the cavalry to participate in Meade's useless advance, but shifted it out toward the left to the road running from Deatonsville to Rice's station, Crook leading and Merritt close up. Before long the enemy's trains were discovered on this road, but Crook could make but little impression on them, they were so strongly guarded; so, leaving Stagg's brigade and Miller's battery about three miles southwest of Deatonsville - where the road forks, with a branch leading north toward the Appomattox - to harass the retreating column and find a vulnerable point, I again shifted the rest of the cavalry toward the left, across-country, but still keeping parallel to the enemy's line of march.

Just after crossing Sailor's Creek, a favorable

opportunity offering, both Merritt and Crook attacked vigorously, gained the Rice's Station road, destroyed several hundred wagons, made many prisoners, and captured sixteen pieces of artillery. This was important, but more valuable still was the fact that we were astride the enemy's line of retreat, and had cut off from joining Longstreet, waiting at Rice's Station, a corps of Confederate infantry under General Ewell, composed of Anderson's, Kershaw's, and Custis Lee's divisions. Stagg's brigade and Miller's battery, which, as I have said, had been left at the forks of the Deatonsville road, had meanwhile broken in between the rear of Ewell's column and the head of Gordon's, forcing Gordon to abandon his march for Rice's Station, and to take the right-hand road at the forks, on which he was pursued by General Humphreys.

The complete isolation of Ewell from Longstreet in his front and Gordon in his rear led to the battle of Sailor's Creek, one of the severest conflicts of the war, for the enemy fought with desperation to escape capture, and we, bent on his destruction, were no less eager and determined. The capture of Ewell, with six of his generals and most of his troops, crowned our success, but the fight was so overshadowed by the stirring events of the surrender three days later, that the battle has never been accorded the prominence it deserves.

The small creek from which the field takes its name flows in a northwesterly direction across the road leading from Deatonsville to Rice's Station. By shifting to the left, Merritt gained the Rice's Station road west of the creek, making havoc of the wagon-trains, while Crook struck them further on and planted himself square across the road. This blocked Ewell, who, advancing Anderson to some high ground west of the creek, posted him behind barricades, with the intention of making a hard fight there, while the main body should escape through the woods in a westerly direction to roads that led to Farmville. This was prevented, however, by Crook forming his division, two brigades dismounted and one mounted, and at once assaulting all along Anderson's front and overlapping his right, while Merritt fiercely attacked to the right of Crook. The enemy being thus held, enabled the Sixth Corps-which in the meantime I had sent for - to come upon the ground, and Ewell, still contending with the cavalry, found himself suddenly beset by this new danger from his rear. To meet it, he placed Kershaw to the right and Custis Lee to the left of the Rice's Station road, facing them north toward and some little distance from Sailor's Creek, supporting Kershaw with Commander Tucker's Marine brigade. Ewell's skirmishers held the line of Sailor's Creek, which runs through a gentle valley, the north slope of which was cleared ground.

By General Grant's directions the Sixth Corps had been following my route of march since the discovery, about 9 o'clock in the morning, that Lee had decamped from Amelia Court House. Grant had promptly informed me of this in a note, saying, "The Sixth Corps will go in with a vim any place you may dictate," so when I sent word to Wright of the enemy's isolation, and asked him to hurry on with all speed, his gallant corps came as fast as legs could carry them, he sending to me successively Major McClellan and Colonel Franklin, of his staff, to report his approach.

I was well advised as to the position of the enemy through information brought me by an intelligent young soldier, William A. Richardson, Company "A," Second Ohio, who, in one of the cavalry charges on Anderson, had cleared the barricades and made his way back to my front through Ewell's line. Richardson had told me just how the main body of the enemy was posted, so as Seymour's division arrived I directed General Wright to put it on the right of the road, while Wheaton's men, coming up all hot and out of breath, promptly formed on Seymour's left. Both

divisions thus aligned faced southwest toward
Sailor's Creek, and the artillery of the corps being
massed to the left and front of the Hibbon house,
without waiting for Getty's division-for I feared
that if we delayed longer the enemy might effect
his escape toward Farmville-the general attack
was begun. Seymour and Wheaton, moving forward together, assailed the enemy's front and left,
and Stagg's brigade, too, which in the mean time
had been placed between Wheaton's left and
Devin's right, went at him along with them, Merritt and Crook resuming the fight from their positions in front of Anderson. The enemy, seeing
little chance of escape, fought like a tiger at bay,
but both Seymour and Wheaton pressed him vigorously, gaining ground at all points except just
to the right of the road, where Seymour's left was
checked. Here the Confederates burst back on us
in a counter-charge, surging down almost to the
creek, but the artillery, supported by Getty, who
in the mean time had come on the ground, opened
on them so terribly that this audacious and furious onset was completely broken, though the gallant fellows fell back to their original line dog-
gedly, and not until after they had almost gained
the creek. Ewell was now hemmed in on every
side, and all those under his immediate command
were captured. Merritt and Crook had also broken

up Anderson by this time, but he himself, and about two thousand disorganized men escaped by making their way through the woods toward the Appomattox River before they could be entirely enveloped.   Night had fallen when the fight was entirely over, but Devin was pushed on in pursuit for about two miles, part of the Sixth Corps following to clinch a victory which not only led to the annihilation of one corps of Lee's retreating army, but obliged Longstreet to move up to Farmville, so as to take a road north of the Appomattox River toward Lynchburg instead of continuing toward Danville.

At the close of the battle I sent one of my staff - Colonel Redwood Price - to General Grant to report what had been done; that we had taken six generals and from nine to ten thousand prisoners.   On his way Price stopped at the headquarters of General Meade, where he learned that not the slightest intelligence of the occurrence on my line had been received, for I not being under Meade's command, he had paid no attention to my movements.   Price gave the story of the battle, and General Meade, realizing its importance, sent directions immediately to General Wright to make his report of the engagement to the headquarters of the Army of the Potomac, assuming that Wright was operating independently of me in the face

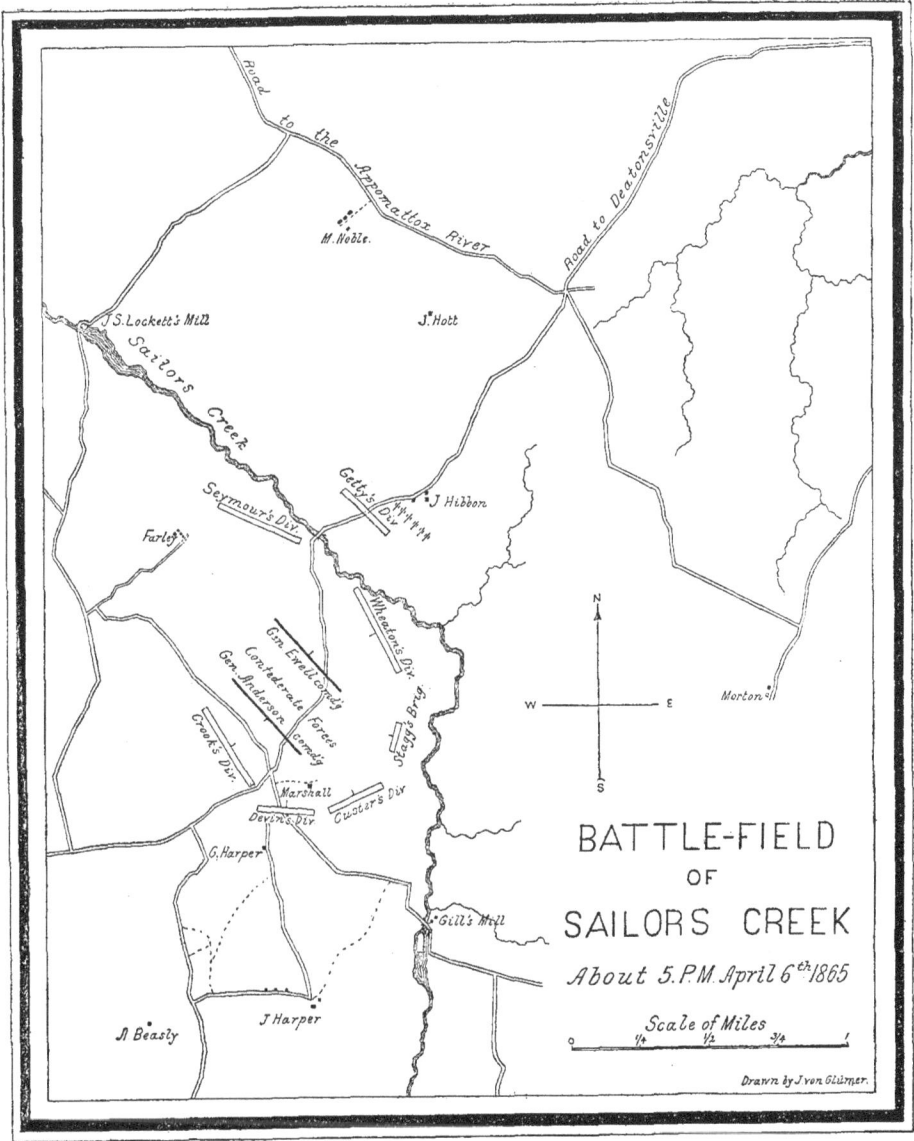

Road to the Appomattox River

Road to Deatonsville

M. Noble.

J. Hott

J. S. Lockett's Mill

Sailors Creek

Seymour's Div.

Getty's Div.

J. Hibbon

Farley

Wheaton's Div.

Gen. Ewell comdg.
Confederate Forces
Gen. Anderson comdg.

Crook's Div.

Seymour's Brig.

Marshall
Devin's Div.
Custer's Div.

G. Harper

Gill's Mill

J. Beasly

J. Harper

N
W   E
S

Morton

BATTLE-FIELD
OF
SAILORS CREEK

About 5. P.M. April 6th 1865

Scale of Miles

0   ¼   ½   ¾   1

of Grant's despatch of 2 o'clock, which said that Wright was following the cavalry and would "go in with a vim" wherever I dictated. Wright could not do else than comply with Meade's orders in the case, and I, being then in ignorance of Meade's reasons for the assumption, could say nothing. But General Grant plainly intending, and even directing, that the corps should be under my command, remedied this phase of the matter, when informed of what had taken place, by requiring Wright to send a report of the battle through me. What he then did, and what his intentions and orders were, are further confirmed by a reference to the episode in his "Memoirs,"* where he gives his reasons for ordering the Sixth Corps to abandon the move on Amelia Court House and pass to the left of the army. On the same page he also says, referring to the 6th of April: "The Sixth Corps now remained with the cavalry under Sheridan's direct command until after the surrender." He unquestionably intended all of this, but his purpose was partly frustrated by General Meade's action next morning in assuming direction of the movements of the corps; and before General Grant became aware of the actual conditions the surrender was at hand.

*Page 473, Vol. II., Grant's "Memoirs."

CHAPTER VIII.

T HE first report of the battle of Sailors Creek
that General Grant received was, as already
stated, an oral message carried by Colonel Price,
of my staff. Near midnight I sent a despatch giving the names of the generals captured. These
were Ewell, Kershaw, Barton, Corse, Dubose, and
Custis Lee. In the same despatch I wrote: "If
the thing is pressed, I think that Lee will surrender." When Mr. Lincoln, at City Point, received
this word from General Grant, who was transmit-
ting every item of news to the President, he telegraphed Grant the laconic message: "Let the
thing be pressed." The morning of the 7th we
moved out at a very early hour, Crooks division
marching toward Farmville in direct pursuit,
while Merritt and Mackenzie were ordered to
Prince Edwards Court House to anticipate any

effort Lee might make to escape through that place toward Danville, since it had been discovered that Longstreet had slipped away already from the front of General Ord's troops at Rice's Station. Crook overtook the main body of the Confederates at Farmville, and promptly attacked their trains on the north side of the Appomattox with Gregg's brigade, which was fiercely turned upon and forced to recross the river with the loss of a number of prisoners, among them Gregg himself.

When Crook sent word of this fight, it was clear that Lee had abandoned all effort to escape to the southwest by way of Danville. Lynchburg was undoubtedly his objective point now: so, resolving to throw my cavalry again across his path, and hold him till the infantry could over. take him, I directed everything on Appomattox depot, recalling Crook the night of the 7th to Prospect Station, while Merritt camped at Buffalo Creek, and Mackenzie made a reconnoissance along the Lynchburg railroad.

At break of day, April 8, Merritt and Mackenzie united with Crook at Prospect Station, and the cavalry all moved then toward Appomattox depot. Hardly had it started when one of the scouts -Sergeant White - informed me that there were four trains of cars at the depot loaded with supplies for Lee's army; these had been sent from

Lynchburg, in compliance with the telegram of Lee's commissary-general, which message, it will be remembered, was captured and transmitted to Lynchburg by two of Young's scouts on the 4th. Sergeant White, who had been on the lookout for the trains ever since sending the despatch, found them several miles west of Appomattox depot, feeling their way along, in ignorance of Lee's exact position. As he had the original despatch with him, and took pains to dwell upon the pitiable condition of Lee's army, he had little difficulty in persuading the men in charge of the trains to bring them east of Appomattox Station, but fearing that the true state of affairs would be learned before long, and the trains be returned to Lynchburg, he was painfully anxious to have them cut off by breaking the track west of the station.

The intelligence as to the trains was immediately despatched to Crook, and I pushed on to join him with Merritt's command. Custer having the advance, moved rapidly, and on nearing the station detailed two regiments to make a detour southward to strike the railroad some distance beyond and break the track. These regiments set off at a gallop, and in short order broke up the railroad enough to prevent the escape of the trains, Custer meanwhile taking possession of the station, but none too soon, for almost at the moment he did so the advance-guard of Lee's army appeared, bent on securing the trains. Without halting to look after the cars further, Custer attacked this advance-guard and had a spirited fight, in which he drove the Confederates away from the station, captured twenty-five pieces of artillery, a hospital train, and a large park of wagons, which, in the hope that they would reach Lynchburg next day, were being pushed ahead of Lee's main body.

Devin coming up a little before dusk, was put in on the right of Custer, and one of Crook's brigades was sent to our left and the other two held in reserve. I then forced the enemy back on the Appomattox road' to the vicinity of the Court House, and that the Confederates might have no rest, gave orders to continue the skirmishing throughout the night. Meanwhile the captured trains had been taken charge of by locomotive engineers, soldiers of the command, who were delighted evidently to get back at their old calling. They amused themselves by running the trains to and fro, creating much confusion, and keeping up such an unearthly screeching with the whistles that I was on the point of ordering the cars burned. They finally wearied of their fun, however, and ran the trains off to the east toward General Ord's column.

The night of the 8th I made my headquarters

at a little frame house just south of the station. I did not sleep at all, nor did anybody else, the entire command being up all night long; indeed, there had been little rest in the cavalry for the past eight days. The necessity of getting Ord's column up was so obvious now that staff-officer after staff-officer was sent to him and to General Grant requesting that the infantry be pushed on, for if it could get to the front, all knew that the rebellion would be ended on the morrow. Merritt, Crook, Custer, and Devin were present at frequent intervals during the night, and everybody was overjoyed at the prospect that our weary work was about to end so happily. Before sun-up General Ord arrived, and informed me of the approach of his column, it having been marching the whole night. As he ranked me, of course I could give him no orders, so after a hasty consultation as to where his troops should be placed we separated, I riding to the front to overlook my line near Appomattox Court House, while he went back to urge along his weary troops.

The night before General Lee had held a council with his principal generals, when it was arranged that in the morning General Gordon should undertake to break through my cavalry, and when I neared my troops this movement was beginning, a heavy line of infantry bearing down on us from the direction of the village. In front of Crook and Mackenzie firing had already begun, so riding to a slight elevation where a good view of the Confederates could be had, I there came to the conclusion that it would be unwise to offer more resistance than that necessary to give Ord time to form, so I directed Merritt to fall back, and in retiring to shift Devin and Custer to the right so as to make room for Ord, now in the woods to my rear. Crook, who with his own and Mackenzie's divisions was on my extreme left covering some by-roads, was ordered to hold his ground as long as practicable without sacrificing his men, and, if forced to retire, to contest with obstinacy the enemy's advance.

As already stated, I could not direct General Ord's course, he being my senior, but hastily galloping back to where he was, at the edge of the timber, I explained to him what was taking place at the front.   Merritt's withdrawal inspired the Confederates, who forthwith began to press Crook, their line of battle advancing with confidence till it reached the crest whence I had reconnoitred them. From this ground they could see Ord's men emerging from the woods, and the hopelessness of a further attack being plain, the gray lines instinctively halted, and then began to retire toward a ridge immediately fronting Appomattox Court House, while Ord, joined on his right by the Fifth Corps, advanced on them over the ground that Merritt had abandoned.

I now directed my steps toward Merritt, who, having mounted his troopers, had moved them off to the right, and by the time I reached his headquarters flag he was ready for work, so a move on the enemy's left was ordered, and every guidon was bent to the front. As the cavalry marched along parallel with the Confederate line, and in toward its left, a heavy fire of artillery opened on us, but this could not check us at such a time, and we soon reached some high ground about half a mile from the Court House, and from here I could see in the low valley beyond the village the bivouac undoubtedly of Lee's army. The troops did not seem to be disposed in battle order, but on the other side of the bivouac was a line of battle - a heavy rear-guard -confronting, presumably, General Meade.

I decided to attack at once, and formations were ordered at a trot for a charge by Custer's and Devin's divisions down the slope leading to the camps. Custer was soon ready, but Devin's division being in rear its formation took longer, since he had to shift further to the right; Devin's preparations were, therefore, but partially completed when an aide-de-camp galloped up to me with the word from Custer, "Lee has surrendered; do not charge; the white flag is up. "The enemy perceiving that Custer was forming for attack, had sent the flag out to his front and stopped the charge just in time.   I at once sent word of the truce to General Ord, and hearing nothing more from Custer himself, I supposed that he had gone down to the Court House to join a mounted group of Confederates that I could see near there, so I, too, went toward them, galloping down a narrow ridge, staff and orderlies following; but we had not got half way to the Court House when, from a skirt of timber to our right, not more than three hundred yards distant, a musketry fire was opened on us. This halted us, when, waving my hat, I called out to the firing party that we were under a truce, and they were violating it.   This did not stop them, however, so we hastily took shelter in a ravine so situated as to throw a ridge between us and the danger.

We traveled in safety down this depression to its mouth, and thence by a gentle ascent approached the Court House. I was in advance, followed by a sergeant carrying my battle-flag. When I got within about a hundred and fifty yards of the enemy's line, which was immediately in front of the Court House, some of the Confed-

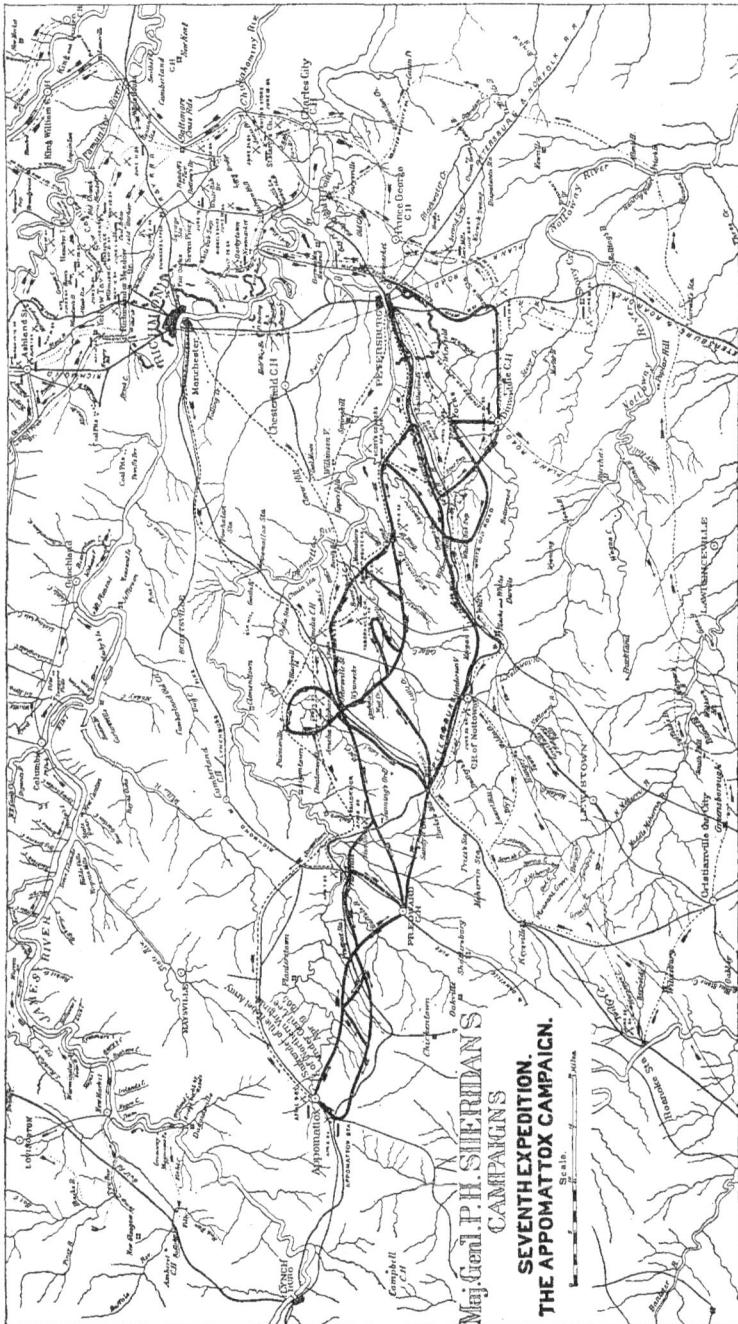

Maj. Gen. P. H. SHERIDAN'S
CAMPAIGNS

SEVENTH EXPEDITION.
THE APPOMATTOX CAMPAIGN.

Scale.

erates leveled their pieces at us, and I again halted. Their officers kept their men from firing, however, but meanwhile a single-handed contest had
begun behind me, for on looking back I heard a
Confederate soldier demanding my battle-flag
from the color-bearer, thinking, no doubt, that we
were coming in as prisoners. The sergeant had
drawn his sabre and was about to cut the man
down, but at a word from me he desisted and
carried the flag back to my staff, his assailant
quickly realizing that the boot was on the
other leg.

These incidents determined me to remain where
I was till the return of a staff-officer whom I had
sent over to demand an explanation from the
group of Confederates for which I had been heading. He came back in a few minutes with apologies for what had occurred, and informed me
that General Gordon and General Wilcox were
the superior officers in the group. As they wished
me to join them I rode up with my staff, but we
had hardly met when in front of Merritt firing
began. At the sound I turned to General Gordon,
who seemed embarrassed by the occurrence, and
remarked: "General, your men fired on me as I
was coming over here, and undoubtedly they are
treating Merritt and Custer the same way. We
might as well let them fight it out," He replied,

"There must be some mistake." I then asked, "Why not send a staff-officer and have your people cease firing; they are violating the flag." He answered, "I have no staff-officer to send." Whereupon I said that I would let him have one of mine, and calling for Lieutenant Vanderbilt Allen, I directed him to carry General Gordon's orders to General Geary, commanding a small brigade of South Carolina cavalry, to discontinue firing. Allen dashed off with the message and soon delivered it, but was made a prisoner, Geary saying, "I do not care for white flags: South Carolinians never surrender." By this time Merritt's patience being exhausted, he ordered an attack, and this in short order put an end to General Geary's "last ditch" absurdity, and extricated Allen from his predicament.

When quiet was restored Gordon remarked: "General Lee asks for a suspension of hostilities pending the negotiations which he is having with General Grant." I rejoined: "I have been constantly informed of the progress of the negotiations, and think it singular that while such discussions are going on, General Lee should have continued his march and attempted to break through my lines this morning. I will entertain no terms except that General Lee shall surrender to General Grant on his arrival here. If these terms are not accepted we will renew hostilities." Gordon replied: "General Lee's army is exhausted. There is no doubt of his surrender to General Grant."

It was then that General Ord joined us, and after shaking hands all around, I related the situation to him, and Gordon went away agreeing to meet us again in half an hour. When the time was up he came back accompanied by General Longstreet, who brought with him a despatch, the duplicate of one that had been sent General Grant through General Meade's lines back on the road over which Lee had been retreating.

General Longstreet renewed the assurances that already had been given by Gordon, and I sent Colonel Newhall with the despatch to find General Grant and bring him to the front. When Newhall started, everything on our side of the Appomattox Court House was quiet, for inevitable surrender was at hand, but Longstreet feared that Meade, in ignorance of the new conditions on my front might attack the Confederate rearguard. To prevent this I offered to send Colonel J. W. Forsyth through the enemy's lines to let Meade know of my agreement, for he too was suspicious that by a renewed correspondence Lee was endeavoring to gain time for escape. My offer being accepted, Forsyth set out accompanied

by Colonel Fairfax, of Longstreet's staff, and had
no difficulty in accomplishing his mission.
About five or six miles from Appomattox, on
the road toward Prospect Station near its intersection with the Walker's Church road, my adjutant-general, Colonel Newhall, met General Grant,
he having started from north of the Appomattox
River for my front the morning of April 9, in
consequence of the following despatches which
had been sent him the night before, after we had
captured Appomattox Station and established a
line intercepting Lee:

"CAVALRY HEADQUARTERS, April 8, 1865 - 9:20 P.M.
"LIEUTETANT-GENERAL U. S. GRANT,
    "Commanding Armies of the U. S.
"General: I marched early this morning from Buffalo Creek
and Prospect Station on Appomattox Station, where my scouts had
reported trains of cars with supplies for Lee's army.   A short time
before dark General Custer, who had the advance, made a dash at
the station, capturing four trains of supplies, with locomotives. One
of the trains was burned and the others were run back toward
Farmville for security.   Custer then pushed on toward Appomattox Court House, driving the enemy - who kept up a heavy fire
of artillery - charging them repeatedly and capturing, as far as
reported, twenty-five pieces of artillery and a number of prisoners and wagons.   The First Cavalry Division supported him on
the right.   A reconnoissance sent across the Appomattox reports
the enemy moving on the Cumberland road to Appomattox Station, where they expect to get supplies.   Custer is still pushing
on.   If General Gibbon and the Fifth Corps can get up to-night,
we will perhaps finish the job in the morning.   I do not think
Lee means to surrender until compelled to do so.
                    "P. H. SHERIDAN, Major-General."

"HEADQUARTERS CAVALRY, April 8, 1865 - 9:40 P.M.
"LIEUTENANT-GENERAL U. S. GRANT.
   "Commanding Armies U. S.
   "GENERAL: Since writing the accompanying despatch, General Custer reports that his command has captured in all thirty-five pieces of artillery, one thousand prisoners - including one general officer - and from one hundred and fifty to two hundred wagons.
                    "P. H. SHERIDAN, Major-General."

In attempting to conduct the lieutenant-general and staff back by a short route, Newhall lost his bearings for a time, inclining in toward the enemy's lines too far, but regained the proper direction without serious loss of time. General Grant arrived about 1 o'clock in the afternoon, Ord and I, dismounted, meeting him at the edge of the town, or crossroads, for it was little more. He remaining mounted, spoke first to me, saying simply, "How are you, Sheridan?" I assured him with thanks that I was "first-rate," when, pointing toward the village, he asked, "Is General Lee up there?" and I replied, "There is his army down in that valley, and he himself is over in that house (designating McLean's house) waiting to surrender to you." The General then said, "Come, let us go over," this last remark being addressed to both Ord and me. We two then mounted and joined him, while our staff-officers followed, intermingling with those of the general-in-chief as the cavalcade took its way to McLean's house near by, and where General Lee had arrived some time before, in consequence of a message from General Grant consenting to the interview asked for by Lee through Meade's front that morning-the consent having been carried by Colonel Babcock.

When I entered McLean's house General Lee was standing, as was also his military secretary, Colonel Marshall, his only staff-officer present. General Lee was dressed in a new uniform and wore a handsome sword. His tall, commanding form thus set off contrasted strongly with the short figure of General Grant, clothed as he was in a soiled suit, without sword or other insignia of his position except a pair of dingy shoulder-straps. After being presented, Ord and I, and nearly all of General Grant's staff, withdrew to await the agreement as to terms, and in a little while Colonel Babcock came to the door and said, "The surrender had been made; you can come in again."

When we re-entered General Grant was writing; and General Lee, having in his hand two despatches, which I that morning requested might be returned, as I had no copies of them, addressed me with the remark: "I am sorry. It is probable that my cavalry at that point of the line did not fully understand the agreement." These despatches had been sent in the forenoon, after the fighting had been stopped, notifying General Lee that some of his cavalry in front of Crook was violating the suspension of hostilities by withdrawing. About 3 o'clock in the afternoon the terms of surrender were written out and accepted, and General Lee left the house, as he departed cordially shaking hands with General Grant. A moment later he mounted his chunky gray horse, and lifting his hat as he passed out of the yard, rode off toward his army, his arrival there being announced to us by cheering, which, as it progressed, varying in loudness, told he was riding through the bivouac of the Army of Northern Virginia.

The surrender of General Lee practically ended the war of the rebellion. For four years his army had been the main-stay of the Confederacy; and the marked ability with which he directed its operations is evidenced both by his frequent successes and the length of time he kept up the contest. Indeed, it may be said that till General Grant was matched against him, he never met an opponent he did not vanquish, for while it is true that defeat was inflicted on the Confederates at Antietam and Gettysburg, yet the fruits of these victories were not gathered, for after each of these battles Lee was left unmolested till he had a chance to recuperate.

The assignment of General Grant to the command of the Union armies in the winter of 1863-64 gave presage of success from the start, for his eminent abilities had already been proved, and be-sides, he was a tower of strength to the Govern-ment, because he had the confidence of the people. They knew that henceforth systematic direction would be given to our armies in every section of the vast territory over which active operations were being prosecuted, and further, that this co-herence, this harmony of plan, was the one thing needed to end the war, for in the three preceding years there had been illustrated most lamentable effects of the absence of system. From the mo-ment he set our armies in motion simultaneously, in the spring of 1864, it could be seen that we should be victorious ultimately, for though on different lines we were checked now and then, yet we were harassing the Confederacy at so many vital points that plainly it must yield to our blows. Against Lee's army, the forefront of the Confederacy, Grant pitted himself ; and it may be said that the Confederate commander was now, for the first time, overmatched, for against all his devices - the products of a mind fertile in defense - General Grant brought to bear not only the wealth of ex-pedient which had hitherto distinguished him, but also an imperturbable tenacity, particularly in the Wilderness and on the march to the James, with-

out which the almost insurmountable obstacles of
that campaign could not have been overcome.
During it and in the siege of Petersburg he met
with many disappointments - on several occasions
the shortcomings of generals, when at the point of
success, leading to wretched failures. But so far
as he was concerned, the only apparent effect of
these discomfitures was to make him all the more
determined to discharge successfully the stupendous trust committed to his care, and to bring into
play the manifold resources of his well - ordered
military mind. He guided every subordinate then,
and in the last days of the rebellion, with a fund
of common sense and superiority of intellect, which
have left an impress so distinct as to exhibit his
great personality. When his military history is
analyzed after the lapse of years, it will show, even
more clearly than now, that during these as well
as in his previous campaigns he was the steadfast
centre about and on which everything else turned.

CHAPTER IX.

ORDERED TO GREENSBORO, N. C. - MARCH TO THE DAN
RIVER - ASSIGNED TO THE COMMAND WEST OF
THE MISSISSIPPI - LEAVING WASHINGTON - FLIGHT
OF GENERAL EARLY - MAXIMILIAN - MAKING
DEMONSTRATIONS ON THE UPPER RIO GRANDE-
CONFEDERATES JOIN MAXIMILIAN - THE FRENCH
INVASION OF MEXICO AND ITS RELATIONS TO THE
REBELLION - ASSISTING THE LIBERALS - RESTORA-
TION OF THE REPUBLIC.

T HE surrender at Appomattox put a stop to all
military operations on the part of General
Grant's forces, and the morning of April 10 my
cavalry began its march to Petersburg, the men
anticipating that they would soon be mustered
out and returned to their homes. At Nottoway
Court House I heard of the assassination of the
President. The first news came to us the night
after the dastardly deed, the telegraph operator
having taken it from the wires while in transmis-
sion to General Meade. The despatch ran that
Mr. Lincoln had been shot at 10 o'clock that
morning at Willard's Hotel, but as I could conceive of nothing to take the President there I set
the story down as a canard, and went to bed with-

out giving it further thought. Next morning, however, an official telegram confirmed the fact of the assassination, though eliminating the distorted circumstances that had been communicated the night before.

When we reached Petersburg my column was halted, and instructions given me to march the cavalry and the Sixth Corps to Greensboro', North Carolina, for the purpose of aiding General Sherman (the surrender of General Johnston having not yet been effected), so I made the necessary preparations and moved on the 24th of April, arriving at South Boston, on the Dan River, the 28th, the Sixth Corps having reached Danville meanwhile. At South Boston I received a despatch from General Halleck, who immediately after Lee's surrender had been assigned to command at Richmond, informing me that General Johnston had been brought to terms. The necessity for going farther south being thus obviated we retraced our steps to Petersburg, from which place I proceeded by steamer to Washington, leaving the cavalry to be marched thither by easy stages.

The day after my arrival in Washington an important order was sent me, accompanied by the following letter of instructions, transferring me to a new field of operations:

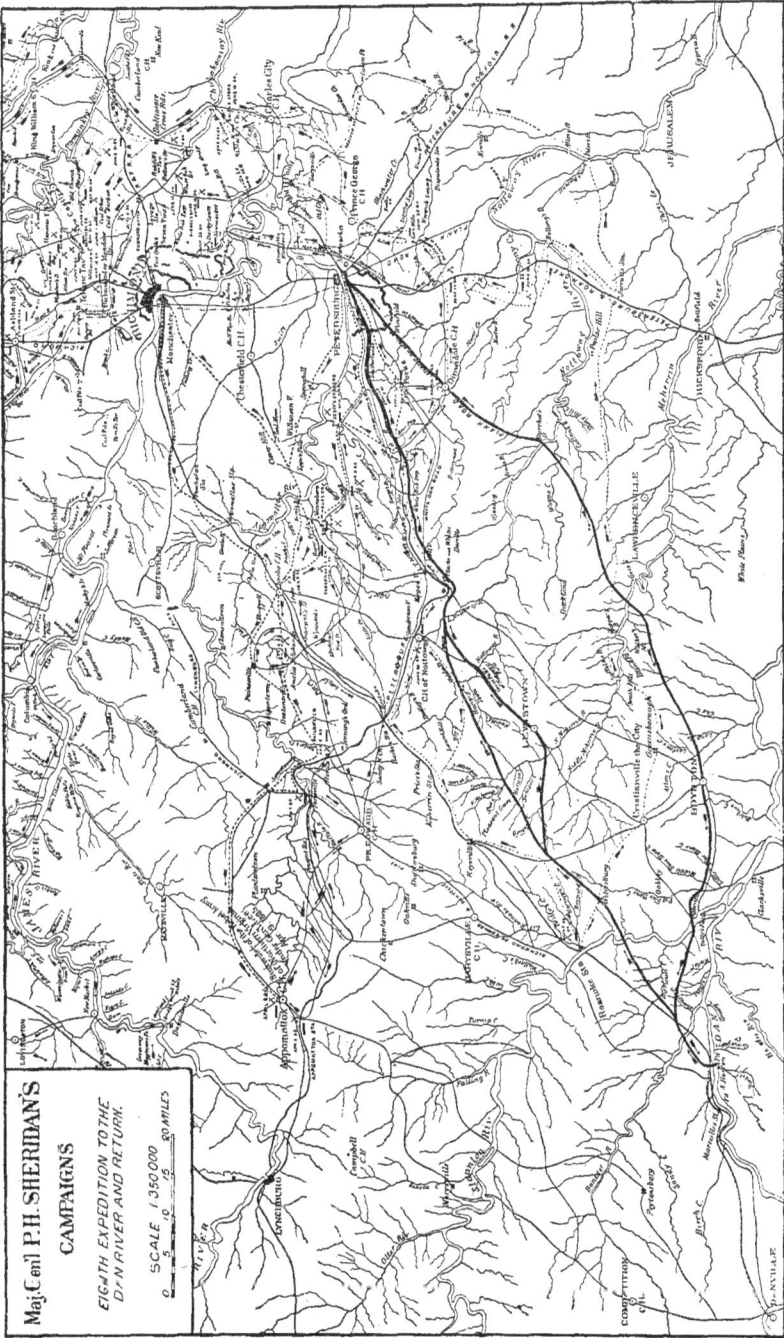

Maj.Genl P.H.SHERIDAN'S
CAMPAIGNS

EIG-4TH EXPEDITION TO THE
DI-N RIVER AND RETURN.

SCALE 1:350,000

5   0   5   10   20 MILES

"HEADQUARTERS ARMIES OF THE UNITED STATES.
"Washington, D. C., May 17, 1865.

"GENERAL: Under the orders relieving you from the command of the Middle Military Division and assigning you to command west of the Mississippi, you will proceed without delay to the West to arrange all preliminaries for your new field of duties.

"Your duty is to restore Texas, and that part of Louisiana held by the enemy, to the Union in the shortest practicable time, in a way most effectual for securing permanent peace.

"To do this, you will be given all the troops that can be spared by Major-General Canby, probably twenty-five thousand men of all arms; the troops with Major-General J. J. Reynolds, in Arkansas, say twelve thousand, Reynolds to command; the Fourth Army Corps, now at Nashville, Tennessee, awaiting orders; and the Twenty-Fifth Army Corps, now at City Point, Virginia, ready to embark.

"I do not wish to trammel you with instructions; I will state, however, that if Smith holds out, without even an ostensible government to receive orders from or to report to, he and his men are not entitled to the considerations due to an acknowledged belligerent. Theirs are the conditions of outlaws, making war against the only Government having an existence over the territory where war is now being waged.

"You may notify the rebel commander west of the Mississippi - holding intercourse with him in person, or through such officers of the rank of major-general as you may select - that he will be allowed to surrender all his forces on the same terms as were accorded to Lee and Johnston. If he accedes, proceed to garrison the Red River as high up as Shreveport, the seaboard at Galveston, Malagorda Bay, Corpus Christi, and mouth of the Rio Grande.

"Place a strong force on the Rio Grande, holding it at least to a point opposite Camargo, and above that if supplies can be procured.

"In case of an active campaign (a hostile one) I think a heavy force should be put on the Rio Grande as a first preliminary. Troops for this might be started at once. The Twenty-Fifth

Corps is now available, and to it should be added a force of white troops, say those now under Major-General Steele.

"To be clear on this last point, I think the Rio Grande should be strongly held, whether the forces in Texas surrender or not, and that no time should be lost in getting troops there. If war is to be made, they will be in the right place; if Kirby Smith surrenders, they will be on the line which is to be strongly garrisoned.

"Should any force be necessary other than those designated, they can be had by calling for them on Army Headquarters.

"U. S. GRANT,
"Lieutenant-General.
"To MAJOR-GENERAL P. H. SHERIDAN,
"United States Army."

On receipt of these instructions I called at once on General Grant, to see if they were to be considered so pressing as to preclude my remaining in Washington till after the Grand Review, which was fixed for the 23d and 24th of May, for naturally I had a strong desire to head my command on that great occasion. But the General told me that it was absolutely necessary to go at once to force the surrender of the Confederates under Kirby Smith. He also told me that the States lately in rebellion would be embraced in two or three military departments, the commanders of which would control civil affairs until Congress took action about restoring them to the Union, since that course would not only be economical and simple, but would give the Southern people confidence, and encourage them to go to work, instead of distracting them with politics.

At this same interview he informed me that there was an additional motive in sending me to the new command, a motive not explained by the instructions themselves, and went on to say that, as a matter of fact, he looked upon the invasion of Mexico by Maximilian as a part of the rebellion itself, because of the encouragement that invasion had received from the Confederacy, and that our success in putting down secession would never be complete till the French and Austrian invaders were compelled to quit the territory of our sister republic.   With regard to this matter, though, he said it would be necessary for me to act with great circumspection, since the Secretary of State, Mr. Seward, was much opposed to the use of our troops along the border in any active way that would be likely to involve us in a war with European powers.

Under the circumstances, my disappointment at not being permitted to participate in the review had to be submitted to, and I left Washington without an opportunity of seeing again in a body the men who, while under my command, had gone through so many trials and unremittingly pursued and assailed the enemy, from the beginning of the campaign of 1864 till the white flag came into their hands at Appomattox Court House.

I went first to St. Louis, and there took the

steamboat for New Orleans, and when near the mouth of the Red River received word from General Canby that Kirby Smith had surrendered under terms similar to those accorded Lee and Johnston. But the surrender was not carried out in good faith, particularly by the Texas troops, though this I did not learn till some little time afterward, when I was informed that they had marched off to the interior of the State in several organized bodies, carrying with them their camp equipage, arms, ammunition, and even some artillery, with the ultimate purpose of going to Mexico. In consequence of this, and also because of the desire of the Government to make a strong showing of force in Texas, I decided to traverse the State with two columns of cavalry, directing one to San Antonio under Merritt, the other to Houston under Custer.

Both commands were to start from the Red River - Shreveport and Alexandria being the respective initial points - and in organizing the columns, to the mounted force already on the Red River were added several regiments of cavalry from the east bank of the Mississippi, and in a singular way one of these fell upon the trail of my old antagonist, General Early. While crossing the river somewhere below Vicksburg some of the men noticed a suspicious looking party being ferried over in a rowboat, behind which two horses were swimming in tow. Chase was given, and the horses, being abandoned by the party, fell into the hands of our troopers, who, however, failed to capture or identify the people in the boat. As subsequently ascertained, the men were companions of Early, who was already across the Mississippi, hidden in the woods, on his way with two or three of these followers to join the Confederates in Texas, not having heard of Kirby Smith's surrender. A week or two later I received a letter from Early describing the affair, and the capture of the horses, for which he claimed pay, on the ground that they were private property, because he had taken them in battle. The letter also said that any further pursuit of Early would be useless, as he "expected to be on the deep blue sea" by the time his communication reached me. The unfortunate man was fleeing from imaginary dangers, however, for striking his trail was purely ac--cidental, and no effort whatever was being made to arrest him personally. Had this been specially desired it might have been accomplished very readily just after Lee's surrender, for it was an open secret that Early was then not far away, pretty badly disabled with rheumatism.

By the time the two columns were ready to set out for San Antonio and Houston, General Frank Herron, with one division of the Thirteenth Corps, occupied Galveston, and another division under General Fred Steele had gone to Brazos Santiago, to hold Brownsville and the line of the Rio Grande, the object being to prevent, as far as possible, the escaping Confederates from joining Maximilian. With this purpose in view, and not forgetting Grant's conviction that the French invasion of Mexico was linked with the rebellion, I asked for an increase of force to send troops into Texas - in fact, to concentrate at available points in the State an army strong enough to move against the invaders of Mexico if occasion demanded. The Fourth and Twenty-fifth army corps being ordered to report to me accordingly, I sent the Fourth Corps to Victoria and San Antonio, and the bulk of the Twenty-fifth to Brownsville. Then came the feeding and caring for all these troops -a difficult matter - for those at Victoria and San Antonio had to be provisioned overland from Indianola across the "hog-wallow prairie," while the supplies for the forces at Brownsville and along the Rio Grande must come by way of Brazos Santiago, from which point I was obliged to construct, with the labor of the men, a railroad to Clarksville, a distance of about eighteen miles.

The latter part of June 1 repaired to Brownsville myself to impress the Imperialists, as much as possible, with the idea that we intended hostilities, and took along my chief of scouts - Major Young - and four of his most trusty men, whom I had had sent from Washington. From Brownsville I despatched all these men to important points in northern Mexico, to glean information regarding the movements of the Imperial forces, and also to gather intelligence about the ex-Confederates who had crossed the Rio Grande. On information furnished by these scouts, I caused General Steele to make demonstrations all along the lower Rio Grande, and at the same time demanded the return of certain munitions of war that had been turned over by ex-Confederates to the Imperial General (Mejia) commanding at Matamoras. These demands, backed up as they were by such a formidable show of force, created much agitation and demoralization among the Imperial troops, and measures looking to the abandonment of northern Mexico were forthwith adopted by those in authority - a policy that would have resulted in the speedy evacuation of the entire country by Maximilian, had not our Government weakened; contenting itself with a few pieces of the contraband artillery varnished over with the Imperial apologies. A golden opportunity was lost, for we had ample excuse for crossing the boundary, but Mr. Seward, being, as I have already stated, unalterably opposed to any act

likely to involve us in war, insisted on his course
of negotiation with Napoleon.

As the summer wore away, Maximilian, under
Mr. Seward's policy, gained in strength till finally
all the accessible sections of Mexico were in his
possession, and the Republic under President
Juarez almost succumbed. Growing impatient at
this, in the latter part of September I decided to
try again what virtue there might be in a hostile
demonstration, and selected the upper Rio Grande
for the scene of my attempt. Merritt's cavalry
and the Fourth Corps still being at San Antonio,
I went to that place and reviewed these troops,
and having prepared them with some ostentation
for a campaign, of course it was bruited about
that we were going to invade Mexico. Then, escorted by a regiment of horse I proceeded hastily
to Fort Duncan, on the Rio Grande just opposite
the Mexican town of Piedras Negras. Here I
opened communication with President Juarez,
through one of his staff, taking care not to do this
in the dark, and the news, spreading like wildfire,
the greatest significance was ascribed to my action, it being reported most positively and with
many specific details that I was only awaiting the
arrival of the troops, then under marching orders
at San Antonio, to cross the Rio Grande in behalf
of the Liberal cause.

Ample corroboration of the reports then circulated was found in my inquiries regarding the quantity of forage we could depend upon getting in Mexico, our arrangements for its purchase, and my sending a pontoon train to Brownsville, together with which was cited the renewed activity of the troops along the lower Rio Grande. These reports and demonstrations resulted in alarming the Imperialists so much that they withdrew the French and Austrian soldiers from Matamoras, and practically abandoned the whole of northern Mexico as far down as Monterey, with the exception of Matamoras, where General Mejia continued to hang on with a garrison of renegade Mexicans.

The abandonment of so much territory in northern Mexico encouraged General Escobedo and other Liberal leaders to such a degree that they collected a considerable army of their followers at Comargo, Mier, and other points. At the same time that unknown quantity, Cortinas, suspended his freebooting for the nonce, and stoutly harassing Matamoras, succeeded in keeping its Imperial garrison within the fortifications. Thus countenanced and stimulated, and largely supplied with arms and ammunition, which we left at convenient places on our side of the river to fall into their hands, the Liberals, under General Escobedo - a man of much force of character - were enabled in northern Mexico to place the affairs of the Republic on a substantial basis.

But in the midst of what bade fair to cause a final withdrawal of the foreigners, we were again checked by our Government, as a result of representations of the French Minister at Washington. In October, he wrote to Mr. Seward that the United States troops on the Rio Grande were acting "in exact opposition to the repeated assurances Your Excellency has given me concerning the desire of the Cabinet at Washington to preserve the most strict neutrality in the events now taking place in Mexico," and followed this statement with an emphatic protest against our course. Without any investigation whatever by our State Department, this letter of the French Minister was transmitted to me, accompanied by directions to preserve a strict neutrality; so, of course, we were again debarred from anything like active sympathy.

After this, it required the patience of Job to abide the slow and poky methods of our State Department, and, in truth, it was often very difficult to restrain officers and men from crossing the Rio Grande with hostile purpose. Within the knowledge of my troops, there had gone on formerly the transfer of organized bodies of ex-Confederates to Mexico, in aid of the Imperialists, and at this period it was known that there was in preparation an immigration scheme having in view the colonizing, at Cordova and one or two other places, of all the discontented elements of the defunct Confederacy - Generals Price, Magruder, Maury, and other high personages being promoters of the enterprise, which Maximilian took to readily. He saw in it the possibilities of a staunch support to his throne, and therefore not only sanctioned the project, but encouraged it with large grants of land, inspirited the promoters with titles of nobility, and, in addition, instituted a system of peonage, expecting that the silver hook thus baited would be largely swallowed by the Southern people.

The announcement of the scheme was followed by the appointment of commissioners in each of the Southern States to send out emigrants; but before any were deluded into starting, I made to General Grant a report of what was going on, with the recommendation that measures be taken, through our State Department, looking to the suppression of the colony; but, as usual, nothing could be effected through that channel; so, as an alternative, I published, in April, 1866, by authority of General Grant, an order prohibiting the embarkation from ports in Louisiana and Texas, for ports in Mexico, of any person without a permit from my headquarters. This dampened the ardor of everybody in the Gulf States who had planned to go to Mexico; and although the projectors of the Cordova Colonization Scheme - the name by which it was known - secured a few innocents from other districts, yet this set-back led ultimately to failure.

Among the Liberal leaders along the Rio Grande during this period there sprang up many factional differences from various causes, some personal, others political, and some, I regret to say, from downright moral obliquity - as, for example, those between Cortinas and Canales - who, though generally hostile to the Imperialists, were freebooters enough to take a shy at each other frequently, and now and then even to join forces against Escobedo, unless we prevented them by coaxing or threats. A general who could unite these several factions was therefore greatly needed, and on my return to New Orleans I so telegraphed General Grant, and he, thinking General Caravajal (then in Washington seeking aid for the Republic) would answer the purpose, persuaded him to report to me in New Orleans. Caravajal promptly appeared, but he did not impress me very favorably. He was old and cranky, yet, as he seemed anxious to do his best, I sent him over to Brownsville, with credentials, authorizing him to cross into Mexico, and followed him myself by the next boat. When I arrived in Brownsville, matters in Matamoras had already reached a crisis. General Mejia, feeling keenly the moral support we were giving the Liberals, and hard pressed by the harassing attacks of Cortinas and Canales, had abandoned the place, and Caravajal, because of his credentials from our side, was in command, much to the dissatisfaction of both those chiefs whose differences it was intended he should reconcile.

The day after I got to Brownsville I visited Matamoras, and had a long interview with Caravajal. The outcome of this meeting was, on my part, a stronger conviction than ever that he was unsuitable, and I feared that either Canales or Cortinas would get possession of the city. Caravajal made too many professions of what he would do -in short, bragged too much - but as there was no help for the situation, I made the best of it by trying to smooth down the ruffled feathers of Canales and Cortinas. In my interview with Caravajal I recommended Major Young as a confidential man, whom he could rely upon as a "go-between" for communicating with our people at Brownsville, and whom he could trust to keep him informed of the affairs of his own country as well.

A day or two afterward I recrossed the Gulf to New Orleans, and then, being called from my headquarters to the interior of Texas, a fortnight passed before I heard anything from Brownsville. In the meanwhile Major Young had come to New Orleans, and organized there a band of men to act as a body-guard for Caravajal, the old wretch having induced him to accept the proposition by representing that it had my concurrence. I at once condemned the whole business, but Young, having been furnished with seven thousand dollars to recruit the men and buy their arms, had already secured both, and was so deeply involved in the transaction, he said, that he could not withdraw without dishonor, and with tears in his eyes he besought me to help him. He told me he had entered upon the adventure in the firm belief that I would countenance it; that the men and their equipment were on his hands; that he must make good his word at all hazards; and that while I need not approve, yet I must go far enough to consent to the departure of the men, and to loan him the money necessary to provision his party and hire a schooner to carry them to Brazos. It was hard indeed to resist the appeals of this man, who had served me so long and so well, and the result of his pleading was that I gave him permission to sail, and also loaned him the sum asked for; but

I have never ceased to regret my consent, for misfortune fell upon the enterprise almost from its inception.

By the time the party got across the Gulf and over to Brownsville, Caravajal had been deposed by Canales, and the latter would not accept their services. This left Young with about fifty men to whom he was accountable, and as he had no money to procure them subsistence, they were in a bad fix. The only thing left to do was to tender their services to General Escobedo, and with this in view the party set out to reach the General's camp, marching up the Rio Grande on the American side, intending to cross near Ringgold Barracks. In advance of them, however, had spread far and wide the tidings of who they were, what they proposed to do, and where they were going, and before they could cross into Mexico they were attacked by a party of ex-Confederates and renegade Mexican rancheros. Being on American soil, Young forbade his men to return the fire, and bent all his efforts to getting them over the river; but in this attempt they were broken up, and became completely demoralized. A number of the men were drowned while swimming the river, Young himself was shot and killed, a few were captured, and those who escaped - about twenty in all - finally joined Escobedo, but in such a plight as to be of little use. With this distressing affair came to an end pretty much all open participation of American sympathizers with the Liberal cause, but the moral support afforded by the presence of our forces continued, and this was frequently supplemented with material aid in the shape of munitions of war, which we liberally supplied, though constrained to do so by the most secret methods.

The term of office of Juarez as President of the Mexican Republic expired in December, 1865, but to meet existing exigencies he had continued himself in office by proclamation, a course rendered necessary by the fact that no elections could be held on account of the Imperial occupation of most of the country. The official who, by the Mexican Constitution, is designated for the succession in such an emergency, is the President of the Supreme Court, and the person then eligible under this provision was General Ortega, but in the interest of the Imperialists he had absented himself from Mexico, hence the patriotic course of Juarez in continuing himself at the head of affairs was a necessity of the situation. This action of the President gave the Imperialists little concern at first, but with the revival of the Liberal cause they availed themselves of every means to divide its supporters, and Ortega, who had been lying low in the United States, now came forward to claim the Presidency. Though ridiculously late for such a step, his first act was to issue a manifesto protesting against the assumption of the executive authority by Juarez. The protest had little effect, however, and his next proceeding was to come to New Orleans, get into correspondence with other disaffected Mexicans, and thus perfect his plans. When he thought his intrigue ripe enough for action, he sailed for Brazos, in tending to cross the Rio Grande and assert his claims with arms. While he was scheming in-New Orleans, however, I had learned what he was up to, and in advance of his departure had sent instructions to have him arrested on American soil. Colonel Sedgwick, commanding at Brownsville, was now temporary master of Matamoras also, by reason of having stationed some American troops there for the protection of neutral merchants, so when Ortega appeared at Brazos, Sedgwick quietly arrested him and held him till the city of Matamoras was turned over to General Escobedo, the authorized representative of Juarez; then Escobedo took charge of Ortega, and with ease prevented his further machinations.

During the winter and spring of 1866 we continued covertly supplying arms and ammunition to the Liberals - sending as many as 30,000 mus-

BELLE-GROVE HOUSE. GENERAL SHERIDAN'S HEADQUARTERS AT CEDAR CREEK

kets from Baton Rouge Arsenal alone - and by mid-summer Juarez, having organized a pretty good sized army, was in possession of the whole line of the Rio Grande, and, in fact, of nearly the whole of Mexico down to San Louis Potosi. Then thick and fast came rumors pointing to the tottering condition of Maximilians Empire - first, that Orizaba and Vera Cruz were being fortified; then, that the French were to be withdrawn; and later came the intelligence that the Empress Carlotta had gone home to beg assistance from Napoleon, the author of all of her husbands troubles. But the situation forced Napoleon to turn a deaf ear to Carlottas prayers. The broken-hearted woman besought him on her knees, but his fear of losing an army made all pleadings vain. In fact, as I ascertained by the following cablegram which came into my hands, Napoleons instructions for the French evacuation were in Mexico at the very time of this pathetic scene between him and Carlotta. The despatch was in cipher when I received it, but was translated by the telegraph operator at my headquarters, who long before had mastered the key of the French cipher:

"PARIS, January 10, 1867.
"FRENCH CONSUL, New Orleans, La.
"To GENERAL CASTELNAU, at Mexico.
"Received your despatch of the 9th December. Do not compel the Emperor to abdicate, but do not delay the departure of

the troops; bring back all those who will not remain there. Most of the fleet has left.

"NAPOLEON."

This meant the immediate withdrawal of the French. The rest of the story-which has necessarily been but an outline - is soon told. Maximilian, though deserted, determined to hold out to the last, and with the aid of disloyal Mexicans stuck to his cause till the spring. When taken prisoner at Queretaro, he was tried and executed under circumstances that are well known. From promptings of humanity Secretary Seward tried hard to save the Imperial prisoner, but without success. The Secretary's plea for mercy was sent through me at New Orleans, and to make speed I hired a steamer to proceed with it across the Gulf to Tampico. The document was carried by Sergeant White, one of my scouts, who crossed the country from Tampico, and delivered it to Escobedo at Queretaro; but Mr. Seward's representations were without avail - refused probably because little mercy had been shown certain Liberal leaders unfortunate enough to fall into Maximilian's hands during the prosperous days of his Empire.

At the close of our war there was little hope for the Republic of Mexico. Indeed, till our troops were concentrated on the Rio Grande there was none. Our appearance in such force along the border permitted the Liberal leaders, refugees from their homes, to establish rendezvous whence they could promulgate their plans in safety, while the countenance thus given the cause, when hope was wellnigh gone, incited the Mexican people to renewed resistance. Beginning again with very scant means, for they had lost about all, the Liberals saw their cause, under the influence of such significant and powerful backing, progress and steadily grow so strong that within two years imperialism had received its death-blow. I doubt very much whether such results could have been achieved without the presence of an American army on the Rio Grande, which, be it remembered, was sent there because, in General Grant's words, the French invasion of Mexico was so closely related to the rebellion as to be essentially a part of it.

CHAPTER X.

ALTHOUGH in 1865-66 much of my attention was directed to international matters along the Rio Grande, the civil affairs of Texas and Louisiana required a certain amount of military supervision also in the absence of regularly established civil authority. At the time of Kirby Smith's surrender the National Government had formulated no plan with regard to these or the other States lately in rebellion, though a provisional Government had been set up in Louisiana as early as 1864. In consequence of this lack of system, Governor Pendleton Murray, of Texas, who was elected under Confederate rule, continued to discharge the duties of Governor till President Johnson, on June 17, in harmony with his amnesty proclamation of May 29, 1865, appointed A. J. Hamilton provisional Governor. Hamilton was empowered by the President to call a Constitutional convention, the delegates to which were to be elected, under certain prescribed qualifications, for the purpose of organizing the political affairs of the State, the Governor to be guided by instructions similar to those given the provisional Governor of North Carolina (W. W. Holden), when appointed in May.

The convening of this body gave rise to much dissatisfaction among the people of Texas. They had assumed that affairs were to go on as of old, and that the reintegration of the State was to take place under the administration of Governor Murray, who, meanwhile, had taken it upon himself, together with the Legislature, to authorize the election of delegates to a State Convention, without restriction as to who should be entitled to vote. Thus encouraged, the element but lately in armed rebellion was now fully bent on restoring the State to the Union without any intervention whatever of the Federal Government; but the advent of Hamilton put an end to such illusions, since his proclamation promptly disfranchised the element in question, whose consequent disappoint-

ment and chagrin were so great as to render this
factor of the community almost uncontrollable.
The provisional Governor at once rescinded the
edict of Governor Murray, prohibited the assembling of his convention, and shortly after called
one himself,. the delegates to which were to be
chosen by voters who could take the amnesty
oath. The proclamation convening this assemblage also announced the policy that would be pursued in governing the State until its affairs were
satisfactorily reorganized, defined in brief the
course to be followed by the Judiciary, and provided for the appointment, by the Governor, of
county officials to succeed those known to be
disloyal. As this action of Hamilton's disfranchised all who could not take the amnesty oath,
and of course deprived them of the offices, it met
at once with pronounced and serious opposition,
and he quickly realized that he had on his hands
an arduous task to protect the colored people,
particularly as in the transition state of society
just after the close of the war there prevailed
much lawlessness, which vented itself chiefly on
the freedmen. It was greatly feared that political rights were to be given those so recently in
servitude, and as it was generally believed that
such enfranchisement would precipitate a race war
unless the freedmen were overawed and kept in a

state of subjection, acts of intimidation were soon reported from all parts of the State.

Hamilton, an able, determined, and fearless man, tried hard to curb this terrorism, but public opinion being strong against him, he could accomplish little without military aid. As department commander, I was required, whenever called upon, to assist his government, and as these requisitions for help became necessarily very frequent, the result was that shortly after he assumed his duties, detachments of troops were stationed in nearly every county of the State. By such disposition of my forces fairly good order was maintained under the administration of Hamilton, and all went well till the inauguration of J. W. Throckmorton, who, elected Governor in pursuance of an authorization granted by the convention which Hamilton had called together, assumed the duties of the office August 9, 1866.

One of Governor Throckmorton's first acts was to ask the withdrawal or non-interference of the military. This was not all granted, but under his ingenious persuasion President Johnson, on the 13th of August, 1866, directed that the new State officials be entrusted with the unhampered control of civil affairs, and this was more than enough to revive the bulldozing methods that had characterized the beginning of Hamilton's administration. Oppressive legislation in the shape of certain apprentice and vagrant laws quickly followed, developing a policy of gross injustice toward the colored people on the part of the courts, and a reign of lawlessness and disorder ensued which, throughout the remote districts of the State at least, continued till Congress, by what are known as the Reconstruction Acts, took into its own hands the rehabilitation of the seceded States.

In the State of Louisiana a provisional government, chosen by the loyal element, had been put in operation, as already mentioned, as early as 1864. This was effected under encouragement given by President Lincoln, through the medium of a Constitutional convention, which met at New Orleans in April, 1864, and adjourned in July. The constitution then agreed upon was submitted to the people, and in September, 1864, was ratified by a vote of the few loyal residents of the State.

The government provided under this constitution being looked upon as provisional merely, was never recognized by Congress, and in 1865 the returned Confederates, restored to citizenship by the President's amnesty proclamation, soon got control of almost all the State. The Legislature was in their hands, as well as most of the State and municipal offices; so, when the President, on the 20th of August, 1866, by proclamation, extended his previous instructions regarding civil affairs in Texas so as to have them apply to all the seceded States, there at once began in Louisiana a system of discriminative legislation directed against the freedmen, that led to flagrant wrongs in the enforcement of labor contracts, and in the remote parishes to numbers of outrages and murders.

To remedy this deplorable condition of things, it was proposed, by those who had established the government of 1864, to remodel the constitution of the State; and they sought to do this by reassembling the convention, that body before its adjournment having provided for reconvening under certain conditions, in obedience to the call of its president. Therefore, early in the summer of 1866, many members of this convention met in conference at New Orleans, and decided that a necessity existed for reconvening the delegates, and a proclamation was issued accordingly by B. K. Howell, President *pro tempore.*

Mayor John T. Monroe and the other officials of New Orleans looked upon this proposed action as revolutionary, and by the time the convention assembled (July 30), such bitterness of feeling prevailed that efforts were made by the mayor and city police to suppress the meeting. A bloody riot followed, resulting in the killing and wounding of about a hundred and sixty persons.

I happened to be absent from the city at the time, returning from Texas, where I had been called by affairs on the Rio Grande. On my way up from the mouth of the Mississippi I was met on the night of July 30 by one of my staff, who reported what had occurred, giving the details of the massacre - no milder term is fitting - and informing me that, to prevent further slaughter, General Baird, the senior military officer present, had assumed control of the municipal government. On reaching the city I made an investigation, and that night sent the following report of the affair:

"HEADQUARTERS MILITARY DIVISION OF THE GULF,
"NEW ORLEANS, LA., Aug. 1, 1866.

" GENERAL U. S. GRANT :

"You are doubtless aware of the serious riot which occurred in this city on the 30th. A political body, styling themselves the Convention of 1864, met on the 30th, for, as it is alleged, the purpose of remodeling the present constitution of the State. The leaders were political agitators and revolutionary men, and the action of the convention was liable to produce breaches of the public peace. I had made up my mind to arrest the head men, if the proceedings of the convention were calculated to disturb the tranquility of the Department; but I had no cause for action until they committed the overt act. In the meantime official duty called me to Texas, and the mayor of the city, during my absence, suppressed the convention by the use of the police force, and in so doing attacked the members of the convention, and a party of two hundred negroes, with fire-arms, clubs, and knives, in a manner so unnecessary and atrocious as to compel me to say that it was murder. About forty whites and blacks were thus killed, and about one hundred and sixty wounded. Everything is now quiet, but I deem it best to maintain a military supremacy in the city for a few days, until the affair is fully investigated. I believe the sentiment of the general community is great regret at this unnecessary cruelty, and that the police could have made any arrest they saw fit without sacrificing lives.

"P. H. SHERIDAN,
"Major-General   Commanding."

On receiving the telegram, General Grant immediately submitted it to the President. Much clamor being made at the North for the publication of the despatch, Mr. Johnson pretended to give it to the newspapers. It appeared in the issues of August 4, but with this paragraph omitted, viz.:

"I had made up my mind to arrest the head men, if the proceedings of the convention were calculated to disturb the tranquility of the Department, but I had no cause for action until they committed the overt act. In the mean time official duty called me to Texas, and the mayor of the city, during my absence, suppressed the convention by the use of the police force, and in so doing attacked the members of the convention, and a party of two hundred negroes, with fire-arms, clubs, and knives, in a manner so unnecessary and atrocious as to compel me to say it was murder."

Against this garbling of my report - done by the President́s own order - I strongly demurred; and this emphatic protest marks the beginning of

Mr. Johnson's well-known personal hostility toward me. In the mean time I received (on August 3) the following despatch from General Grant approving my course :

"HEADQUARTERS ARMIES OF THE UNITED STATES,
"WAR DEPT., WASHINGTON, D. C.,
"August 3, 1866 - 5 P. M.
"MAJOR-GENERAL P. H. SHERIDAN,
"Commanding Mil. Div. of the Gulf,
"New Orleans, La.:
"Continue to enforce martial law, so far as may be necessary to preserve the peace; and do not allow any of the civil authorities to act, if you deem such action dangerous to the public safety. Lose no time in investigating and reporting the causes that led to the riot, and the facts which occurred.
"U. S. GRANT,
"Lieutenant-General."

In obedience to the President's directions, my report of August I was followed by another, more in detail, which I give in full, since it tells the whole story of the riot:

"HEADQUARTERS MILITARY DIVISION OF THE GULF,
"NEW ORLEANS, LA., August 6, 1866.
"HIS EXCELLENCY ANDREW JOHNSON,
"President United States:
"I have the honor to make the following reply to your despatch of August 4. A very large number of colored people marched in procession on Friday night, July twenty-seven (27), and were addressed from the steps of the City Hall by Dr. Dostie, ex-Governor Hahn, and others. The speech of Dostie was intemperate in language and sentiment. The speeches of the others, so far as I can learn, were characterized by moderation.

I have not given you the words of Dostie's speech, as the version published was denied; but from what I have learned of the man, I believe they were intemperate.

"The convention assembled at twelve (12) M. on the thirtieth (30), the timid members absenting themselves because the tone of the general public was ominous of trouble. I think there were about twenty-six (26) members present. In front of the Mechanics Institute, where the meeting was held, there were assembled some colored men, women, and children, perhaps eighteen (18) or twenty (20), and in the Institute a number of colored men, probably one hundred and fifty (150).   Among those outside and inside there might have been a pistol in the possession of every tenth (IO) man.

"About one (1) P. M. a procession of say from sixty (60) to one hundred and thirty (130) colored men marched up Burgundy Street and across Canal Street toward the convention, carrying an American flag. These men had about one pistol to every ten men, and canes and clubs in addition.   While crossing Canal Street a row occurred. There were many spectators on the street, and their manner and tone toward the procession unfriendly. A shot was fired, by whom I am not able to state, but believe it to have been by a policeman, or some colored man in the procession.   This led to other shots and a rush after the procession. On arrival at the front of the Institute there was some throwing of brickbats by both sides.   The police, who had been held well in hand, were vigorously marched to the scene of disorder. The procession entered the Institute with the flag, about six (6) or eight (8) remaining outside.   A row occurred between a policeman and one of these colored men, and a shot was again fired by one of the parties, which led to an indiscriminate fire on the building through the windows by the policemen. This had been going on for a short time, when a white flag was displayed from the windows of the Institute, whereupon the firing ceased, and the police rushed into the building.

"From the testimony of wounded men, and others who were inside the building, the policemen opened an indiscriminate fire upon the audience until they had emptied their revolvers, when they retired, and those inside barricaded the doors. The door was broken in, and the firing again commenced, when many of the colored and white people either escaped throughout the door or were passed out by the policemen inside; but as they came out the policemen who formed the circle nearest the building fired upon them, and they were again fired upon by the citizens that formed the outer circle. Many of those wounded and taken prisoners, and others who were prisoners and not wounded, were fired upon by their captors and by citizens. The wounded were stabbed while lying on the ground, and their heads beaten with brickbats. In the yard of the building, whither some of the colored men had escaped and partially secreted themselves, they were fired upon and killed or wounded by policemen. Some were killed and wounded several squares from the scene. Members of the convention were wounded by the police while in their hands as prisoners - some of them mortally.

"The immediate cause of this terrible affair was the assemblage of this Convention; the remote cause was the bitter and antagonistic feeling which has been growing in this community since the advent of the present Mayor, who, in the organization of his police force, selected many desperate men, and some of them known murderers. People of clear views were overawed by want of confidence in the Mayor, and fear of the thugs, many of which he had selected for his police force. I have frequently been spoken to by prominent citizens on this subject, and have heard them express fear, and want of confidence in Mayor Monroe. Ever since the intimation of this last convention movement I must condemn the course of several of the city papers for supporting, by their articles, the bitter feeling of bad men. As to the merciless manner in which the convention was broken up, I feel obliged to confess strong repugnance.

"It is useless to disguise the hostility that exists on the part of a great many here toward Northern men, and this unfortunate affair has so precipitated matters that there is now a test of what shall be the status of Northern men - whether they can live here without being in constant dread or not, whether they can be protected in life and property, and have justice in the courts. If this matter is permitted to pass over without a thorough and determined prosecution of those engaged in it, we may look out for frequent scenes of the same kind, not only here, but in other places.   No steps have as yet been taken by the civil authorities to arrest citizens who were engaged in this massacre, or policemen who perpetrated such cruelties.   The members of the convention have been indicted by the grand jury, and many of them arrested and held to bail.   As to whether the civil authorities can mete out ample justice to the guilty parties on both sides, I must say it is my opinion, unequivocally, that they cannot.   Judge Abell, whose course I have closely watched for nearly a year, I now consider one of the most dangerous men that we have here to the peace and quiet of the city.   The leading men of the convention - King, Cutler, Hahn, and others - have been political agitators, and are bad men.   I regret to say that the course of Governor Wells has been vacillating, and that during the late trouble he has shown very little of the man.

"P. H. SHERIDAN,
"Major-General   Commanding."

Subsequently a military commission investigated the subject of the riot, taking a great deal of testimony.   The commission substantially confirmed the conclusions given in my despatches, and still later there was an investigation by a select committee of the House of Representatives, of which the Honorables Samuel Shellabarger, of Ohio, W. L. Elliot, of Massachusetts, and B. M. Boyer, of Pennsylvania, were the members.   The majority report of the committee also corrobora, ted, in all essentials, my reports of the distressing occurrence.   The committee likewise called attention to a violent speech made by Mr. Johnson at St. Louis in September, 1866, charging the origin of the riot to Congress, and went on to say of the speech that "it was an unwarranted and unjust expression of hostile feeling, without pretext or foundation in fact." A list of the killed and wounded was embraced in the committees report, and among other conclusions reached were the following: "That the meeting of July 30 was a meeting of quiet citizens, who came together without arms and with intent peaceably to discuss questions of public concern. . . . There has been no occasion during our National history when a riot has occurred so destitute of justifiable cause, resulting in a massacre so inhuman and fiendlike, as that which took place at New Orleans on the 30th of July last. This riotous attack upon the convention, with its terrible results of massacre and murder, was not an accident. It was the determined purpose of the mayor of the city of New Orleans to break up this convention by armed force."

The statement is also made, that "He [the President] knew that 'rebels' and 'thugs' and disloyal men had controlled the election of Mayor Monroe, and that such men composed chiefly his police force."

The committee held that no legal government existed in Louisiana, and recommended the temporary establishment of a provisional government therein; the report concluding that "in the meantime the safety of all Union men within the State demands that such government be formed for their protection, for the well being of the nation and the permanent peace of the Republic."

The New Orleans riot agitated the whole country, and the official and other reports served to intensify and concentrate the opposition to President Johnson's policy of reconstruction, a policy resting exclusively on and inspired solely by the executive authority - for it was made plain, by his language and his acts, that he was seeking to rehabilitate the seceded States under conditions differing not a whit from those existing before the rebellion; that is to say, without the slightest constitutional provision regarding the status of the emancipated slaves, and with no assurances of protection for men who had remained loyal in the war.

In December, 1866, Congress took hold of the subject with such vigor as to promise relief from all these perplexing disorders, and, after much investigation and a great deal of debate, there resulted the so-called "Reconstruction Laws," which, for a clear understanding of the powers conferred on the military commanders, I deem best to append in full:

AN ACT to provide for the more efficient government of the rebel States.

Whereas, no legal State governments or adequate protection for life or property now exist in the rebel States of Virginia, North Carolina, South Carolina, Georgia, Mississippi, Alabama, Louisiana, Florida, Texas, and Arkansas; and whereas, it is necessary that peace and good order should be enforced in said States until loyal and republican State governments can be legally established; therefore,

Be it enacted by the Senate and House of Representatives of the United States of America in Congress assembled, That said rebel States shall be divided into military districts and made subject to the military authority of the United States as hereinafter prescribed; and for that purpose Virginia shall constitute the first district; North Carolina and South Carolina, the second district; Georgia, Alabama, and Florida, the third district; Mississippi and Arkansas, the fourth district; and Louisiana and Texas, the fifth district.

SEC. 2. *And be it further enacted,* That it shall be the duty of the President to assign to the command of each of said districts an officer of the army not below the rank of brigadier-general, and to detail a sufficient military force to enable such officer to perform his duties and enforce his authority within the district to which he is assigned.

SEC. 3. *And be it further enacted,* That it shall be the duty of each officer assigned as aforesaid to protect all persons in their rights of person and property, to suppress insurrection, disorder, and violence, and to punish, or cause to be punished, all disturbers of the public peace and criminals, and to this end he may allow local civil tribunals to take jurisdiction of and to try offenders, or, when in his judgment it may be necessary for the trial of offenders, he shall have power to organize military commissions or tribunals for that purpose, and all interference, under cover of State authority, with the exercise of military authority under this act, shall be null and void.

SEC. 4. *And be it further enacted,* That all persons put under military arrest by virtue of this act shall be tried without unnecessary delay, and no cruel or unjust punishment shall be inflicted;

and no sentence of any military commission or tribunal hereby authorized affecting the life or liberty of any person, shall be executed until it is approved by the officer in command of the district; and the laws and regulations for the government of the army shall not be affected by this act. except in so far as they conflict with its provisions: *Provided,* That no sentence of death, under the provisions of this act, shall be carried into effect without the approval of the President.

Sec. 5. *And be it further enacted.* That when the people of any one of said rebel States shall have formed a constitution of government in conformity with the Constitution of the United States in all respects, framed by a convention of delegates elected by the male citizens of said State twenty-one years old and upward, of whatever race, color, or previous condition, who have been resident in said State for one year previous to the day of such election, except such as may be disfranchised for participation in the rebellion, or for felony at common law; and when such constitution shall provide that the elective franchise shall be enjoyed by all such persons as have the qualifications herein stated for electors of delegates; and when such constitution shall be ratified by a majority of the persons voting on the question of ratification who are qualified as electors for delegates, and when such constitution shall have been submitted to Congress for examination and approval, and Congress shall have approved the same; and when said State, by a vote of its legislature elected under said constitution, shall have adopted the amendment to the Constitution of the United States proposed by the Thirty-ninth Congress, and known as article fourteen; and when said article shall have become a part of the Constitution of the United States, said State shall be declared entitled to representation in Congress, and senators and representatives shall be admitted therefrom on their taking the oath prescribed by law; and then and thereafter the preceding sections of this act shall be inoperative in said State: *Provided,* That no person excluded from the privilege of holding office by said proposed amendment to the Constitution of the United States shall be eligible to election as a member of the convention to frame a constitution for any of said rebel States, nor shall any such person vote for members of such convention.

SEC. 6. *And be it further enacted,* That until the people of said rebel States shall be by law admitted to representation in the Congress of the United States, any civil government which may exist there in shall be deemed provisional only, and in all respects subject to the paramount authority of the United States at any time to abolish, modify, control, or supersede the same; and in all elections to any office under such provisional governments all persons shall be entitled to vote, and none others, who are entitled to vote under the fifth section of this act; and no person shall be eligible to any office under any such provisional governments who would be disqualified from holding office under the provisions of the third article of said constitutional amendment.

SCHUYLER COLFAX,

Speaker of the House of Representatives.

LAFAYETTE S. FOSTER,

President of the Senate pro tempore.

AN ACT supplementary to an act entitled "An act to provide for the more efficient government of the rebel States," passed March second, eighteen hundred and sixty-seven, and to facilitate restoration.

Be it enacted by the Senate and House of Representatives of the United States of America in Congress assembled, That before the first day of September, eighteen hundred and sixty-seven, the commanding general in each district defined by an act entitled "An act to provide for the more efficient government of the rebel States," passed March second, eighteen hundred and sixty-seven, shall cause a registration to be made of the male citizens of the United States, twenty-one years of age and upwards, resident in each county or parish in the State or States included in his district, which registration shall include only those persons who are qualified to vote for delegates by the act aforesaid, and who shall have taken and subscribed the following oath or affirmation: "I, – do solemnly swear (or affirm), in the presence of the Almighty God, that I am a citizen of the State of – ; that I have resided in said State for - months next preceding this day, and now reside in the county of – , or the parish of – , in said State, (as the case may be); that I am twenty-one years old; that I have not been disfranchised for participation in any rebellion or civil war against the United States, nor for felony committed against the laws of any State or of the United States; that I have never been a member of any State Legislature, nor held any executive or judicial office in any State, and afterwards engaged in insurrection or rebellion against the United States, or given aid or comfort to the enemies thereof; that I have never taken an oath as a member of Congress of the United States, or as an officer of the United States, or as a member of any State Legislature, or as an executive or judicial officer of any State, to support the Constitution of the United States, and afterwards engaged in insurrection or rebellion against the United States or given aid or comfort to the enemies thereof; that I will faithfully support the Constitution and obey the laws of the United States, and will, to the best of my ability, encourage others so to do: so help me God"; which oath or affirmation may be administered by any registering officer.

SEC. 2. *And be it further enacted,* That after the completion of the registration hereby provided for in any State, at such time and places therein as the commanding general shall appoint and direct, of which at least thirty days' public notice shall be given, an election shall be held of delegates to a convention for the purpose of establishing a constitution and civil government for such State loyal to the Union, said convention in each State, except Virginia, to consist of the same number of members as the most numerous branch of the State Legislature of such State in the year eighteen hundred and sixty, to be apportioned among the several districts, counties, or parishes of such State by the commanding general, giving each representation in the ratio of voters registered as aforesaid as nearly as may be.   The convention in Virginia shall consist of the same number of members as represented the territory now constituting Virginia in the most numerous branch of the Legislature of said State in the year eighteen hundred and sixty, to be apportioned as aforesaid.

SEC. 3. *And be it further enacted,* That at said election the registered voters of each State shall vote for or against a convention to form a constitution therefor under this act.   Those voting in favor of such a convention shall have written or printed on the

ballots by which they vote for delegates, as aforesaid, the words
"For a convention," and those voting against such a convention
shall have written or printed on such ballot the words "Against
a convention." The persons appointed to superintend said election, and to make return of the votes given thereat, as herein
provided, shall count and make return of the votes given for and
against a convention; and the commanding general to whom the
same shall have been returned shall ascertain and declare the
total vote in each State for and against a convention. If a majority of the votes given on that question shall be for a convention,
then such convention shall be held as hereinafter provided; but
if a majority of said votes shall be against a convention, then no
such convention shall be held under this act: *Provided,* That such
convention shall not be held unless a majority of all such registered voters shall have voted on the question of holding such convention.

SEC. 4. *And be it further enacted,* That the commanding general
of each district shall appoint as many boards of registration as
may be necessary, consisting of three loyal officers or persons, to
make and complete the registration, superintend the election,
and make return to him of the votes, list of voters, and of the
persons elected as delegates by a plurality of the votes cast at
said election; and upon receiving said returns he shall open the
same, ascertain the persons elected as delegates, according to
the returns of the officers who conducted said election, and make
proclamation thereof; and if a majority of the votes given on
that question shall be for a convention, the commanding general,
within sixty days from the date of election, shall notify the delegates to assemble in convention, at a time and place to be mentioned in the notification, and said convention, when organized,
shall proceed to frame a constitution and civil government
according to the provisions of this act, and the act to which it is
supplementary; and when the same shall have been so framed,
said constitution shall be submitted by the convention for ratification to the persons registered under the provisions of this act
at an election to be conducted by the officers or persons appointed or to be appointed by the commanding general, as herein-
before provided, and to be held after the expiration of thirty days

from the date of notice thereof, to be given by said convention; and the returns thereof shall be made to the commanding general of the district.

SEC. 5. *And be it further enacted,* That if, according to said returns, the constitution shall be ratified by a majority of the votes of the registered electors qualified as herein specified, cast at said election, at least one-half of all the registered voters voting upon the question of such ratification, the president of the convention shall transmit a copy of the same, duly certified, to the President of the United States, who shall forthwith transmit the same to Congress, if then in session, and if not in session, then immediately upon its next assembling; and if it shall moreover appear to Congress that the election was one at which all the registered and qualified electors in the State had an opportunity to vote freely, and without restraint, fear, or the influence of fraud, and if the Congress shall be satisfied that such constitution meets the approval of a majority of all the qualified electors in the State, and if the said constitution shall be declared by Congress to be in conformity with the provisions of the act to which this is supplementary, and the other provisions of said act shall have been complied with, and the said constitution shall be approved by Congress, the State shall be declared entitled to representation, and senators and representatives shall be admitted therefrom as therein provided.

SEC. 6. *And be it further enacted,* That all elections in the States mentioned in the said "Act to provide for the more efficient government of the rebel States" shall, during the operation of said act, be by ballot; and all officers making the said registration of voters and conducting said elections, shall, before entering upon the discharge of their duties, take and subscribe the oath prescribed by the act approved July second, eighteen hundred and sixty-two, entitled "An act to prescribe an oath of office": Provided, That if any person shall knowingly and falsely take and subscribe any oath in this act prescribed, such person so offending and being thereof duly convicted, shall be subject to the pains, penalties, and disabilities which by law are provided for the punishment of the crime of wilful and corrupt perjury.

SEC. 7. *And be it further enacted,* That all expenses incurred by the several commanding generals, or by virtue of any orders issued, or appointments made, by them, under or by virtue of this act, shall be paid out of any moneys in the treasury not otherwise appropriated.

SEC. 8. *And be it further enacted,* That the convention for each State shall prescribe the fees, salary, and compensation to be paid to all delegates and other officers and agents herein authorized or necessary to carry into effect the purposes of this act not herein otherwise provided for, and shall provide for the levy and collection of such taxes on the property in such State as may be necessary to pay the same.

SEC. 9. *And be it further enacted,* That the word "article," in the sixth section of the act to which this is supplementary, shall be construed to mean "section."

SCHUYLER COLFAX,
Speaker of the House of Representatives.
B. F. WADE,
President of the Senate *pro tempore.*

CHAPTER XI.

PASSAGE OF THE RECONSTRUCTION ACT OVER THE PRES-
IDENTS VETO - PLACED IN COMMAND OF THE
FIFTH MILITARY DISTRICT - REMOVING OFFICERS-
MY REASONS FOR SUCH ACTION - AFFAIRS IN
LOUISIANA AND TEXAS - REMOVAL OF GOVERNOR.
WELLS - REVISION OF THE JURY LISTS - RELIEVED
FROM THE COMMAND OF THE FIFTH MILITARY
DISTRICT.

T HE first of the Reconstruction laws was passed
March 2, 1867, and though vetoed by the
President, such was the unanimity of loyal sentiment and the urgency demanding the measure,
that the bill became a law over the veto the day
the President returned it to Congress. March the
11th this law was published in General Orders
No. 10, from the Headquarters of the Army, the
same order assigning certain officers to take charge
of the five military districts into which the States
lately in rebellion were subdivided, I being announced as the commander of the Fifth Military
District, which embraced Louisiana and Texas, a
territory that had formed the main portion of my
command since the close of the war.

Between the date of the Act and that of my assignment, the Louisiana Legislature, then in special session, had rejected a proposed repeal of an Act it had previously passed providing for an election of certain municipal officers in New Orleans. This election was set for March 11, but the mayor and the chief of police, together with General Mower, commanding the troops in the city, having expressed to me personally their fears that the public peace would be disturbed by the election, I, in this emergency, though not yet assigned to the district, assuming the authority which the Act conferred on district commanders, declared that the election should not take place; that no polls should be opened on the day fixed; and that the whole matter would stand postponed till the district commander should be appointed, or special instructions be had. This, my first official act under the Reconstruction laws, was rendered necessary by the course of a body of obstructionists, who had already begun to give unequivocal indications of their intention to ignore the laws of Congress.

A copy of the order embodying the Reconstruction law, together with my assignment, having reached me a few days after, I regularly assumed control of the Fifth Military District on March 19, by an order wherein I declared the State and. municipal governments of the district to be provisional only, and, under the provisions of the sixth section of the Act, subject to be controlled, modified, superseded, or abolished. I also announced that no removals from office would be made unless the incumbents failed to carry out the provisions of the law or impeded reorganization, or unless willful delays should necessitate a change, and added: "Pending the reorganization, it is desirable and intended to create as little disturbance in the machinery of the various branches of the provisional governments as possible, consistent with the law of Congress and its successful execution, but this condition is dependent upon the disposition shown by the people, and upon the length of time required for reorganization."

Under these limitations Louisiana and Texas retained their former designations as military districts, the officers in command exercising their military powers as heretofore. In addition, these officers were to carry out in their respective commands all provisions of the law except those specially requiring the action of the district commander, and in cases of removals from and appointment to office.

In the course of legislation the first Reconstruction act, as I have heretofore noted, had been vetoed. On the very day of the veto, however, despite the President's adverse action, it passed

each House of Congress by such an overwhelming majority as not only to give it the effect of
law, but to prove clearly that the plan of reconstruction presented was, beyond question, the policy
endorsed by the people of the country. It was,
therefore, my determination to see to the law's
zealous execution in my district, though I felt
certain that the President would endeavor to embarrass me by every means in his power, not only
on account of his pronounced personal hostility,
but also because of his determination not to execute
but to obstruct the measures enacted by Congress.

Having come to this conclusion, I laid down, as
a rule for my guidance, the principle of non-interference with the provisional State governments,
and though many appeals were made to have me
rescind rulings of the courts, or interpose to fore-
stall some presupposed action to be taken by
them, my invariable reply was that I would not
take cognizance of such matters, except in cases
of absolute necessity. The same policy was announced also in reference to municipal affairs
throughout the district, so - long as the action of
the local officers did not conflict with the law.

In a very short time, however, I was obliged to
interfere in municipal matters in New Orleans,
for it had become clearly apparent that several
of the officials were, both by acts of omission and

commission, ignoring the law, so on the 27th of March I removed from office the Mayor, John T. Monroe; the Judge of the First District Court, E. Abell; and the Attorney-General of the State, Andrew S. Herron; at the same time appointing to the respective offices thus vacated Edward Heath, W. W. Howe, and B. L. Lynch. The officials thus removed had taken upon themselves from the start to pronounce the Reconstruction acts unconstitutional, and to advise such a course of obstruction that I found it necessary at an early day to replace them by men in sympathy with the law, in order to make plain my determination to have its provisions enforced. The President at once made inquiry, through General Grant, for the cause of the removal, and I replied:

"HEADQUARTERS FIFTH MILITARY DISTRICT,
"New Orleans, La., April 19, 1867.

"GENERAL: On the 27th day of March last I removed from office Judge E. Abell, of the Criminal Court of New Orleans; Andrew S. Herron, Attorney-General of the State of Louisiana; and John T. Monroe, Mayor of the City of New Orleans. These removals were made under the powers granted me in what is usually termed the 'military bill,' passed March 2, 1867, by the Congress of the United States.

"I did not deem it necessary to give any reason for the removal of these men, especially after the investigations made by the military board on the massacre of July 30, 1866, and the report of the congressional committee on the same massacre; but as some inquiry has been made for the cause of removal, I would respectfully state as follows:

"The court over which Judge Abell presided is the only criminal court in the city of New Orleans, and for a period of at least nine months previous to the riot of July 30 he had been educating a large portion of the community to the perpetration of this outrage, by almost promising no prosecution in his court against the offenders, in case such an event occurred. The records of his court will show that he fulfilled his promise, as not one of the guilty has been prosecuted.

"In reference to Andrew J. Herron, Attorney-General of the State of Louisiana, I considered it his duty to indict these men before this criminal court. This he failed to do, but went so far as to attempt to impose on the good sense of the whole nation by indicting the victims of the riot instead of the rioters; in other words, making the innocent guilty and the guilty innocent. He was therefore, in my belief, an able coadjutor with Judge Abell in bringing on the massacre of July 30.

"Mayor Monroe controlled the element engaged in this riot, and when backed by an attorney-general who would not prosecute the guilty, and a judge who advised the grand jury to find the innocent guilty and let the murderers go free, felt secure in engaging his police force in the riot and massacre.

"With these three men exercising a large influence over the worst elements of the population of this city, giving to those elements an immunity for riot and bloodshed, the general-in-chief will see how insecurely I felt in letting them occupy their respective positions in the troubles which might occur in registration and voting in the reorganization of this State.

"I am, General, very respectfully, your obedient servant,

"P. H. SHERIDAN,
"Major-General U. S. A.

"GENERAL U. S. GRANT,
"Commanding Armies of the United States,
"Washington, D. C."

To General Grant my reasons were satisfactory, but not so to the President, who took no steps, however, to rescind my action, for he knew that the removals were commended by wellnigh the entire community in the city, for it will be understood that Mr. Johnson was, through his friends and adherents in Louisiana and Texas, kept constantly advised of every step taken by me. Many of these persons were active and open opponents of mine, while others were spies, doing their work so secretly and quickly that sometimes Mr. Johnson knew of my official acts before I could report them to General Grant.

The supplemental Reconstruction act which defined the method of reconstruction became a law despite the President's veto on March 23. This was a curative act, authorizing elections and prescribing methods of registration. When it reached me officially I began measures for carrying out its provisions, and on the 28th of March issued an order to the effect that no elections for the State, parish, or municipal officers would be held in Louisiana until the provisions of the laws of Congress entitled "An act to provide for the more efficient government of the rebel States," and of the act supplemental thereto, should have been complied with. I also announced that until elections were held in accordance with these acts, the law of the Legislature of the State providing for the holding over of those persons whose terms of office otherwise would have expired, would govern in all cases excepting only those special ones in which I myself might take action. There was one parish, Livingston, which this order did not reach in time to prevent the election previously ordered there, and which therefore, took place, but by a supplemental order this election was declared null and void.

In April I began the work of administering the Supplemental Law, which, under certain conditions of eligibility, required a registration of the voters of the State, for the purpose of electing delegates to a Constitutional convention. It therefore became necessary to appoint Boards of Registration throughout the election districts, and on April 10 the boards for the Parish of Orleans were given out, those for the other parishes being appointed ten days later. Before announcing these boards, I had asked to be advised definitely as to what persons were disfranchised by the law, and was directed by General Grant to act upon my own interpretation of it, pending an opinion expected shortly from the Attorney-General - Mr. Henry Stanbery -so, for the guidance of the boards, I gave the following instructions:

"HEADQUARTERS FIFTH MILITARY DISTRICT.
"New Orleans, La., April 10, 1867.
"Special Orders, No. 15.

"2. In obedience to the directions contained in the first section of the Law of Congress entitled 'An Act supplemental to

an Act entitled "An Act to provide for the more efficient government of the rebel States," the registration of the legal voters,
according to that law in the Parish of Orleans, will be commenced
on the 15th instant, and must be completed by the 15th of May.

"The four municipal districts of the City of New Orleans and
the Parish of Orleans, right bank (Algiers), will each constitute
a Registration district. Election precincts will remain as at present constituted.

*   *   *   *   *   *   *   *

"Each member of the Board of Registers, before commencing
his duties, will file in the office of the Assistant-Inspector-General
at these headquarters, the oath required in the sixth section of
the Act referred to, and be governed in the execution of his duty
by the provisions of the first section of that Act, faithfully administering the oath therein prescribed to each person registered.

"Boards of Registers will immediately select suitable offices
within their respective districts, having reference to convenience
and facility of registration, and will enter upon their duties on
the day designated. Each Board will be entitled to two clerks.
Office-hours for registration will be from 8 o'clock till 12 A. M.,
and from 4 till 7 P. M.

"When elections are ordered, the Board of Registers for each
district will designate the number of polls and the places where
they shall be opened in the election precincts within its district,
appoint the commissioners and other officers necessary for properly conducting the elections, and will superintend the same.

"They will also receive from the commissioners of elections of
the different precincts the result of the vote, consolidate the
same, and forward it to the commanding general.

"Registers and all officers connected with elections will be
held to a rigid accountability and will be subject to trial by
military commission for fraud, or unlawful or improper conduct
in the performance of their duties. Their rate of compensation
and manner of payment will be in accordance with the provisions
of sections six and seven of the supplemental act.

*   *   *   *   *   *   *   *

"Every male citizen of the United States, twenty-one years
old and upward, of whatever race, color, or previous condition,

who has been resident in the State of Louisiana for one year and Parish of Orleans for three months previous to the date at which he presents himself for registration, and who has not been disfranchised by act of Congress or for felony at common law, shall, after having taken and subscribed the oath prescribed in the first section of the act herein referred to, be entitled to be, and shall be, registered as a legal voter in the Parish of Orleans and State of Louisiana.

"Pending the decision of the Attorney-General of the United States on the question as to who are disfranchised by law, registers will give the most rigid interpretation to the law, and exclude from registration every person about whose right to vote there may be a doubt. Any person so excluded who may, under the decision of the Attorney-General, be entitled to vote, shall be permitted to register after that decision is received, due notice of which will be given.

"By command of Major-General P. H. SHERIDAN,

"GEO. L. HARTSUFF,

"Assistant Adjutant-General."

The parish Boards of Registration were composed of three members each. Ability to take what was known as the "iron-clad oath" was the qualification exacted of the members, and they were prohibited from becoming candidates for office. In the execution of their duties they were to be governed by the provisions of the supplemental act. It was also made one of their functions to designate the number and location of the polling-places in the several districts, to appoint commissioners for receiving the votes and in general to attend to such other matters as were necessary, in order properly to conduct the vot-

ing, and afterward to receive from the commissioners the result of the vote and forward it to
my headquarters.   These registers, and all other
officers having to do with elections, were to be
held to a rigid accountability, and be subject to
trial by military commission for fraud or unlawful or improper conduct in the performance of
their duties; and in order to be certain that the
Registration Boards performed their work faithfully and intelligently, officers of the army were
appointed as supervisors.   To this end the parishes were grouped together conveniently in temporary districts, each officer having from three to
five parishes to supervise. The programme thus
mapped out for carrying out the law in Louisiana
was likewise adhered to in Texas, and indeed was
followed as a model in some of the other military
districts.

Although Military Commissions were fully
authorized by the Reconstruction acts, yet I did
not favor their use in governing the district, and
probably would never have convened one had
these acts been observed in good faith.   I much
preferred that the civil courts, and the State and
municipal authorities already in existence, should
perform their functions without military control
or interference, but occasionally, because the civil
authorities neglected their duty, I was obliged to

resort to this means to ensure the punishment of offenders. At this time the condition of the negroes in Texas and Louisiana was lamentable, though, in fact, not worse than that of the few white loyalists who had been true to the Union during the war. These last were singled out as special objects of attack, and were, therefore, obliged at all times to be on the alert for the protection of their lives and property. This was the natural outcome of Mr. Johnson's defiance of Congress, coupled with the sudden conversion to his cause of persons in the North who but a short time before had been his bitterest enemies; for all this had aroused among the disaffected element new hopes of power and place, hopes of being at once put in political control again, with a resumption of their functions in State and National matters without any preliminary authorization by Congress. In fact, it was not only hoped, but expected, that things were presently to go on just as if there had been no war.

In the State of Texas there were in 1865 about 200,000 of the colored race - roughly, a third of the entire population - while in Louisiana there were not less than 350,000, or more than one-half of all the people in the State. Until the enactment of the Reconstruction laws these negroes were without rights, and though they had been liberated by the war, Mr. Johnson's policy now proposed that they should have no political status at all, and consequently be at the mercy of a people who, recently their masters, now seemed to look upon them as the authors of all the misfortunes that had come upon the land. Under these circumstances the blacks naturally turned for protection to those who had been the means of their liberation, and it would have been little less than inhuman to deny them sympathy. Their freedom had been given them, and it was the plain duty of those in authority to make it secure, and screen them from the bitter political resentment that beset them, and to see that they had a fair chance in the battle of life. Therefore, when outrages and murders grew frequent, and the aid of the military power was an absolute necessity for the protection of life, I employed it unhesitatingly - the guilty parties being brought to trial before military commissions - and for a time, at least, there occurred a halt in the march of terrorism inaugurated by the people whom Mr. Johnson had deluded.

The first Military Commission was convened to try the case of John W. Walker, charged with shooting a negro in the parish of St. John. The proper civil authorities had made no effort to arrest Walker, and even connived at his escape, so I had him taken into custody in New Orleans, and ordered him tried, the commission finding him guilty, and sentencing him to confinement in the penitentiary for six months. This shooting was the third occurrence of the kind that had taken place in St. Johns parish, a negro being wounded in each case, and it was plain that the intention was to institute there a practice of intimidation which should be effective to subject the freedmen to the will of their late masters, whether in making labor contracts, or in case these newly enfranchised negroes should evince a disposition to avail themselves of the privilege to vote.

The trial and conviction of Walker, and of one or two others for similiar outrages, soon put a stop to every kind of "bull-dozing" in the country parishes; but about this time I discovered that many members of the police force in New Orleans were covertly intimidating the freedmen there, and preventing their appearance at the registration offices, using milder methods than had obtained in the country, it is true, but none the less effective.

Early in 1866 the Legislature had passed an act which created for the police of New Orleans a residence qualification, the object of which was to discharge and exclude from the force ex-Union soldiers. This of course would make room for the appointment of ex-Confederates, and Mayor Monroe had not been slow in enforcing the provisions of the law. It was, in fact, a result of this enactment that the police was so reorganized as to become the willing and efficient tool which it proved to be in the riot of 1866; and having still the same personnel, it was now in shape to prevent registration by threats, unwarranted arrests, and by various other influences, all operating to keep the timid blacks away from the registration places.

That the police were taking a hand in this practice of repression, I first discovered by the conduct of the assistant to the chief of the body, and at once removed the offender, but finding this ineffectual I annulled that part of the State law fixing the five years' residence restriction, and restored the two years' qualification, thus enabling Mayor Heath, who by my appointment had succeeded Monroe, to organize the force anew, and take about one-half of its members from ex-Union soldiers who when discharged had settled in New Orleans. This action put an end to intimidation in the parish of Orleans; and now were put in operation in all sections the processes provided by the supplemental Reconstruction law for the summoning of a convention to form a Constitution preparatory to the readmission of the State, and I was full of hope that there would now be much less difficulty in administering the trust imposed by Congress.

During the two years previous great damage had been done the agricultural interests of Louisiana by the overflow of the Mississippi, the levees being so badly broken as to require extensive repairs, and the Legislature of 1866 had appropriated for the purpose $4,000,000, to be raised by an issue of bonds. This money was to be disbursed by a Board of Levee Commissioners then in existence, but the term of service of these commissioners, and the law creating the board, would expire in the spring of 1867. In order to overcome this difficulty the Legislature passed a bill continuing the commissioners in office, but as the act was passed inside of ten days before the adjournment of the Legislature, Governor Wells pocketed the bill, and it failed to become a law. The Governor then appointed a board of his own, without any warrant of law whatever. The old commissioners refused to recognize this new board, and of course a conflict of authority ensued, which, it was clear, would lead to vicious results if allowed to continue; so, as the people of the State had no confidence in either of the boards, I decided to end the contention summarily by appointing an entirely new commission, which would disburse the money honestly, and further the real purpose for which it had been appropriated. When I took this course the legislative board acquiesced, but Governor Wells immediately requested the President to revoke my order, which, however, was not done, but meanwhile the Secretary of War directed me to suspend all proceedings in the matter, and make a report of the facts. I complied in the following telegram:

" HEADQUARTERS   FIFTH MILITARY DISTRICT,
" NEW ORLEANS, La., June 3, 1867.

"SIR: I have the honor to acknowledge the receipt of your telegram of this date in reference to the Levee Commissioners in this State.

"The following were my reasons for abolishing the two former boards, although I intended that my order should be sufficiently explanatory:

"Previous to the adjournment of the Legislature last winter it passed an act continuing the old Levee board in office, so that the four millions of dollars ($4,000,000) in bonds appropriated by the Legislature might be disbursed by a board of rebellious antecedents.

"After its adjournment the Governor of the State appointed a board of his own, in violation of this act, and made the acknowledgment to me in person that his object was to disburse the money in the interest of his own party by securing for it the vote of the employés at the time of election.

"The board continued in office by the Legislature refused to turn over to the Governor's board, and each side appealed to me to sustain it, which I would not do. The question must then have gone to the courts, which, according to the Governor's judgment when he was appealing to me to be sustained, would require one year for decision. Meantime the State was overflowed, the Levee boards tied up by political chicanery, and nothing done to relieve the poor people, now fed by the charity of the Government and charitable associations of the North.

"To obviate this trouble, and to secure to the overflowed districts of the State the immediate relief which the honest disbursement of the four millions ($4,000,000) would give, my order dissolving both boards was issued.

"I say now, unequivocally, that Governor Wells is a political trickster and a dishonest man. I have seen him myself, when I first came to this command, turn out all the Union men who had supported the Government, and put in their stead rebel soldiers who had not yet doffed their gray uniform. I have seen him again, during the July riot of 1866, skulk away where I could not find him to give him a guard, instead of coming out as a manly representative of the State and joining those who were preserving the peace. I have watched him since, and his conduct has been as sinuous as the mark left in the dust by the movement of a snake.

"I say again that he is dishonest, and that dishonesty is more than must be expected of me.

"P. H. SHERIDAN,
"Major-General, U. S. A.

"Hon. E. M. STANTON,
"Secretary of War, Washington, D. C."

The same day that I sent my report to the Secretary of War I removed from office Governor Wells himself, being determined to bear no longer with the many obstructions he had placed in the way of reorganizing the civil affairs of the State. I was also satisfied that he was unfit to retain the place, since he was availing himself of every opportunity to work political ends beneficial to himself. In this instance Wells protested to me against his removal, and also appealed to the President for an opinion of the Attorney-General as to my power in the case; and doubtless he would have succeeded in retaining his office, but for the fact that the President had been informed by General James B. Steadman* and others placed to watch me that Wells was wholly unworthy.

I appointed Mr. Thomas J. Durant as Wells's successor, but he declining, I then appointed Mr. Benjamin F. Flanders, who, after I had sent a staff-officer to forcibly eject Wells in case of necessity, took possession of the Governor's office. Wells having vacated, Governor Flanders began immediately the exercise of his duties in sympathy with the views of Congress, and I then notified General Grant that I thought he need have no further apprehension about the condition of affairs in Louisiana, as my appointee was a man of such integrity and ability that I already felt relieved of half my labor. I also stated in the same despatch that nothing would answer in Louisiana but a

---

*"NEW ORLEANS June 19, 1867,
"ANDREW JOHNSON, President United States,
"Washington City:

"Lewis D. Campbell leaves New Orleans for home this evening. Want of respect for Governor Wells personally, alone represses the expression of indignation felt by all honest and sensible men at the unwarranted usurpation of General Sheridan in removing the civil officers of Louisiana. It is believed here that you will reinstate Wells. He is a bad man, and has no influence.

"I believe Sheridan made the removals to embarrass you, believing the feeling at the North would sustain him. My conviction is that on account of the bad character of Wells and Monroe, you ought not to reinstate any who have been removed, because you cannot reinstate any without reinstating all, but you ought to prohibit the exercise of this power in the future.

"Respectfully yours,
" JAMES B. STEADMAN."

bold and firm course, and that in taking such a one I felt that I was strongly supported; a statement that was then correct, for up to this period the better classes were disposed to accept the Congressional plan of reconstruction.

During the controversy over the Levee Commissioners, and the correspondence regarding the removal of Governor Wells, registration had gone on under the rules laid down for the boards. The date set for closing the books was the 30th of June, but in the parish of Orleans the time was extended till the 15th of July. This the President considered too short a period, and therefore directed the registry lists not to be closed before the 1st of August, unless there was some good reason to the contrary. This was plainly designed to keep the books open in order that under the Attorney-General's interpretation of the Reconstruction laws, published June 20, many persons who had been excluded by the registration boards could yet be registered, so I decided to close the registration, unless required by the President unconditionally, and in specific orders, to extend the time. My motives were manifold, but the main reasons were that as two and a half months had been given already, the number of persons who, under the law, were qualified for registry was about exhausted, and because of the expense I did not feel warranted in keeping up the boards longer, as I said, "to suit new issues coming in at the eleventh hour," which would but open a "broad macadamized road for perjury and fraud."

When I thus stated what I intended to do, the opinion of the Attorney-General had not yet been received. When it did reach me it was merely in the form of a circular signed by Adjutant-General Townsend, and had no force of law. It was not even sent as an order, nor was it accompanied by any instructions, or by anything except the statement that it was transmitted to the "respective military commanders for their information, in order that there might be uniformity in the execution " of the Reconstruction acts. To adopt Mr. Stanbery's interpretation of the law and reopen registration accordingly, would defeat the purpose of Congress, as well as add to my perplexities. Such a course would also require that the officers appointed by me for the performance of specified duties, under laws which I was empowered to interpret and enforce, should receive their guidance and instructions from an unauthorized source, so on communicating with General Grant as to how I should act, he directed me to enforce my own construction of the military bill until ordered to do otherwise.

Therefore the registration continued as I had originally directed, and nothing having been definitely settled at Washington in relation to my extending the time, on the 10th of July I ordered all the registration boards to select, immediately, suitable persons to act as commissioners of election, and at the same time specified the number of each set of commissioners, designated the polling-places, gave notice that two days would be allowed for voting, and followed this with an order discontinuing registration the 31st of July, and then another appointing the 27th and 28th of September as the time for the election of delegates to the State convention.

In accomplishing the registration there had been little opposition from the mass of the people, but the press of New Orleans, and the office-holders and office-seekers in the State generally, antagonized the work bitterly and violently, particularly after the promulgation of the opinion of the Attorney-General. These agitators condemned everybody and everything connected with the Congressional plan of reconstruction; and the pernicious influence thus exerted was manifested in various ways, but most notably in the selection of persons to compose the jury lists in the country parishes. It also tempted certain municipal officers in New Orleans to perform illegal acts that would seriously have affected the credit of the city had matters not been promptly corrected by the summary removal from office of the comptroller and the treasurer, who had already issued a quarter of a million dollars in illegal certificates. On learning of this unwarranted and unlawful proceeding, Mayor Heath demanded an investigation by the Common Council, but this body, taking its cue from the evident intention of the President to render abortive the Reconstruction acts, refused the mayor's demand. Then he tried to have the treasurer and comptroller restrained by injunction, but the city attorney, under the same inspiration as the council, declined to sue out a writ, and the attorney being supported in this course by nearly all the other officials, the mayor was left helpless in his endeavors to preserve the city's credit. Under such circumstances he took the only step left him - recourse to the military commander; and after looking into the matter carefully I decided, in the early part of August, to give the mayor officials who would not refuse to make an investigation of the illegal issue of certificates, and to this end I removed the treasurer, surveyor, comptroller. city attorney, and twenty-two of the aldermen; these officials, and all of their assistants, having reduced the financial credit of New Orleans to a disordered condition, and also having made efforts

General Horatio G. Wright.

- and being then engaged in such - to hamper the execution of the Reconstruction laws.

This action settled matters in the city, but subsequently I had to remove some officials in the parishes - among them a justice of the peace and a sheriff in the parish of Rapides; the justice for refusing to permit negro witnesses to testify in a certain murder case, and for allowing the murderer, who had foully killed a colored man, to walk out of his court on bail in the insignificant sum of five hundred dollars; and the sheriff, for conniving at the escape from jail of another alleged murderer. Finding, however, even after these removals, that in the country districts murderers and other criminals went unpunished, provided the offenses were against negroes merely (since the jurors were selected exclusively from the whites, and often embraced those excluded from the exercise of the election franchise), I, having full authority under the Reconstruction laws, directed such a revision of the jury lists as would reject from them every man not eligible for registration as a voter. This order* was issued August

* "Headquarters Fifth Military District,
"New Orleans, La., August 24, 1867.
"Special Orders, No. 125.

"The registration of voters of the State of Louisiana, according to the law of Congress, being complete, it is hereby ordered that no person who is not registered in accordance with said law shall be considered as ' a duly qualified

24, and on its promulgation the President relieved me from duty and assigned General Hancock as my successor.

Pending the arrival of General Hancock, I
turned over the command of the district September 1 to General Charles Griffin; but he dying
of yellow fever, General J. A. Mower succeeded
him, and retained command till November 29,
on which date General Hancock assumed control.
Immediately after Hancock took charge, he re-
voked my order of August 24 providing for a
revision of the jury lists; and, in short, President
Johnson's policy now became supreme, till Hancock himself was relieved in March, 1868.

My official connection with the reconstruction
of Louisiana and Texas practically closed with
this order concerning the jury lists. In my judgment this had become a necessity, for the disaffected element, sustained as it was by the open
sympathy of the President, had grown so determined in its opposition to the execution of the Reconstruction acts that I resolved to remove from

voter of the State of Louisiana.' All persons duly registered as above, and no
others, are consequently eligible, under the laws of the State of Louisiana, to
serve as jurors in any of the courts of the State.

"The necessary revision of the jury lists will immediately be made by the
proper officers.

"All the laws of the State respecting exemptions, &c., from jury duty will
remain in force.

     "By command of Major-General P. H. Sheridan.
      "Geo. L. Hartsuff, Asst. Adjt-General."

place and power all obstacles; for the summer's experience had convinced me that in no other way could the law be faithfully administered.

The President had long been dissatisfied with my course ; indeed, he had harbored personal enmity against me ever since he perceived that he could not bend me to an acceptance of the false position in which he had tried to place me by garbling my report of the riot of 1866. When Mr. Johnson decided to remove me, General Grant protested in these terms, but to no purpose:

" HEADQUARTERS ARMIES OF THE UNITED STATES,
"WASHINGTON, D. C., August 17, 1867.

"SIR: I am in receipt of your order of this date directing the assignment of General G. H. Thomas to the command of the Fifth Military District, General Sheridan to the Department of the Missouri, and General Hancock to the Department of the Cumberland; also your note of this date (enclosing these instructions), saying: Before you issue instructions to carry into effect the enclosed order, I would be pleased to hear any suggestions you may deem necessary respecting the assignments to which the order refers.'

"I am pleased to avail myself of this invitation to urge - earnestly urge - urge in the name of a patriotic people, who have sacrificed hundreds of thousands of loyal lives and thousands of millions of treasure to preserve the integrity and union of this country - that this order be not insisted on.   It is unmistakably the expressed wish of the country that General Sheridan should not be removed from his present command.

"This is a republic where the will of the people is the law of the land.   I beg that their voice may be heard.

"General Sheridan has performed his civil duties faithfully and intelligently.   His removal will only be regarded as an effort to defeat the laws of Congress. It will be interpreted by the unreconstructed element in the South - those who did all they could to break up this Government by arms, and now wish to be the only element consulted as to the method of restoring order - as a triumph. It will embolden them to renewed opposition to the will of the loyal masses, believing that they have the Executive with them.

"The services of General Thomas in battling for the Union entitle him to some consideration. He has repeatedly entered his protest against being assigned to either of the five military districts, and especially to being assigned to relieve General Sheridan.

"There are military reasons, pecuniary reasons, and above all, patriotic reasons, why this should not be insisted upon.

"I beg to refer to a letter marked ʃprivate,ʃ which I wrote to the President when first consulted on the subject of the change in the War Department. It bears upon the subject of this removal, and I had hoped would have prevented it.

"I have the honor to be, with great respect, your obedient servant,

"U. S. GRANT,
"General U. S. A., Secretary of War *ad interim.*
"His Excellency A. JOHNSON,
"President of the United States."

I was ordered to command the Department of the Missouri (General Hancock, as already noted, finally becoming my successor in the Fifth Military District), and left New Orleans on the 5th of September. I was not loath to go. The kind of duty I had been performing in Louisiana and Texas was very trying under the most favorable circumstances, but all the more so in my case, since I had to contend against the obstructions which the President placed in the way from persistent opposition to the acts of Congress as well as from antipathy to me - which obstructions he interposed with all the boldness and aggressiveness of his peculiar nature.

On more than one occasion while I was exercising this command, impurity of motive was imputed to me, but it has never been truthfully shown (nor can it ever be) that political or corrupt influences of any kind controlled me in any instance. I simply tried to carry out, without fear or favor, the Reconstruction acts as they came to me. They were intended to disfranchise certain persons, and to enfranchise certain others, and, till decided otherwise, were the laws of the land; and it was my duty to execute them faithfully, without regard, on the one hand, for those upon whom it was thought they bore so heavily, nor, on the other, for this or that political party, and certainly without deference to those persons sent to Louisiana to influence my conduct of affairs.

Some of these missionaries were high officials, both military and civil, and I recall among others a visit made me in 1866 by a distinguished friend of the President, Mr. Thomas A. Hendricks. The purpose of his coming was to convey to me assurances of the very high esteem in which I was held by the President, and to explain personally Mr. Johnson's plan of reconstruction, its flawless constitutionality, and so on. But being on the ground, I had before me the exhibition of its practical working, saw the oppression and excesses growing out of it, and in the face of these experiences even Mr. Hendrickss persuasive eloquence was powerless to convince me of its beneficence. Later General Lovell H. Rousseau came down on a like mission, but was no more successful than Mr. Hendricks.

During the whole period that I commanded in Louisiana and Texas my position was a most unenviable one. The service was unusual, and the nature of it scarcely to be understood by those not entirely familiar with the conditions existing immediately after the war. In administering the affairs of those States, I never acted except by authority, and always from conscientious motives. I tried to guard the rights of everybody in accordance with the law. In this I was supported by General Grant and opposed by President Johnson. The former had at heart, above every other consideration, the good of his country, and always sustained me with approval and kind suggestions. The course pursued by the President was exactly the opposite, and seems to prove that in the whole matter of reconstruction he was governed less by patriotic motives than by personal ambitions. Add to this his natural obstinacy of character and personal enmity toward me, and no surprise should be occasioned when I say that I heartily welcomed the order that lifted from me my unsought burden.

CHAPTER XII.

THE headquarters of the military department to which I was assigned when relieved from duty at New Orleans was at Fort Leavenworth, Kansas, and on the 5th of September I started for that post. In due time I reached St. Louis, and stopped there a day to accept an ovation tendered in approval of the course I had pursued in the Fifth Military District - a public demonstration apparently of the most sincere and hearty character.

From St. Louis to Leavenworth took but one night, and the next day I technically complied with my orders far enough to permit General Hancock to leave the department, so that he might go immediately to New Orleans if he so desired, but

on account of the yellow fever epidemic then prevailing, he did not reach the city till late in November.

My new command was one of the four military
departments that composed the geographical division then commanded by Lieutenant-General
Sherman. This division had been formed in 1866,
with a view to controlling the Indians west of the
Missouri River, they having become very restless and troublesome because of the building of
the Pacific railroads through their hunting-grounds,
and the encroachments of pioneers, who began settling in middle and western Kansas and eastern
Colorado immediately after the war.

My department embraced the States of Missouri
and Kansas, the Indian Territory, and New Mexico.
Part of this section of country-western Kansas
particularly - had been frequently disturbed and
harassed during two or three years past, the savages every now and then massacring an isolated
family, boldly attacking the surveying and construction parties of the Kansas-Pacific railroad,
sweeping down on emigrant trains, plundering and
burning stage-stations and the like along the
Smoky Hill route to Denver and the Arkansas
route to New Mexico.

However, when I relieved Hancock, the department was comparatively quiet. Though some

military operations had been conducted against the hostile tribes in the early part of the previous summer, all active work was now suspended in the attempt to conclude a permanent peace with the Cheyennes, Arapahoes, Kiowas, and Comanches, in compliance with the act of Congress creating what was known as the Indian Peace Commission of 1867.

Under these circumstances there was little necessity for my remaining at Leavenworth, and as I was much run down in health from the Louisiana climate, in which I had been obliged to live continuously for three summers (one of which brought epidemic cholera, and another a scourge of yellow fever), I took a leave of absence for a few months, leaving Colonel A. J. Smith, of the Seventh Cavalry, temporarily in charge of my command.

On this account I did not actually go on duty in the department of the Missouri till March, 1868. On getting back I learned that the negotiations of the Peace Commissioners - held at Medicine Lodge, about seventy miles south of Fort Larned - had resulted in a treaty with the Cheyennes, Arapahoes, Kiowas, and Comanches, by which agreement it was supposed all troubles had been settled. The compact, as concluded, contained numerous provisions, the most important to us being one which practically relinquished the country between the Arkansas and Platte rivers for white settlement; another permitted the peaceable construction of the Pacific railroads through the same region; and a third requiring the tribes signing the treaty to retire to reservations allotted them in the Indian Territory. Although the chiefs and head-men were wellnigh unanimous in ratifying these concessions, it was discovered in the spring of 1868 that many of the young men were bitterly opposed to what had been done, and claimed that most of the signatures had been obtained by misrepresentation and through proffers of certain annuities, and promises of arms and ammunition to be issued in the spring of 1868. This grumbling was very general in extent, and during the winter found outlet in occasional marauding, so, fearing a renewal of the pillaging and plundering at an early day, to prepare myself for the work evidently ahead the first thing I did on assuming permanent command was to make a trip to Fort Larned and Fort Dodge, near which places the bulk of the Indians had congregated on Pawnee and Walnut creeks. I wanted to get near enough to the camps to find out for myself the actual state of feeling among the savages, and also to familiarize myself with the characteristics of the Plains Indians, for my previous experience had been mainly with mountain tribes on the Pacific coast. Fort Larned I found too near the camps for my purpose, its proximity too readily inviting unnecessary "talks," so I remained here but a day or two, and then went on to Dodge, which, though considerably farther away from the camps, was yet close enough to enable us to obtain easily information of all that was going on.

It took but a few days at Dodge to discover that great discontent existed about the Medicine Lodge concessions, to see that the young men were chafing and turbulent, and that it would require much tact and good management on the part of the Indian Bureau to persuade the four tribes to go quietly to their reservations, under an agreement which, when entered into, many of them protested had not been fully understood.

A few hours after my arrival a delegation of prominent chiefs called on me and proposed a council, where they might discuss their grievances, and thus bring to the notice of the Government the alleged wrongs done them; but this I refused, because Congress had delegated to the Peace Commission the whole matter of treating with them, and a council might lead only to additional complications. My refusal left them without hope of securing better terms, or of even delaying matters longer; so henceforth they were more than ever reckless and defiant. Denunciations of the treaty became outspoken, and as the young braves grew more and more insolent every day, it amounted to conviction that, unless by some means the irritation was allayed, hostilities would surely be upon us when the buffalo returned to their summer feeding-grounds between the Arkansas and the Platte.

The principal sufferers in this event would be the settlers in middle and western Kansas, who, entirely ignorant of the dangers hanging over them, were laboring to build up homes in a new country. Hence the maintenance of peace was much to be desired, if it could be secured without too great concessions, and although I would not meet the different tribes in a formal council, yet, to ward off from settlers as much as possible the horrors of savage warfare, I showed, by resorting to persuasive methods, my willingness to temporize a good deal. An abundant supply of rations is usually effective to keep matters quiet in such cases, so I fed them pretty freely, and also endeavored to control them through certain men who, I found, because of former associations, had their confidence. These men, employed as scouts or interpreters, were Mr. William Comstock, Mr. Abner S. Grover, and Mr. Richard Parr. They had lived on the Plains for many years with different tribes of Indians, had trapped and hunted with them, and knew all the principal chiefs and headmen. Through such influences, I thought I saw good chances of preserving peace, and of inducing the discontented to go quietly to their reservations in the Indian Territory as soon as General Hazen, the representative of the Peace Commissioners, was ready to conduct them there from Fort Larned.

Before returning to Leavenworth I put my mediators (as I may call them) under charge of an officer of the army, Lieutenant F. W. Beecher, a very intelligent man, and directed him to send them out to visit among the different tribes, in order to explain what was intended by the treaty of Medicine Lodge, and to make every effort possible to avert hostilities. Under these instructions Comstock and Grover made it their business to go about among the Cheyennes - the most warlike tribe of all - then camping about the headwaters of Pawnee and Walnut creeks, and also to the north and west of Fort Wallace, while Parr spent his time principally with the Kiowas and Comanches.

From the different posts - Wallace, Dodge, and Larned - Lieutenant Beecher kept up communication with ail three scouts, and through him I heard from them at least once a week. Every now and then some trouble along the railroad or stage routes would be satisfactorily adjusted and quiet restored, and matters seemed to be going on very well, the warm weather bringing the grass and buffalo in plenty, and still no outbreak, nor any act of downright hostility. So I began to hope that we should succeed in averting trouble till the favorite war season of the Indians was over, but the early days of August rudely ended our fancied tranquility.

In July the encampments about Fort Dodge began to break up, each band or tribe moving off to some new location north of the Arkansas, instead of toward its proper reservation to the south of that river. Then I learned presently that a party of Cheyennes had made a raid on the Kaws - a band of friendly Indians living near Council Grove - and stolen their horses, and also robbed the houses of several white people near Council Grove. This raid was the beginning of the Indian war of 1868. Immediately following it, the Comanches and Kiowas came to Fort Larned to receive their annuities, expecting to get also the arms and ammunition promised them at Medicine Lodge, but the raid to Council Grove having been reported to the Indian Department, the issue of arms was suspended till reparation was made. This action of the Department greatly incensed the savages, and the agents offer of the annuities without guns and pistols was insolently refused, the Indians sulking back to their camps, the young men giving themselves up to war-dances, and to pow-wows with "medicine-men," till all hope of control was gone.

Brevet Brigadier-General Alfred Sully, an officer of long experience in Indian matters, who at this time was in command of the District of the Arkansas, which embraced Forts Larned and Dodge, having notified me of these occurrences at Larned, and expressed the opinion that the Indians were bent on mischief, I directed him there immediately to act against them. After he reached Larned, the chances for peace appeared more favorable. The Indians came to see him, and protested that it was only a few bad young men who had been depredating, and that all would be well and the young men held in check if the agent would but issue the arms and ammunition. Believing their promises, Sully thought that the delivery of the arms would solve all the difficulties, so on his advice the agent turned them over along with the annuities, the Indians this time condescendingly accepting.

This issue of arms and ammunition was a fatal mistake; Indian diplomacy had overreached Sul-

lys experience, and even while the delivery was
in progress a party of warriors had already begun
a raid of murder and rapine, which for acts of
devilish cruelty perhaps has no parallel in savage
warfare. The party consisted of about two hundred Cheyennes and a few Arapahoes, with
twenty Sioux who had been visiting their friends,
the Cheyennes. As near as could be ascertained,
they organized and left their camps along Pawnee
Creek about the 3d of August. Traveling northeast, they skirted around Fort Harker, and made
their first appearance among the settlers in the
Saline Valley, about thirty miles north of that
post. Professing friendship and asking food at
the farm-houses, they saw the unsuspecting occupants comply by giving all they could spare from
their scanty stores. Knowing the Indians inordi-
nate fondness for coffee, particularly when well
sweetened, they even served him this luxury
freely. With this the demons began their devilish
work. Pretending to be indignant because it was
served them in tin cups, they threw the hot con-
tents into the women's faces, and then, first making prisoners of the men, they, one after another,
ravished the women till the victims became
insensible. For some inexplicable reason the two
farmers were neither killed nor carried off, so
after the red fiends had gone, the unfortunate

women were brought in to Fort Harker, their arrival being the first intimation to the military that hostilities had actually begun.

Leaving the Saline, this war-party crossed over to the valley of the Solomon, a more thickly settled region, and where the people were in better circumstances, their farms having been started two or three years before. Unaware of the hostile character of the raiders, the people here received them in the friendliest way, providing food, and even giving them ammunition, little dreaming of what was impending. These kindnesses were requited with murder and pillage, and worse, for all the women who fell into their hands were subjected to horrors indescribable by words. Here also the first murders were committed, thirteen men and two women being killed. Then, after burning five houses and stealing all the horses they could find, they turned back toward the Saline, carrying away as prisoners two little girls named Bell, who have never been heard of since.

It was probably the intention to finish, as they marched back to the south, the devilish work begun on the Saline, but before they reached that valley on the return, the victims left there originally had fled to Fort Harker, as already explained, and Captain Benteen was now nearing the little settlement with a troop of cavalry, which he had hurriedly marched from Fort Zarah. The savages were attacking the house of a Mr. Schermerhorn, where a few of the settlers had collected for defense, when Benteen approached. Hearing the firing, the troopers rode toward the sound at a gallop, but when they appeared in view, coming over the hills, the Indians fled in all directions, escaping punishment through their usual tactics of scattering over the Plains, so as to leave no distinctive trail.

When this frightful raid was taking place, Lieutenant Beecher, with his three scouts - Comstock, Grover, and Parr - was on Walnut Creek. Indefinite rumors about troubles on the Saline and Solomon reaching him, he immediately sent Comstock and Grover over to the headwaters of the Solomon, to the camp of a band of Cheyennes, whose chief was called "Turkey Leg," to see if any of the raiders belonged there; to learn the facts, and make explanations, if it was found that the white people had been at fault. For years this chief had been a special friend of Comstock and Grover. They had trapped, hunted, and lived with his band, and from this intimacy they felt confident of being able to get "Turkey Leg" to quiet his people, if any of them were engaged in the raid; and, at all events, they expected, through him and his band, to influence the rest of the

Cheyennes. From the moment they arrived in the Indian village, however, the two scouts met with a very cold reception. Neither friendly pipe nor food was offered them, and before they could recover from their chilling reception, they were peremptorily ordered out of the village, with the intimation that when the Cheyennes were on the war-path the presence of whites was intolerable. The scouts were prompt to leave, of course, and for a few miles were accompanied by an escort of seven young men, who said they were sent with them to protect the two from harm. As the party rode along over the prairie, such a depth of attachment was professed for Comstock and Grover that, notwithstanding all the experience of their past lives, they were thoroughly deceived, and in the midst of a friendly conversation some of the young warriors fell suddenly to the rear and treacherously fired on them.

At the volley Comstock fell from his horse, instantly killed. Grover, badly wounded in the shoulder, also fell to the ground near Comstock. Seeing his comrade was dead, Grover made use of his friend's body to protect himself, lying close behind it. Then took place a remarkable contest, Grover, alone and severely wounded, obstinately fighting the seven Indians, and holding them at bay for the rest of the day. Being an expert shot, and having a long-range repeating rifle, he "stood off" the savages till dark. Then cautiously crawling away on his belly to a deep ravine, he lay close, suffering terribly from his wound, till the following night, when, setting out for Fort Wallace, he arrived there the succeeding day, almost crazed from pain and exhaustion.

Simultaneously with the fiendish atrocities committed on the Saline and Solomon rivers and the attack on Comstock and Grover, the pillaging and murdering began on the Smoky Hill stage-route, along the upper Arkansas River and on the headwaters of the Cimarron. That along the Smoky Hill and north of it was the exclusive work of the Cheyennes, a part of the Arapahoes, and the few Sioux allies heretofore mentioned, while the raiding on the Arkansas and Cimarron was done principally by the Kiowas under their chief, Satanta, aided by some of the Comanches. The young men of these tribes set out on their bloody work just after the annuities and guns were issued at Larned, and as soon as they were well on the road the rest of the Comanches and Kiowas escaped from the post and fled south of the Arkansas. They were at once pursued by General Sully with a small force, but by the time he reached the Cimarron the war-party had finished its raid on the upper Arkansas, and so many Ind-

ians combined against Sully that he was compelled to withdraw to Fort Dodge, which he
reached not without considerable difficulty, and
after three severe fights.

These, and many minor raids which followed,
made it plain that a general outbreak was upon us.
The only remedy, therefore, was to subjugate the
savages immediately engaged in the forays by
forcing the several tribes to settle down on the
reservations set apart by the treaty of Medicine
Lodge. The principal mischief-makers were the
Cheyennes. Next in deviltry were the Kiowas,
and then the Arapahoes and Comanches. Some
few of these last two tribes continued friendly, or
at least took no active part in the raiding, but
nearly all the young men of both were the constant allies of the Cheyennes and Kiowas. All
four tribes together could put on the war-path a
formidable force of about 6,000 warriors. The
subjugation of this number of savages would be
no easy task, so to give the matter my undivided
attention I transferred my headquarters from
Leavenworth to Fort Hays, a military post near
which the prosperous town of Hays City now
stands.

Fort Hays was just beyond the line of the most
advanced settlements, and was then the terminus
of the Kansas-Pacific railroad. For this reason it

could be made a dépôt of supplies, and was a good
point from which to supervise matters in the section of country to be operated in, which district is
a part of the Great American Plains, extending
south from the Platte River in Nebraska to the
Red River in the Indian Territory, and westward
from the line of frontier settlements to the foot-
hills of the Rocky Mountains, a vast region embracing an area of about 150,000 square miles.
With the exception of a half-dozen military posts
and a few stations on the two overland emigrant
routes - the Smoky Hill to Denver, and the Arkansas to New Mexico - this country was an un-
settled waste known only to the Indians and a
few trappers. There were neither roads nor well-
marked trails, and the only timber to be found -
which generally grew only along the streams -
was so scraggy and worthless as hardly to deserve
the name. Nor was water by any means plentiful,
even though the section is traversed by important
streams, the Republican, the Smoky Hill, the Arkansas, the Cimarron, and the Canadian all flow-
ing eastwardly, as do also their tributaries in the
main. These feeders are sometimes long and
crooked, but as a general thing the volume of
water is insignificant except after rain-falls. Then,
because of unimpeded drainage, the little streams
fill up rapidly with torrents of water, which quickly

flows off or sinks into the sand, leaving only an occasional pool without visible inlet or outlet.

At the period of which I write, in 1868, the Plains were covered with vast herds of buffalo - the number has been estimated at 3,000,000 head - and with such means of subsistence as this everywhere at hand, the 6,000 hostiles were wholly unhampered by any problem of food-supply. The savages were rich too according to Indian standards, many a lodge owning from twenty to a hundred ponies; and consciousness of wealth and power, aided by former temporizing, had made them not only confident but defiant. Realizing that their thorough subjugation would be a difficult task, I made up my mind to confine operations during the grazing and hunting season to protecting the people of the new settlements and on the overland routes, and then, when winter came, to fall upon the savages relentlessly, for in that season their ponies would be thin, and weak from lack of food, and in the cold and snow, without strong ponies to transport their villages and plunder, their movements would be so much impeded that the troops could overtake them.

At the outbreak of hostilities I had in all, east of New Mexico, a force of regulars numbering about 2,600 men - 1,200 mounted and 1,400 foot troops. The cavalry was composed of the Seventh

and Tenth regiments; the infantry, of the Third
and Fifth regiments and four companies of the
Thirty-Eighth. With these few troops all the
posts along the Smoky Hill and Arkansas had to
be garrisoned, emigrant trains escorted, and the
settlements and routes of travel and the, construction parties on the Kansas-Pacific railway protected. Then, too, this same force had to furnish
for the field small movable columns, that were
always on the go, so it will be rightly inferred
that every available man was kept busy from the
middle of August till November; especially as
during this period the hostiles attacked over forty
widely dispersed places, in nearly all cases stealing
horses, burning houses, and killing settlers. It was
of course impossible to foresee where these de-
scents would be made, but as soon as an attack
was heard of assistance was always promptly rendered, and every now and then we succeeded in
killing a few savages. As a general thing, though,
the raiders escaped before relief arrived, and when
they had a few miles the start, all efforts to catch
them were futile. I therefore discouraged long
pursuits, and, in fact, did not approve of making
any at all unless the chances of obtaining paying
results were very evident, otherwise the troops
would be worn out by the time the hard work of
the winter was demanded from them.

To get ready for a winter campaign of six months gave us much to do. The thing most needed was more men, so I asked for additional cavalry, and all that could be spared - seven troops of the Fifth Cavalry - was sent to me. Believing this reinforcement insufficient, to supplement it I applied for a regiment of Kansas volunteers, which request being granted, the organization of the regiment was immediately begun at Topeka. It was necessary also to provide a large amount of transportation and accumulate quantities of stores, since the campaign probably would not end till spring. Another important matter was to secure competent guides for the different columns of troops, for, as I have said, the section of country to be operated in was comparatively unknown.

In those days the railroad town of Hays City was filled with so-called "Indian scouts," whose common boast was of having slain scores of redskins, but the real scout - that is, a guide and trailer knowing the habits of the Indians-was very scarce, and it was hard to find anybody familiar with the country south of the Arkansas, where the campaign was to be made. Still, about Hays City and the various military posts there was some good material to select from, and we managed to employ several men, who, from their experience on the Plains in various capacities, or from natural instinct and aptitude, soon became excellent guides and courageous and valuable scouts, some of them, indeed, gaining much distinction. Mr. William F. Cody ("Buffalo Bill"), whose renown has since become world-wide, was one of the men thus selected. He received his sobriquet from his marked success in killing buffaloes for a contractor, to supply fresh meat to the construction parties on the Kansas-Pacific railway. He had given up this business, however, and was now in the employ of the quartermaster's department of the army, and was first brought to my notice by distinguishing himself in bringing me an important despatch from Fort Larned to Fort Hays, a distance of sixty-five miles, through a section infested with Indians. The despatch informed me that the Indians near Larned were preparing to decamp, and this intelligence required that certain orders should be carried to Fort Dodge, ninety-five miles south of Hays. This too being a particularly dangerous route - several couriers having been killed on it - it was impossible to get one of the various "Petes," "Jacks," or "Jims" hanging around Hays City to take my communication. Cody learning of the strait I was in, manfully came to the rescue, and proposed to make the trip to Dodge, though he had just finished his long and perilous ride from Larned. I gratefully accepted his offer, and after four or five hours' rest he mounted a fresh horse and hastened on his journey, halting but once to rest on the way, and then only for an hour, the stop being made at Coon Creek, where he got another mount from a troop of cavalry. At Dodge he took six hours' sleep, and then continued on to his own post - Fort Larned - with more despatches. After resting twelve hours at Larned, he was again in the saddle with tidings for me at Fort Hays, General Hazen sending him, this time, with word that the villages had fled to the south of the Arkansas. Thus, in all, Cody rode about 350 miles in less than sixty hours, and such an exhibition of endurance and courage was more than enough to convince me that his services would be extremely valuable in the campaign, so I retained him at Fort Hays till the battalion of the Fifth Cavalry arrived, and then made him chief of scouts for that regiment.

The information brought me by Cody on his second trip from Larned indicated where the villages would be found in the winter, and I decided to move on them about the 1st of November. Only the women and children and the decrepit old men were with the villages, however - enough, presumably, to look after the plunder -

most of the warriors remaining north of the Arkansas to continue their marauding. Many severe
fights occurred between our troops and these
marauders, and in these affairs, before November
I over a hundred Indians were killed, yet from
the ease with which the escaping savages would
disappear only to fall upon remote settlements
with pillage and murder, the results were by no
means satisfactory. One of the most noteworthy
of these preliminary affairs was the gallant fight
made on the Republican River the 17th of September by my Aide, Colonel George A. Forsyth,
and party, against about seven hundred Cheyennes and Sioux. Forsyth, with Lieutenant Beecher,
and Doctor J. H. Mooers as surgeon, was in
charge of a company of citizen scouts, mostly expert rifle-shots, but embracing also a few Indian
fighters, among these Grover and Parr. The company was organized the latter part of August for
immediate work in defense of the settlements, and
also for future use in the Indian Territory when
the campaign should open there. About the time
the company had reached its complement - it was
limited to forty-seven men and three officers - a
small band of hostiles began depredations near
Sheridan City, one of the towns that grew up
over-night on the Kansas-Pacific railway. Forsyth
pursued this party, but failing to overtake it,

made his way into Fort Wallace for rations, intending to return from there to Fort Hays. Before
he started back, however, another band of Indians
appeared near the post and stole some horses
from the stage company. This unexpected raid
made Forsyth hot to go for the marauders, and he
telegraphed me for permission, which I as promptly gave him. He left the post on the 10th of September, the command consisting of himself, Lieutenant Beecher, Acting Assistant Surgeon Mooers,
and the full strength, forty-seven men, with a
few pack mules carrying about ten days' rations.

He headed north toward the Republican River.
For the first two days the trail was indistinct and
hard to follow. During the next three it continued
to grow much larger, indicating plainly that the
number of Indians ahead was rapidly increasing.
Of course this sign meant a fight as soon as a
large enough force was mustered, but as this was
what Forsyth was after, he pushed ahead with
confidence and alacrity. The night of the 16th of
September he encamped on the Arickaree branch
of the Republican, not far from the forks of the
river, with the expectation of resuming the march
as usual next day, for the indications were that
the main body of the savages must be still a long
way off, though in the preceding twenty-four
hours an occasional Indian had been seen.

But the enemy was much nearer than was thought, for at daybreak on the morning of the 17th he made known his immediate presence by a sudden dash at Forsyth's horses, a few of which were stampeded and captured before the scouts could reach them. This dash was made by a small party only to get the horses, so those engaged in it were soon driven off, but a few minutes later hundreds of savages - it was afterward learned that seven hundred warriors took part in the fight - hitherto invisible, showed themselves on the hills overlooking the camp and so menacingly as to convince Forsyth that his defense must be one of desperation. The only place at hand that gave any hope of successful resistance was a small island in the Arickaree, the channel on one side being about a foot deep while on the other it was completely dry; so to this position a hurried retreat was made. All the men and the remaining animals reached the island in safety, but on account of the heavy fire poured in from the neighboring hills the packs containing the rations and medicines had to be abandoned.

On seeing Forsyth's hasty move, the Indians, thinking they had him, prepared to overwhelm the scouts by swooping down on one side of the island with about five hundred mounted warriors, while about two hundred, covered by the tall

grass in the river-bottom attacked the other side,
dismounted.   But the brave little band sadly disappointed them.   When the charge came it was
met with such a deadly fire that a large number of
the fiends were killed, some of them even after
gaining the bank of the island. This check had the
effect of making the savages more wary, but they
were still bold enough to make two more assaults
before mid-day.   Each of these ending like the
first, the Indians thereafter contented themselves
with shooting all the horses, which had been tied
up to some scraggy little cottonwood-trees, and
then proceeded to lay siege to the party.

The first man struck was Forsyth himself.   He
was hit three times in all - twice in one leg, both
serious wounds, and once on the head, a slight
abrasion of the scalp.   A moment later Beecher
was killed and Doctor Mooers mortally wounded;
and in addition to these misfortunes the scouts
kept getting hit, till several were killed, and the
whole number of casualties had reached twenty-
one in a company of forty-seven.   Yet with all
this, and despite the seeming hopelessness of the
situation, the survivors kept up their pluck undi-
minished, and during a lull succeeding the third repulse dug into the loose soil till the entire party
was pretty well protected by rifle-pits.   Thus
covered they stood off the Indians for the next

three days, although of course their condition became deplorable from lack of food, while those who were hurt suffered indescribable agony, since no means were at hand for dressing their wounds.

By the third day the Indians, seeming to despair of destroying the beleaguered party before succor might arrive, began to draw off, and on the fourth wholly disappeared. The men were by this time nearly famished for food. Even now there was nothing to be had except horse-meat from the carcasses of the animals killed the first day, and this, though decidedly unpalatable, not to say disgusting, had to be put up with, and so on such unwholesome stuff they managed to live for four days longer, at the end of which time they were rescued by a column of troops under Colonel Bankhead, which had hastened from Fort Wallace in response to calls for help, carried there by two brave fellows - Stilwell and Truedell - who, volunteering to go for relief, had slipped through the Indians, and struck out for that post in the night after the first day's fight.

CHAPTER XIII.

FITTING OUT THE WINTER EXPEDITION - ACCOMPANYING
THE MAIN FORCE - THE OTHER COLUMNS - STRUCK
BY A BLIZZARD - CUSTERS FIGHT ON THE WASHITA
- DEFEAT AND DEATH OF BLACK KETTLE - MAS-
SACRE OF ELLIOTTS PARTY - RELIEF OF COLONEL
CRAWFORD.

T HE end of October saw completed the most
of my arrangements for the winter campaign, though the difficulties and hardships to be
encountered had led several experienced officers
of the army, and some frontiersmen like Mr. James
Bridger, the famous scout and guide of earlier
days, to discourage the project. Bridger even
went so far as to come out from St. Louis to dis-
suade me, but I reasoned that as the soldier was
much better fed and clothed than the Indian, I
had one great advantage, and that, in short, a successful campaign could be made if the operations
of the different columns were energetically conducted.   To see to this I decided to go in person
with the main column, which was to push down
into the western part of the Indian Territory,
having for its initial objective the villages which,

at the beginning of hostilities, had fled toward the head-waters of the Red River, and those also that had gone to the same remote region after decamping from the neighborhood of Larned at the time that General Hazen sent Buffalo Bill to me with the news.

The column which was expected to do the main work was to be composed of the Nineteenth Kansas Volunteer Cavalry, commanded by Colonel Crawford; eleven troops of the Seventh United States Cavalry, under General Custer, and a battalion of five companies of infantry under Brevet Major John H. Page. To facilitate matters, General Sully, the district commander, was ordered to rendezvous these troops and establish a supply dépôt about a hundred miles south of Fort Dodge, as from such a point operations could be more readily conducted. He selected for the dépôt a most suitable place at the confluence of Beaver and Wolf creeks, and on his arrival there with Custer's and Page's commands, named the place Camp Supply.

In conjunction with the main column, two others also were to penetrate the Indian Territory. One of these, which was to march east from New Mexico by way of Fort Bascom, was to be composed of six troops of the Third Cavalry and two companies of infantry, the whole under Colonel A. W. Evans. The other, consisting of seven troops of the Fifth Cavalry, and commanded by Brevet Brigadier-General Eugene A. Carr, was to march southeast from Fort Lyon; the intention being that Evans and Carr should destroy or drive in toward old Fort Cobb any straggling bands that might be prowling through the country west of my own line of march; Carr, as he advanced, to be joined by Brevet Brigadier-General W. H. Penrose, with five troops of cavalry already in the field southeast of Lyon. The Fort Bascom column, after establishing a dépôt of supplies at Monument Creek, was to work down the main Canadian, and remain out as long as it could feed itself from New Mexico; Carr, having united with Penrose on the North Canadian, was to operate toward the Antelope Hills and head-waters of the Red River; while I, with the main column was to move southward to strike the Indians along the Washita, or still farther south on branches of the Red River.

It was no small nor easy task to outfit all these troops by the time cold weather set in, and provide for them during the winter, but by the 1st of November I had enough supplies accumulated at Forts Dodge and Lyon for my own and Carr's columns, and in addition directed subsistence and forage for three months to be sent to Fort Gibson for final delivery at Fort Arbuckle, as I expected to feed the command from this place when we arrived in the neighborhood of old Fort Cobb, but through some mismanagement few of these stores got further than Gibson before winter came on.

November 1, all being ready, Colonel Crawford was furnished with competent guides, and, after sending two troops to Fort Dodge to act as my escort, with the rest of his regiment he started from Topeka November 5, under orders to march straight for the rendezvous at the junction of Beaver and Wolf creeks. He was expected to reach his destination about the 20th, and there unite with the Seventh Cavalry and the battalion of infantry, which in the mean time were on the march from Dodge. A few days later Carr and Evans began their march also, and everything being now in motion, I decided to go to Camp Supply to give the campaign my personal attention, determined to prove that operations could be successfully conducted in spite of winter, and bent on showing the Indians that they were not secure from punishment because of inclement weather - an ally on which they had hitherto relied with much assurance.

We started from Fort Hays on the 15th of November, and the first night out a blizzard struck us and carried away our tents; and as the gale was so violent that they could not be put up again, the rain and snow drenched us to the skin. Shivering from wet and cold, I took refuge under a wagon, and there spent such a miserable night that, when at last morning came, the gloomy predictions of old man Bridger and others rose up before me with greatly increased force. As we took the road the sleet and snow were still falling, but we labored on to Dodge that day in spite of the fact that many of the mules played out on the way. We stayed only one night at Dodge, and then on the 17th, escorted by a troop of cavalry and Forsyth's scouts, now under the command of Lieutenant Lewis Pepoon, crossed the Arkansas and camped the night of the 18th at Bluff Creek, where the two troops of the Nineteenth Kansas, previously detailed as my escort, were awaiting our coming. As, we were approaching this camp some suspicious looking objects were seen moving off at a long distance to the east of us, but as the scouts confidently pronounced them buffalo, we were unaware of their true character till next morning, when we became satisfied that what we had seen were Indians, for immediately after crossing Beaver Creek we struck a trail, leading to the northeast, of a war party that evidently came up from the head-waters of the Washita River.

The evening of November 21 we arrived at the

Camp Supply dépôt having traveled all day in another snow-storm that did not end till twenty-four hours later. General Sully, with Custer's regiment and the infantry battalion, had reached the place several days before, but the Kansas regiment had not yet put in an appearance. All hands were hard at work trying to shelter the stores and troops, but from the trail seen that morning, believing that an opportunity offered to strike an effective blow, I directed Custer to call in his working parties and prepare to move immediately, without waiting for Crawford's regiment, unaccountably absent. Custer was ready to start by the 23d, and he was then instructed to march north to where the trail had been seen near Beaver Creek and follow it on the back track, for, being convinced that the war party had come from the Washita, I felt certain that this plan would lead directly to the villages.

The difficulties attending a winter campaign were exhibited now with their full force, as the march had to be conducted through a snow-storm that hid surrounding objects, and so covered the country as to alter the appearance of the prominent features, making the task of the guides doubly troublesome; but in spite of these obstacles fifteen miles had been traversed when Custer encamped for the night. The next day the storm had ceased, and the weather was clear and cold. The heavy fall of snow had of course obliterated the trail in the bottoms, and everywhere on the level; but, thanks to the wind, that had swept comparatively bare the rough places and high ground, the general direction could be traced without much trouble. The day's march, which was through a country abounding with buffalo, was unattended by any special incident at first, but during the afternoon, after getting the column across the Canadian River - an operation which, on account of the wagons, consumed considerable time - Custer's scouts (friendly Osages) brought back word that, some miles ahead, they had struck fresh signs, a trail coming into the old one from the north, which, in their opinion, indicated that the war party was returning to the villages.

On the receipt of this news, Custer, leaving a guard with the wagons, hastily assembled the rest of his men, and pushing on rapidly, overtook the scouts and a detailed party from his regiment which had accompanied them, all halted on the new trail awaiting his arrival. A personal examination satisfied Custer that the surmises of his scouts were correct; and also that the fresh trail in the deep snow could at night be followed with ease. After a short halt for supper and rest the pursuit was resumed, the Osage scouts in advance, and although the hostile Indians were presumed to be yet some distance off, every precaution was taken to prevent detection and to enable our troops to strike them unawares. The fresh trail, which it was afterward ascertained had been made by raiders from Black Kettle's village of Cheyennes, and by some Arapahoes, led into the valley of the Washita, and growing fresher as the night wore on, finally brought the Osages upon a camp-fire, still smoldering, which, it was concluded, had been built by the Indian boys acting as herders of the ponies during the previous day. It was evident, then, that the village could be but a few miles off; hence the pursuit was continued with redoubled caution until, a few hours before dawn of the 27th, as the leading scouts peered over a rise on the line of march, they discovered a large body of animals in the valley below.

As soon as they reported this discovery, Custer determined to acquaint himself with the situation by making a reconnoissance in person, accompanied by his principal officers. So, sending back word to halt the cavalry, he directed the officers to ride forward with him; then dismounting, the entire party crept cautiously to a high point which overlooked the valley, and from where, by the bright moon then shining, they saw just how the village was situated. It position was such as to

admit of easy approach from all sides. So, to preclude an escape of the Indians, Custer decided to
attack at daybreak, and from four different directions.

The plan having been fully explained to the
officers, the remaining hours of the night were
employed in making the necessary dispositions.
Two of the detachments left promptly, since they
had to make a circuitous march of several miles
to reach the points designated for their attack;
the third started a little later; and then the fourth
and last, under Custer himself, also moved into
position.   As the first light grew visible in the
east, each column moved closer in to the village,
and then, all dispositions having been made according to the prearranged plan, from their appointed places the entire force - to the opening
notes of "Garry Owen," played by the regimental band as the signal for the attack - dashed
at a gallop into the village. The sleeping and
unsuspecting savages were completely surprised
by the onset; yet after the first confusion, during
which the impulse to escape principally actuated
them, they seized their weapons, and from behind
logs and trees, or plunging into the stream and
using its steep bank as a breastwork, they poured
upon their assailants a heavy fire, and kept on
fighting with every exhibition of desperation. In

such a combat mounted men were useless, so Custer directed his troopers to fight on foot, and the Indians were successively driven from one point of vantage to another, until, finally, by 9 o'clock the entire camp was in his possession and the victory complete. Black Kettle and over one hundred of his warriors were killed, and about fifty women and children captured; but most of the non-combatants, as well as a few warriors and boys, escaped in the confusion of the fight. Making their way down the river, these fugitives alarmed the rest of the Cheyennes and Arapahoes, and also the Kiowas and Comanches, whose villages were in close proximity - the nearest not more than two miles off.

Then of course all the warriors of these tribes rallied to attack Custer, who meantime was engaged burning Black Kettle's camp and collecting his herds of ponies. But these new foes were rather wary and circumspect, though they already had partial revenge in an unlooked for way by cutting off Major Elliott and fifteen men, who had gone off in pursuit of a batch of young warriors when the fight was going on at the village. In fact, the Indians had killed Elliott's whole party, though neither the fate of the poor fellows, nor how they happened to be caught, was known till long afterward. It was then ascertained that the detachment pursued a course due south, nearly at right angles to the Washita River, and after galloping a couple of miles over the hills, crossing a small branch of the Washita on the way, they captured some of the fugitives. In bringing the prisoners back, Elliott was in turn attacked on the open prairie by a large number of savages from farther down the Washita, who by this time were swarming to the aid of Black Kettle's village. The little band fought its way gallantly to within rifle-range of the small creek referred to, but could get no farther, for the Indians had taken up a position in the bed of the stream, and from under cover of its banks Elliott and all his remaining men were quickly killed. No relief was sent them, for Custer, not having seen Elliott set out, knew nothing of the direction taken, and, besides, was busy burning the villages and securing the ponies, and deeply concerned, too, with defending himself from the new dangers menacing him. Elliott and his brave little party were thus left to meet their fate alone.

While Custer was burning the lodges and plunder and securing the ponies, the Indians from the villages down the Washita were gathering constantly around him till by mid-day they had collected in thousands, and then came a new problem as to what should be done. If he attacked the other villages, there was great danger of his being overwhelmed, and should he start back to Camp Supply by daylight, he would run the risk of losing his prisoners and the ponies, so, thinking the matter over, he decided to shoot all the ponies, and keep skirmishing with the savages till nightfall, and then, under cover of the darkness, return to Camp Supply; a programme that was carried out successfully, but Custer's course received some severe criticism because no effort was made to discover what had become of Elliott.

Custer had, in all, two officers and nineteen men killed, and two officers and eleven men wounded. The blow struck was a most effective one, and, fortunately, fell on one of the most villanous of the hostile bands that, without any provocation whatever, had perpetrated the massacres on the Saline and Solomon, committing atrocities too repulsive for recital, and whose hands were still red from their bloody work on the recent raid. Black Kettle, the chief, was an old man, and did not himself go with the raiders to the Saline and Solomon, and on this account his fate was regretted by some. But it was old age only that kept him back, for before the demons set out from Walnut Creek he had freely encouraged them by "making medicine," and by other devilish incantations that are gone through with at war and scalp dances.

When the horrible work was over he undertook to shield himself by professions of friendship, but being put to the test by my offering to feed and care for all of his band who would come in to Fort Dodge and remain there peaceably, he defiantly refused. The consequence of this refusal was a merited punishment, only too long delayed.

I received the first news of Custer's fight on the Washita on the morning of November 29. It was brought to me by one of his white scouts, "California Joe," a noted character, who had been experiencing the ups and downs of pioneer life ever since crossing the Plains in 1849. Joe was an invaluable guide and Indian fighter whenever the clause of the statute prohibiting liquors in the Indian country happened to be in full force. At the time in question the restriction was by no means a dead letter, and Joe came through in thirty-six hours, though obliged to keep in hiding during daylight of the 28th. The tidings brought were joyfully received by everybody at Camp Supply, and they were particularly agreeable to me, for, besides being greatly worried about the safety of the command in the extreme cold and deep snows, I knew that the immediate effect of a victory would be to demoralize the rest of the hostiles, which of course would greatly facilitate and expedite our ultimate success. Toward evening the day after Joe arrived the head of Custer's column made its appearance on the distant hills, the friendly Osage scouts and the Indian prisoners in advance. As they drew near, the scouts began a wild and picturesque performance in celebration of the victory, yelling, firing their guns, throwing themselves on the necks and sides of their horses to exhibit their skill in riding, and going through all sorts of barbaric evolutions and gyrations, which were continued till night, when the rejoicings were ended with the hideous scalp dance.

The disappearance of Major Elliott and his party was the only damper upon our pleasure, and the only drawback to the very successful expedition. There was no definite information as to the detachment, and Custer was able to report nothing more than that he had not seen Elliott since just before the fight began. His theory was, however, that Elliott and his men had strayed off on account of having no guide, and would ultimately come in all right to Camp Supply or make their way back to Fort Dodge; a very unsatisfactory view of the matter, but as no one knew the direction Elliott had taken, it was useless to speculate on other suppositions, and altogether too late to make any search for him.

I was now anxious to follow up Custer's stroke

by an immediate move to the south with the entire column, but the Kansas regiment had not yet
arrived. At first its non-appearance did not worry
me much, for I attributed the delay to the bad
weather, and supposed Colonel Crawford had
wisely laid up during the worst storms. Further-
waiting, however, would give the Indians a chance
to recover from the recent dispiriting defeat, so I
sent out scouting parties to look Crawford up and
hurry him along. After a great deal of searching,
a small detachment of the regiment was found
about fifty miles below us on the North Canadian,
seeking our camp. This detachment was in a
pretty bad plight, and when brought in, the officer
in charge reported that the regiment, by not following the advice of the guide sent to conduct
it to Camp Supply, had lost its way. Instead of
relying on the guides, Crawford had undertaken
to strike through the cañons of the Cimarron by
what appeared to him a more direct route, and in
the deep gorges, filled as they were with snow, he
had been floundering about for days without
being able to extricate his command. Then, too,
the men were out of rations, though they had been
able to obtain enough buffalo meat to keep from
starving. As for the horses, since they could get
no grass, about seven hundred of them had already
perished from starvation and exposure. Provi-

sions and guides were immediately sent out to the regiment, but before the relief could reach Crawford his remaining horses were pretty much all gone, though the men were brought in without loss of life. Thus, the regiment being dismounted by this misfortune at the threshold of the campaign, an important factor of my cavalry was lost to me, though as foot-troops the Kansas volunteers continued to render very valuable services till mustered out the next spring.

CHAPTER XIV.

A FEW days were necessarily lost setting up and refitting the Kansas regiment after its rude experience in the Cimarron cañons. This through with, the expedition, supplied with thirty days' rations, moved out to the south on the 7th of December, under my personal command. We headed for the Witchita Mountains, toward which rough region all the villages along the Washita River had fled after Custer's fight with Black Kettle. My line of march was by way of Custer's battle-field, and thence down the Washita, and if the Indians, could not sooner be brought to terms. I intended to follow them into the Witchita Mountains from near old Fort Cobb. The snow was still deep everywhere, and when we started the thermometer was below zero, but the sky being clear and the day very bright, the command was in excellent spirits. The column was made up of ten companies of the Kansas regiment, dismounted; eleven companies of the Seventh Cavalry, Pepoon's scouts, and the Osage scouts. In addition to Pepoon's men and the Osages, there was also "California-Joe," and one or two other frontiersmen besides, to act as guides and interpreters. Of all these the principal one, the one who best knew the country, was Ben Clark, a young man who had lived with the Cheyennes during much of his boyhood, and who not only had a pretty good knowledge of the country, but also spoke fluently the Cheyenne and Arapahoe dialects, and was an adept in the sign language.

The first day we made only about ten miles, which carried us to the south bank of Wolf Creek. A considerable part of the day was devoted to straightening out matters in the command, and allowing time for equalizing the wagon loads, which as a general thing, on a first day's march, are unfairly distributed. And then there was an abundance of fire-wood at Wolf Creek; indeed, here and on Hackberry Creek - where I intended to make my next camp - was the only timber north of the Canadian River; and to select the halting places near a plentiful supply of wood was almost indispensable, for as the men were provided with only shelter-tents, good fires were needed in order to keep warm.

The second day, after marching for hours through vast herds of buffalo, we made Hackberry Creek; but not, however, without several stampedes in the wagon-train, the buffalo frightening the mules so that it became necessary to throw out flankers to shoot the leading bulls and thus turn off the herds. In the wake of every drove invariably followed a band of wolves. This animal is a great coward usually, but hunger had made these so ravenous that they would come boldly up to the column, and as quick as a buffalo was killed, or even disabled, they would fall upon the carcass and eagerly devour it. Antelope also were very numerous, and as they were quite tame - being seldom chased - and naturally very inquisitive, it was not an unfrequent thing to see one of the graceful little creatures run in among the men and be made a prisoner. Such abundance of game relieved the monotony of the march to Hackberry Creek, but still, both men and animals were considerably exhausted by their long tramp, for we made over thirty miles that day.

We camped in excellent shape on the creek, and it was well we did, for a "Norther," or " blizzard," as storms on the Plains are now termed,

struck us in the night. During the continuance of
these blizzards, which is usually about three days,
the cold wind sweeps over the Plains with great
force, and, in the latitude of the Indian Territory,
is weighted with great quantities of sleet and
snow, through which it is often impossible to
travel; indeed, these "Northers" have many times
proved fatal to the unprotected frontiersman.
With our numbers the chance of any one's being
lost, and perishing alone (one of the most common dangers in a blizzard), was avoided; but
under any circumstances such a storm could but
occasion intense suffering to all exposed to it,
hence it would have been well to remain in camp
till the gale was over, but the time could not
be spared.   We therefore resumed the march
at an early hour next morning, with the expectation of making the south bank of the main Canadian and there passing the night, as Clark assured
me that timber was plentiful on that side of the
river.   The storm greatly impeded us, however,
many of the mules growing discouraged, and
some giving out entirely, so we could not get to
Clark's "good camp," for with ten hours of utmost
effort only about half a day's distance could be
covered, when at last, finding the struggle useless,
we were forced to halt for the night in a bleak
bottom on the north bank of the river. But no

one could sleep, for the wind swept over us with unobstructed fury, and the only fuel to be had was a few green bushes. As night fell a decided change of temperature added much to our misery, the mercury, which had risen when the "Norther" began, again falling to zero. It can be easily imagined that under such circumstances the condition of the men was one of extreme discomfort; in truth, they had to tramp up and down the camp all night long to keep from freezing. Anything was a relief to this state of things, so at the first streak of day we quit the dreadful place and took up the march.

A seemingly good point for crossing the Canadian was found a couple of miles down thestream, where we hoped to get our train over on the ice, but an experiment proving that it was not strong enough, a ford had to be made, which was done by marching some of the cavalry through the river, which was about half a mile wide, to break up the large floes when they had been cut loose with axes. After much hard work a passage way was thus opened, and by noon the command was crossed to the south bank, and after thawing out and drying our clothes before big fires, we headed for a point on the Wasia, where Clark said there was plenty of wood, and good water too, to make us comfortable till the blizzard had blown over.

We reached the valley of the Washita a little before dark, and camped some five or six miles above the scene of Custer's fight, where I concluded to remain at least a day, to rest the command and give it a chance to refit. In the mean time I visited the battle-field in company with Custer and several other officers, to see if there was a possibility of discovering any traces of Elliotts party. On arriving at the site of the village, and learning from Custer what dispositions had been made in approaching for the attack, the squadron of the escort was deployed and pushed across the river at the point where Elliott had crossed. Moving directly to the south, we had not gone far before we struck his trail, and soon the whole story was made plain by our finding, on an open level space about two miles from the destroyed village, the dead and frozen bodies of the entire party. The poor fellows were all lying within a circle not more than fifteen or twenty paces in diameter, and the little piles of empty cartridge shells near each body showed plainly that every man had made a brave fight. None were scalped, but most of them were otherwise horribly mutilated, which fiendish work is usually done by the squaws. All had been stripped of their clothing, but their comrades in the escort were able to identify the bodies, which being done, we gave them decent

GENERAL WILLIAM H. EMORY.

burial. Their fate was one that has overtaken many of our gallant army in their efforts to protect the frontiersmen's homes and families from savages who give no quarter, though they have often received it, and where the possibility of defeat in action carries with it the certainty of death and often of preceding torture.

From the meadow where Elliott was found we rode to the Washita, and then down the river through the sites of the abandoned villages, that had been strung along almost continuously for about twelve miles in the timber skirting the stream. On every hand appeared ample evidence that the Indians had intended to spend the winter here, for the ground was littered with jerked meat, bales of buffalo robes, cooking utensils, and all sorts of plunder usually accumulated in a permanent Indian camp. There were, also, lying dead near the villages hundreds of ponies, that had been shot to keep them from falling into our hands, the scant grazing and extreme cold having made them too weak to be driven along in the flight. The wholesale slaughter of these ponies was a most cheering indication that our campaign would be ultimately successful, and we all prayed for at least a couple of months more of cold weather and plenty of snow.

At the Kiowa village we found the body of a

white woman - a Mrs. Blynn - and also that of
her child. These captives had been taken by the
Kiowas near Fort Lyon the previous summer,
and kept close prisoners until the stampede began,
the poor woman being reserved to gratify the bru-
tal lust of the chief, Satanta; then, however, Indian vengeance demanded the murder of the
poor creatures, and after braining the little child
against a tree, the mother was shot through the
forehead, the weapon, which no doubt brought
her welcome release, having been fired so close
that the powder had horribly disfigured her face.
The two bodies were wrapped in blankets and
taken to camp, and afterward carried along in
our march, till finally they were decently interred
at Fort Arbuckle.

At an early hour on December 12 the command
pulled out from its cosy camp and pushed down
the valley of the Washita, following immediately
on the Indian trail which led in the direction of Fort
Cobb, but before going far it was found that the
many deep ravines and cañons on this trail would
delay our train very much, so we moved out of
the valley and took the level prairie on the divide.
Here the traveling was good, and a rapid gait was
kept up till mid-day, when, another storm of sleet
and snow coming on, it became extremely difficult for the guides to make out the proper course;

and fearing that we might get lost. or caught on the open plain without wood or water - as we had been on the Canadian - I turned the command back to the valley, resolved to try no more short-cuts involving the risk of a disaster to the expedition. But to get back was no slight task, for a dense fog just now enveloped us, obscuring all landmarks. However, we were headed right when the fog set in, and we had the good luck to reach the valley before night-fall, though there was a great deal of floundering about, and also much disputing among the guides as to where the river would be found Fortunately we struck the stream right at a large grove of timber, and established ourselves admirably. By dark the ground was covered with twelve or fifteen inches of fresh snow, and as usual the temperature rose very sensibly while the storm was on, but after night-fall the snow ceased and the skies cleared up. Daylight having brought zero weather again, our start on the morning of the 13th was painful work, many of the men freezing their fingers while handling the horse equipments, harness, and tents. However, we got off in fairly good season, and kept to the trail along the Washita notwithstanding the frequent digging and bridging necessary to get the wagons over ravines.

Continuing on this line for three days, we at length came to a point on the Washita where all signs indicated that we were nearing some of the villages. Wishing to strike them as soon as possible, we made a very early start next morning, the 17th. A march of four or five miles brought us to a difficult ravine, and while we were making preparations to get over, word was brought that several Indians had appeared in our front bearing a white flag and making signs that they had a communication to deliver. We signaled back that they would be received, when one of the party came forward alone and delivered a letter, which proved to be from General Hazen, at Fort Cobb. The letter showed that Hazen was carrying on negotiations with the Indians, and stated that all the tribes between Fort Cobb and my column were friendly, but the intimation was given that the Cheyennes and Arapahoes were still hostile, having moved off southward toward the Red River. It was added that Satanta and Lone Wolf - the chiefs of the Kiowas - would give information of the whereabouts of the hostiles; and such a communication coming direct from the representative of the Indian Department, practically took the Kiowas - the village at hand was of that tribe - under its protection, and also the Comanches, who were nearer in to

Cobb. Of course, under such circumstances I was compelled to give up the intended attack, though I afterward regretted that I had paid any heed to the message, because Satanta and Lone Wolf proved, by trickery and double dealing, that they had deceived Hazen into writing the letter.

When I informed the Kiowas that I would respect Hazen's letter provided they all came into Fort Cobb and gave themselves up, the two chiefs promised submission, and, as an evidence of good faith, proposed to accompany the column to Fort Cobb with a large body of warriors, while their villages moved to the same point by easy stages, along the opposite bank of the river-claiming this to be necessary from the poor condition of the ponies. I had some misgivings as to the sincerity of Satanta and Lone Wolf, but as I wanted to get the Kiowas where their surrender would be complete, so that the Cheyennes and Arapahoes could then be pursued, I agreed to the proposition, and the column moved on. All went well that day, but the next it was noticed that the warriors were diminishing, and an investigation showed that a number of them had gone off on various pretexts - the main one being to help along the women and children with the villages. With this I suspected that they were playing me false, and my suspicions grew into certainty when

Satanta himself tried to make his escape by slipping beyond the flank of the column and putting
spurs to his pony. Fortunately, several officers
saw him, and quickly giving chase, overhauled
him within a few hundred yards. I then arrested
both him and Lone Wolf and held them as hos-
tages-a measure that had the effect of bringing
back many of the warriors already beyond our
reach.

When we arrived at Fort Cobb we found some
of the Comanches already there, and soon after
the rest of them, excepting one band, came in to
the post. The Kiowas, however, were not on
hand, and there were no signs to indicate their
coming. At the end of two days it was plain
enough that they were acting in bad faith, and
would continue to unless strong pressure was
brought to bear. Indeed, they had already started
for the Witchita Mountains, so I put on the screws
at once by issuing an order to hang Satanta and
Lone Wolf, if their people did not surrender at
Fort Cobb within forty-eight hours. The two
chiefs promised prompt compliance, but begged
for more time, seeking to explain the non-arrival
of the women and children through the weak
condition of the ponies; but I was tired of their
duplicity, and insisted on my ultimatum.

The order for the execution brought quick fruit.

Runners were sent out with messages, by the two prisoners, appealing to their people to save the lives of their chiefs, and the result was that the whole tribe came in to the post within the specified time. The two manacled wretches thus saved their necks; but it is to be regretted that the execution did not come off; for some years afterward their devilish propensities led them into Texas, where both engaged in the most horrible butcheries.

The Kiowas were now in our hands, and all the Comanches too, except one small band, which, after the Custer fight, had fled toward the headwaters of the Red River. This party was made up of a lot of very bad Indians - outlaws from the main tribe - and we did not hope to subdue them except by a fight, and of this they got their fill; for Evans, moving from Monument Creek toward the western base of the Witchita Mountains on Christmas Day, had the good fortune to strike their village. In the snow and cold his approach was wholly unexpected, and he was thus enabled to deal the band a blow that practically annihilated it. Twenty-five warriors were killed outright, most of the women and children captured, and all the property was destroyed. Only a few of the party escaped, and some of these made their way in to Fort Cobb, to join the rest of their tribe in confinement; while others, later in the season, surrendered at Fort Bascom.

This sudden appearance of Evans in the Red River region also alarmed the Cheyennes and Arapahoes, and their thoughts now began to turn to submission. Food was growing scarce with them, too, as there was but little game to be found either in the Witchita Mountains or on the edge of the Staked Plains, and the march of Carr's column from Antelope Hills precluded their returning to where the buffalo ranged. Then, too, many of their ponies were dead or dying, most of their tepees and robes had been abandoned, and the women and children, having been kept constantly on the move in the winter's storms, were complaining bitterly of their sufferings.

In view of this state of things they intimated, through their Comanche-Apache friends at Fort Cobb, that they would like to make terms. On receiving their messages I entered into negotiations with Little Robe, chief of the Cheyennes, and Yellow Bear, chief of the Arapahoes, and despatched envoys to have both tribes understand clearly that they must recognize their subjugation by surrendering at once, and permanently settling on their reservations in the spring. Of course the usual delays of Indian diplomacy ensued, and it was some weeks before I heard the result.

Then one of my messengers returned with word that Little Robe and Yellow Bear were on their way to see me. They arrived a few days later, and, promptly acceding to the terms, promised to bring their people in, but as many of them would have to come on foot on account of the condition of the ponies, more time was solicited. Convinced of the sincerity of their professions I gave them a reasonable extension, and eventually Yellow Bear made good his word, but Little Robe, in spite of earnest and repeated efforts, was unable to deliver his people till further operations were begun against them.

While these negotiations were in progess I came to the conclusion that a permanent military post ought to be established well down on the Kiowa and Comanche reservation, in order to keep an eye on these tribes in the future, Fort Cobb, being an unsuitable location, because too far to the north to protect the Texas frontier, and too far away from where it was intended to permanently place the Indians. With this purpose in view I had the country thoroughly explored, and afterward a place was fixed upon not far from the base of the Witchita Mountains, and near the confluence of Medicine Bluff and Cash creeks, where building stone and timber could be obtained in plenty, and to this point I decided to move. The

place was named Camp Sill-now Fort Sill - in
honor of my classmate, General Sill, killed at Stone
River; and to make sure of the surrendered Indians, I required them all, Kiowas, Comanches, and
Comanche-Apaches, to accompany us to the new
post, so they could be kept under military control
till they were settled.

During the march to the new camp the weather
was not so cold as that experienced in coming
down from Camp Supply; still, rains were frequent,
and each was invariably followed by a depression
of temperature and high winds, very destructive
to our animals, much weakened by lack of food.
The men fared pretty well, however, for on the
rough march along the Washita, and during our
stay at Fort Cobb, they had learned to protect
themselves materially from the cold. For this
they had contrived many devices, the favorite
means being dugouts - that is, pits dug in the
ground, and roofed over with shelter-tents, and
having at one end a fire-place and chimney ingen-
iously constructed with sod. In these they lived
very snugly - four men in each-and would often
amuse themselves by poking their heads out and
barking at the occupants of adjacent huts in
imitation of the prairie-dog, whose comfortable nests had probably suggested the idea of
dugouts. The men were much better off, in

fact, than many of the officers, for the high winds frequently made havoc with our wall-tents. The horses and mules suffered most of all. They could not be sheltered, and having neither grain nor grass, the poor beasts were in no condition to stand the chilling blasts. Still, by cutting down cottonwood-trees, and letting the animals browse on the small soft branches, we managed to keep them up till, finally even this wretched food beginning to grow scarce, I had all except a few of the strongest sent to Fort Arbuckle, near which place we had been able, fortunately, to purchase some fields of corn from the half-civilized Chickasaws and Choctaws.

Through mismanagement, as previously noted, the greater part of the supplies which I had ordered hauled to Arbuckle the preceding fall had not got farther on the way than Fort Gibson, which post was about four hundred miles off, and the road abominable, particularly east of Arbuckle, where it ran through a low region called "boggy bottom." All along this route were abandoned wagons, left sticking in the mud, and hence the transportation was growing so short that I began to fear trouble in getting subsistence up for the men. Still, it would not do to withdraw, so I made a trip to Arbuckle chiefly for the purpose of reorganizing the transportation, but also with a view to opening a new route to that post, the road to lie on, high ground, so as to avoid the creeks and mud that had been giving us so much trouble. If such a road could be made, I hoped to get up enough rations and grain from the corn-fields purchased to send out a formidable expedition against the Cheyennes, so I set out for Arbuckle accompanied by my quartermaster, Colonel A. J. McGonigle. "California Joe" also went along to guide us through the scrub-oaks covering the ridge, but even the most thorough exploration failed to discover any route more practicable than that already in use; indeed, the high ground was, if anything, worse than the bottom land, our horses in the springy places and quicksands often miring to their knees. The ground was so soft and wet, in fact, that we had to make most of the way on foot, so by the time we reached Arbuckle I was glad to abandon the new road project.

Finding near Arbuckle more fields of corn than those already purchased, I had them bought also, and ordered more of the horses back there to be fed. I next directed every available mule to be put to hauling rations, having discovered that the full capacity of the transportation had not yet been brought into play in forwarding stores from Gibson, and with this regulation of the supply question I was ready to return immediately to Camp Sill. But my departure was delayed by California Joe, who, notwithstanding the prohibitory laws of the Territory, in some unaccountable way had got gloriously tipsy, which caused a loss of time that disgusted me greatly; but as we could not well do without Joe, I put off starting till the next day, by which time it was thought he would sober up. But I might just as well have gone at first, for at the end of the twenty-four hours the incorrigible old rascal was still dead drunk. How he had managed to get the grog to keep up his spree was a mystery which we could not solve, though we had had him closely watched, so I cut the matter short by packing him into my ambulance and carrying him off to Camp Sill.

By the time I got back to Sill, the Arapahoes were all in at the post, or near at hand. The promised surrender of the Cheyennes was still uncertain of fulfillment, however, and although Little Robe and his family had remained with us in evidence of good faith, the messages he sent to his followers brought no assurance of the tribes coming in - the runners invariably returning with requests for more time, and bringing the same old excuse of inability to move because the ponies were so badly off. But more time was just what I was determined not to grant, for I felt sure that if a surrender was not forced before the spring grass came, the ponies would regain their strength, and then it would be doubtful if the Cheyennes came in at all.

To put an end to these delays, Custer proposed to go out and see the Cheyennes himself, taking with him for escort only such number of men as could be fairly well mounted from the few horses not sent back to Arbuckle. At first I was inclined to disapprove Custer's proposition, but he urged it so strongly that I finally consented, though with some misgivings, for I feared that so small a party might tempt the Cheyennes to forget their pacific professions and seek to avenge the destruction of Black Kettle's band. However, after obtaining my approval, Custer, with characteristic energy, made his preparations, and started with three or four officers and forty picked men, taking along as negotiators Yellow Bear and Little Robe, who were also to conduct him to the head-waters of the Red River, where it was supposed the Cheyennes would be found. His progress was reported by couriers every few days, and by the time he got to the Witchita foot-hills he had grown so sanguine that he sent California Joe back to me with word that he was certain of success. Such hopeful anticipation relieved me greatly, of course, but just about the time I expected to hear that his mission had been achieved I was astonished by the party's return.   Inquiring as to the trouble, I learned that out toward the Staked Plains every sign of the Cheyennes had disappeared. Surprised and disappointed at this, and discouraged by the loneliness of his situation - for in the whole region not a trace of animal life was visible - Custer gave up the search, and none too soon, I am inclined to believe, to save his small party from perishing.

This failure put a stop to all expeditions till the latter part of February, by which time I had managed to lay in enough rations to feed the command for about thirty days; and the horses back at Arbuckle having picked up sufficiently for field service they were ordered to Sill, and this time I decided to send Custer out with his own and the Kansas regiment, with directions to insist on the immediate surrender of the Cheyennes, or give them a sound thrashing. He was ordered to get everything ready by March 1, and then move to the mouth of Salt Creek, on the North Fork of the Red River, at which place I proposed to establish a new dépôt for feeding the command.   Trains could reach this point from Camp Supply more readily than from Arbuckle, and wishing to arrange this part of the programme in person, I decided to return at once to

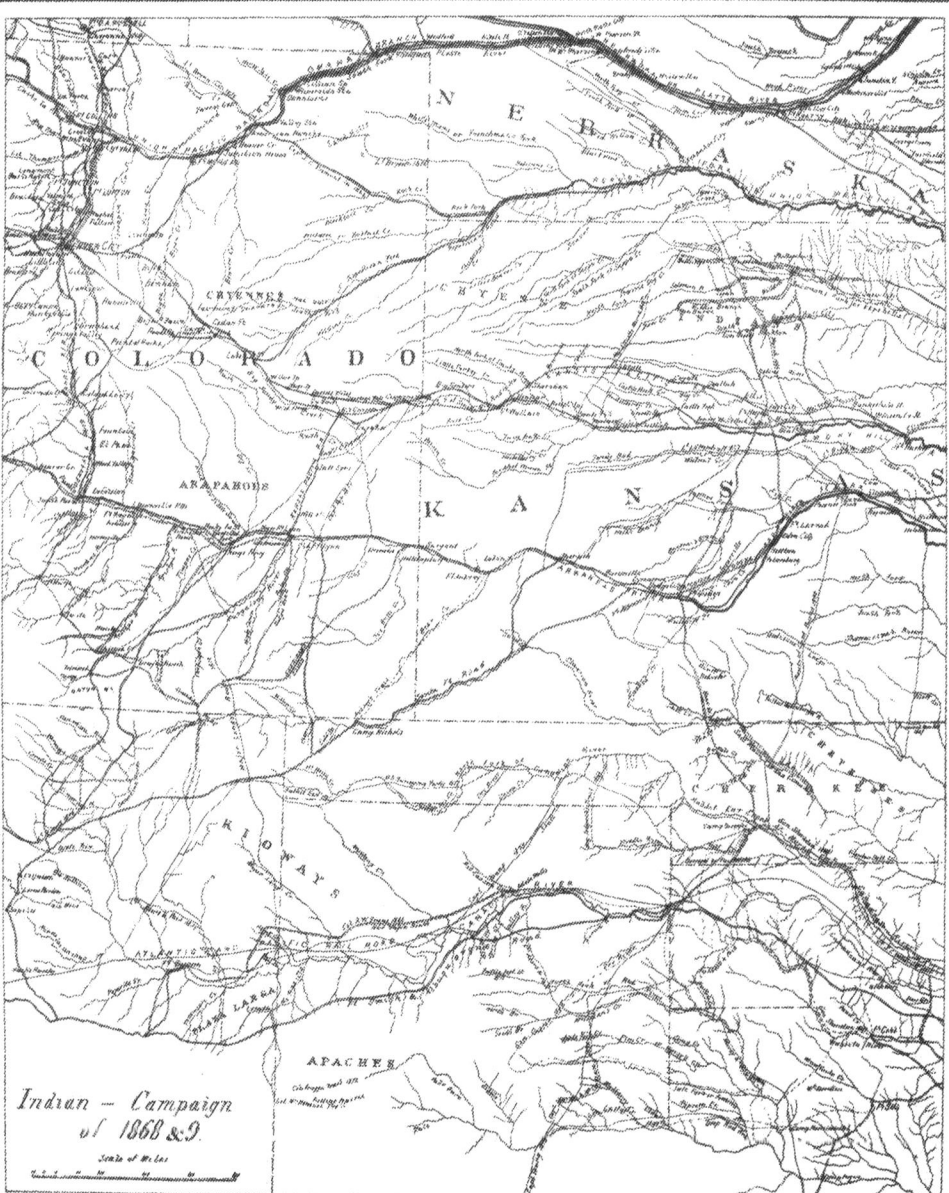

Indian — Campaign
of 1868 & 9.

Scale of Miles

Supply, and afterward rejoin Custer at Salt Creek, on what, I felt sure, was to be the final expedition of the campaign. I made the three hundred and sixty miles from Sill to Supply in seven days, but much to my surprise there found a despatch from General Grant directing me to repair immediately to Washington. These orders precluded, of course, my rejoining the command; but at the appointed time it set out on the march, and within three weeks brought the campaign to a successful close.

In this last expedition, for the first few days Custer's route was by the same trail he had taken in January - that is to say, along the southern base of the Witchita Mountains - but this time there was more to encourage him than before, for, on getting a couple of marches beyond old Camp Radziminski, on all sides were fresh evidences of Indians, and every effort was bent to strike them.

From day to day the signs grew hotter, and toward the latter part of March the game was found. The Indians being in a very forlorn condition, Custer might have destroyed most of the tribe, and certainly all their villages, but in order to save two white women whom, it was discovered, they held as captives, he contented himself with the renewal of the Cheyennes' agreement to come in to Camp Supply. In due time the entire tribe fulfilled its promise except one small band

under "Tall Bull," but this party received a good
drubbing from General Carr on the Republican
early in May.   After this fight all the Indians of
the southern Plains settled down on their reservations, and I doubt whether the peace would ever
again have been broken had they not in after
years been driven to hostilities by most unjust
treatment.

It was the 2d of March that I received at Camp
Supply Grant's despatch directing me to report
immediately in Washington.   It had been my
intention, as I have said, to join Custer on the
North Fork of the Red River, but this new order
required me to recast my plans, so, after arranging
to keep the expedition supplied till the end of the
campaign, I started for Washington, accompanied
by three of my staff - Colonels McGonigle and
Crosby, and Surgeon Asch - and Mr. DeB. Randolph Keim, a representative of the press, who
went through the whole campaign, and in 1870
published a graphic history of it. The day we
left Supply we had another dose of sleet and
snow, but nevertheless we made good time, and by
night-fall reached Bluff Creek. In twenty-four
hours more we made Fort Dodge, and on the 6th
of March arrived at Fort Hays.   Just south of the
Smoky Hill River, a little before we got to the
post, a courier heading for Fort Dodge passed us

at a rapid gait.   Suspecting that he had despatches for me, I directed my outrider to overtake him and find out.   The courier soon turned
back, and riding up to my ambulance handed me
a telegram notifying me that General Grant, on
the day of his inauguration, March 4, 1869, had
appointed me Lieutenant-General of the Army.
When I reported in Washington, the President
desired me to return to New Orleans and resume
command of the Fifth Military District, but this
was not at all to my liking, so I begged off, and
was assigned to take charge of the Division of
the Missouri, succeeding General Sherman, who
had just been ordered to assume command of the
Army.

CHAPTER XV.

A FTER I had for a year been commanding the Division of the Missouri, which embraced the entire Rocky Mountain region, I found it necessary to make an inspection of the military posts in northern Utah and Montana, in order by personal observation to inform myself of their location and needs, and at the same time become acquainted with the salient geographical and topographical features of that section of my division. Therefore in May, 1870, I started west by the Union-Pacific railroad, and on arriving at Corinne Station, the next beyond Ogden, took passage by stage - coach for Helena, the capital of Montana Territory. Helena is nearly five hundred miles north of Corinne, and under ordinary conditions the journey was, in those days, a most tiresome one. As the stage kept jogging on day and night, there was little chance for sleep, and there being with me a sufficient number of staff-officers to justify the proceeding, we chartered the "outfit," stipulating that we were to stop over one night on the road to get some rest. This rendered the journey more tolerable, and we arrived at Helena. without extraordinary fatigue.

Before I left Chicago the newspapers were filled with rumors of impending war between Germany and France. I was anxious to observe the conflict, if it was to occur, but reports made one day concerning the beginning of hostilities would be contradicted the next, and it was not till I reached Helena that the despatches lost their doubtful character, and later became of so positive a nature as to make it certain that the two nations would fight. I therefore decided to cut short my tour of inspection, so that I could go abroad to witness the war, if the President would approve. This resolution limited my stay in Helena to a couple of days, which were devoted to arranging for an exploration of what are now known as the Upper and the Lower Geyser Basins of the Yellowstone Park. While journeying between Corinne and Helena I had gained some vague knowledge of these geysers from an old mountaineer named Atkinson, but his information was very indefinite,

mostly second-hand; and there was such general
uncertainty as to the character of this wonderland
that I authorized an escort of soldiers to go that
season from Fort Ellis with a small party, to make
such superficial explorations as to justify my sending an engineer officer with a well-equipped expedition there next summer to scientifically
examine and report upon the strange country.
When the arrangements for this preliminary expedition were completed I started for Fort Benton,
the head of navigation on the Missouri River, on
the way passing through Fort Shaw, on Sun River.
I expected to take at Benton a steamboat to Fort
Stevenson, a military post which had been established about eighty miles south of Fort Buford,
near a settlement of friendly Mandan and Arickaree Indians, to protect them from the hostile
Sioux.   From there I was to make my way overland, first to Fort Totten near Devils lake in Da-
kota, and thence by way of Fort Abercrombie to
Saint Cloud, Minnesota, the terminus of the railroad.

Luckily I met with no delay in getting a boat
at Benton, and though the water was extremely
low, we steamed down the channel of the Missouri with but slight detention till we got within
fifty miles of Fort Buford.   Here we struck on a
sand bar with such force of steam and current as

to land us almost out of the water from stem to midships. This bad luck was tantalizing, for to land on a bar when your boat is under full headway down- stream in the Missouri River is no trifling matter, especially if you want to make time, for the rapid and turbid stream quickly depositing sand under the hull, makes it commonly a task of several days to get your boat off again. As from our mishap the loss of much time was inevitable, I sent a messenger to Fort Buford for a small escort, and for horses to take my party in to the post. Colonel Morrow, the commandant, came himself to meet us, bringing a strong party of soldiers and some friendly Indian scouts, because, he said, there were then in the region around Buford so many treacherous band of Sioux as to make things exceedingly unsafe.

Desiring to reach the post without spending more than one night on the way, we abandoned our steamer that evening, and set off at an early hour the next morning. We made camp at the end of the day's march within ten miles of Buford, and arrived at the post without having had any incident of moment, unless we may dignify as one a battle with three grizzly bears, discovered by our friendly Indians the morning of our second day's journey. While eating our breakfast - a rather slim one, by the way - spread on a piece of canvas, the Indians, whose bivouac was some distance off, began shouting excitedly, "Bear! bear!" and started us all up in time to see, out on the plain some hundreds of yards away, an enormous grizzly and two almost full-grown cubs. Chances like this for a bear hunt seldom offered, so there was hurried mounting - the horses being already saddled - and a quick advance made on the game from many directions, Lieutenant Townsend, of the escort, and five or six of the Indians going with me. Alarmed by the commotion, bruin and her cubs turned about, and with an awkward yet rapid gait headed for a deep ravine, in which there was brushwood shelter.

My party rode directly across the prairie and struck the trail not far behind the game. Then for a mile or more the chase was kept up, but with such poor shooting because of the "buck fever" which had seized most of us, that we failed to bring down any of the grizzlies, though the cubs grew so tired that the mother was often obliged to halt for their defense, meanwhile urging them on before her. When the ravine was gained she hid the cubs away in the thick brushwood, and then coming out where we could plainly see her, stood on the defense just within the edge of the thicket, beyond the range of our rifles though, unless we went down into the cañon,

which we would have to do on foot, since the precipitous wall precluded going on horseback. For
an adventure like this I confess I had little incli-
nation, and on holding a council of war, I found
that the Indians had still less, but Lieutenant
Townsend, who was a fine shot, and had refrained
from firing hitherto in the hope that I might bag
the game, relieved the embarrassing situation and
saved the credit of the party by going down alone
to attack the enemy. Meanwhile I magnani-
mously held his horse, and the Sioux braves did a
deal of shouting, which they seemed to think of
great assistance.

Townsend, having descended to the bottom of
the ravine, approached within range, when the old
bear struck out, dashing into and out of the
bushes so rapidly, however, that he could not get
fair aim at her, but the startled cubs running into
full view, he killed one at the first shot and at the
second wounded the other. This terribly enraged
the mother, and she now came boldly out to fight,
exposing herself in the open ground so much as
to permit a shot, that brought her down too, with
a broken shoulder. Then the Indians and I, growing very brave, scrambled down to take part in
the fight. It was left for me to despatch the
wounded cub and mother, and having recovered
possession of my nerves, I did the work effective-

ly, and we carried off with us the skins of the three animals as trophies of the hunt and evidence of our prowess.

As good luck would have it, when we reached Buford we found a steamboat there unloading stores, and learned that it would be ready to start down the river the next day. Embarking on her, we got to Stevenson in a few hours, and finding at the post camp equipage that had been made ready for our use in crossing overland to Fort Totten, we set out the following forenoon, taking with us a small escort of infantry, transported in two light wagons, a couple of Mandans and the post interpreter going along as mounted guides.

To reach water we had to march the first day to a small lake forty miles off, and the oppressive heat, together with the long distance traveled, used up one of the teams so much that, when about to start out the second morning, we found the animals unable to go on with any prospect of finishing the trip, so I ordered them to be rested forty-eight hours longer, and then taken back to Stevenson. This diminished the escort by one-half, yet by keeping the Indians and interpreter on the lookout, and seeing that our ambulance was kept closed up on the wagon carrying the rest of the detachment, we could, I thought, stand off any ordinary party of hostile Indians.

About noon I observed that the scouts in advance had left the trail and begun to reconnoitre a low ridge to their right, the sequel of which was that in a few minutes they returned to the wagons on a dead run and reported Sioux just ahead. Looking in the direction indicated, I could dimly see five or six horsemen riding in a circle, as Indians do when giving warning to their camp, but as our halt disclosed that we were aware of their proximity, they darted back again behind the crest of the ridge. Anticipating from this move an immediate attack, we hastily prepared for it by unhooking the mules from the wagon and ambulance, so that we could use the vehicles as a barricade. This done, I told the interpreter to take the Mandan scouts and go over toward the ridge and reconnoitre again. As the scouts neared the crest two of them dismounted, and, crawling slowly on their bellies to the summit, took a hasty look and returned at once to their horses, coming back with word that in the valley beyond was a camp of at least a hundred Sioux lodges, and that the Indians were hurriedly getting ready to attack us. The news was anything but cheering, for with a village of that size the warriors would number two or three hundred, and could assail us from every side.

Still, nothing could be done but stand and take

what was to come, for there was no chance of escape - it being supreme folly to undertake in wagons a race with Indians to Fort Stevenson, sixty miles away. To make the best of the situation, we unloaded the baggage, distributing and adjusting the trunks, rolls of bedding, cracker-boxes, and everything else that would stop a bullet, in such manner as to form a square barricade, two sides of which were the wagons, with the mules haltered to the wheels. Every man then supplied himself with all the ammunition he could carry, and the Mandan scouts setting up the depressing wail of the Indian death-song, we all awaited the attack with the courage of despair.

But no attack came; and time slipping by, and we still unmolested, the interpreter and scouts were sent out to make another reconnaissance. Going through just such precautions as before in approaching the ridge, their slow progress kept us in painful suspense; but when they got to the crest the strain on our nerves was relieved by seeing them first stand up boldly at full height, and then descend beyond. Quickly returning, they brought welcome word that the whole thing was a mistake, and no Sioux were there at all; What had been taken for a hundred Indian lodges turned out to be the camp of a Government train on its way to Fort Stevenson, and the officer in charge seeing

the scouts before they discovered him, and believing them to be Sioux, had sent out to bring his
herds in. It would be hard to exaggerate the
relief that this discovery gave us, and we all
breathed much easier. The scare was a bad one,
and I have no hesitation in saying that, had we
been mounted, it is more than likely that, instead
of showing fight, we would have taken up a lively
pace for Fort Stevenson.

After reciprocal explanations with the officer in
charge of the train, the march was resumed, and
at the close of that day we camped near a small
lake about twenty miles from Fort Totten. From
Totten we journeyed on to Fort Abercrombie.
The country between the two posts is low and
flat, and I verily believe was then the favorite
abiding-place of the mosquito, no matter where
he most loves to dwell now; for myriads of the
pests rose up out of the tall rank grass - more than
I ever saw before or since - and viciously attacked
both men and animals. We ourselves were somewhat protected by gloves and head-nets, provided
us before leaving Totten, but notwithstanding
these our sufferings were wellnigh intolerable;
the annoyance that the poor mules experienced
must, therefore, have been extreme; indeed,
they were so terribly stung that the blood
fairly trickled down their sides. Unluckily, we

had to camp for one night in this region; but we partly evaded the ravenous things by banking up our tent walls with earth, and then, before turning in, sweeping and smoking out such as had got inside. Yet with all this there seemed hundreds left to sing and sting throughout the night. The mules being without protection, we tried hard to save them from the vicious insects by creating a dense smoke from a circle of smothered fires, within which chain the grateful brutes gladly stood; but this relief was only partial, so the moment there was light enough to enable us to hook up we pulled out for Abercrombie in hot haste.

From Abercrombie we drove on. to Saint Cloud, the terminus of the railroad, where, considerably the worse for our hurried trip and truly wretched experience with the mosquitoes, we boarded the welcome cars. Two days later we arrived in Chicago, and having meanwhile received word from General Sherman that there would be no objection to my going to Europe, I began making arrangements to leave, securing passage by the steamship Scotia.

President Grant invited me to come to see him at Long Branch before I should sail, and during my brief visit there he asked which army I wished to accompany, the German or the French. I told

him the German, for the reason that I thought
more could be seen with the successful side, and
that the indications pointed to the defeat of the
French. My choice evidently pleased him greatly,
as he had the utmost contempt for Louis Napoleon, and had always denounced him as a usurper
and a charlatan. Before we separated, the President gave me the following letter to the representatives of our Government abroad, and with it I
not only had no trouble in obtaining permission
to go with the Germans, but was specially favored
by being invited to accompany the headquarters
of the King of Prussia:

"LONG BRANCH, N. J., July 25, 1870.

"Lieutenant-General P. H. Sheridan, of the United States
Army, is authorized to visit Europe, to return at his own pleasure, unless otherwise ordered. He is commended to the good
offices of all representatives of this Government whom he may
meet abroad.

"To citizens and representatives of other Governments I introduce General Sheridan as one of the most skillful, brave and
deserving soldiers developed by the great struggle through which
the United States Government has just passed. Attention paid
him will be duly appreciated by the country he has served so
faithfully and efficiently.

"U. S. GRANT."

Word of my intended trip was cabled to Europe
in the ordinary press despatches, and our Minister
to France, Mr. Elihu B. Washburn, being an intimate friend of mine, and thinking that I might

wish to attach myself to the French army, did me the favor to take preliminary steps for securing the necessary authority. He went so far as to broach the subject to the French Minister of War, but in view of the informality of the request, and an unmistakable unwillingness to grant it being manifested, Mr. Washburn pursued the matter no further. I did not learn of this kindly interest in my behalf till after the capitulation of Paris, when Mr. Washburn told me what he had done of his own motion. Of course I thanked him gratefully, but even had he succeeded in getting the permission he sought I should not have accompanied the French army.

I sailed from New York July 27, one of my aides-de-camp, General James W. Forsyth, going with me. We reached Liverpool August 6, and the next day visited the American Legation in London, where we saw all the officials except our Minister, Mr. Motley, who, being absent, was represented by Mr. Moran, the Secretary of the Legation. We left London August 9 for Brussels, where we were kindly cared for by the American Minister, Mr. Russell Jones, who the same evening saw us off for Germany. Because of the war we secured transportation only as far as Vera, and here we received information that the Prussian Minister of War had telegraphed to the Military Inspector of Railroads to take charge of us on our arrival at Cologne, and send us down to the headquarters of the Prussian army, but the Inspector, for some unexplained reason, instead of doing this, sent us on to Berlin. Here our Minister, Mr. George Bancroft, met us with a telegram from the German Chancellor, Count Bismarck, saying we were expected to come direct to the King's headquarters; and we learned also that a despatch had been sent to the Prussian Minister at Brussels directing him to forward us from Cologne to the army, instead of allowing us to go on to Berlin, but that we had reached and quit Brussels without the Minister's knowledge.

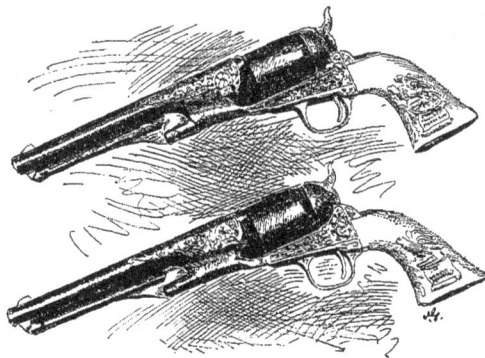

CHAPTER XVI.

LEAVING FOR THE SEAT OF WAR - MEETING WITH PRINCE
BISMARCK - HIS INTEREST IN PUBLIC OPINION IN
AMERICA - HIS INCLINATIONS IN EARLY LIFE -
PRESENTED TO THE KING - THE BATTLE OF GRAVE -
LOTTE - THE GERMAN PLAN - ITS FINAL SUCCESS
-SENDING NEWS OF THE VICTORY - MISTAKEN
FOR A FRENCHMAN.

SHORTLY after we arrived in Berlin the
Queen sent a messenger offering us an opportunity to pay our respects, and fixed an hour
for the visit, which was to take place the next day;
but as the tenor of the despatch Mr. Bancroft had
received from Count Bismarck indicated that
some important event which it was desired I
should witness was about to happen at the theatre
of war, our Minister got us excused from our visit
of ceremony, and we started for the headquarters
of the German army that evening-our stay in
the Prussian capital having been somewhat less
than a day.

Our train was a very long one, of over eighty
cars, and though drawn by three locomotives, its
progress to Cologne was very slow and the jour-

ney most tedious. From Cologne we continued on by rail up the valley of the Rhine to Binge-bruck, near Bingen, and thence across through Saarbrücken to Remilly, where we left the railway and rode in a hay-wagon to Pont-à-Mousson, arriving there August 17, late in the afternoon. This little city had been ceded to France at the Peace of Westphalia, and although originally German, the people had become, in the lapse of so many years, intensely French in sentiment. The town was so full of officers and men belonging to the German army that it was difficult to get lodgings, but after some delay we found quite comfortable quarters at one of the small hotels, and presently, after we had succeeded in getting a slender meal, I sent my card to Count von Bismarck, the Chancellor of the North German Confederation, who soon responded by appointing an hour - about 9 oćlock the same evening - for an interview.

When the Count received me he was clothed in the undress uniform of the Cuirassier regiment, of which he was the colonel. During the interview which ensued, he exhibited at times deep anxiety regarding the conflict now imminent, for it was the night before the battle of Gravelotte, but his conversation was mostly devoted to the state of public sentiment in America, about which he seemed much concerned, inquiring repeatedly as to which side - France or Prussia - was charged with bringing on the war. Expressing a desire to witness the battle which was expected to occur the next day, and remarking that I had not had sufficient time to provide the necessary transportation, he told me to be ready at 4 oʹclock in the morning, and he would take me out in his own carriage and present me to the King, adding that he would ask one of his own staff-officers, who he knew had one or two extra horses, to lend me one. As I did not know just what my status would be, and having explained to the President before leaving America that I wished to accompany the German army unofficially, I hardly knew whether to appear in uniform or not, so I spoke of this matter too, and the Count, after some reflection, thought it best for me to wear my undress uniform, minus the sword, however, because I was a non-combatant.

At 4 oʹclock the next morning, the 18th, I repaired to the Chancellorʹs quarters. The carriage was at the door, also the saddle-horse, but as no spare mount could be procured for General Forsyth, he had to seek other means to reach the battle-field. The carriage was an open one with two double seats, and in front a single one for a messenger; it had also a hand-brake attached.

Count Bismarck and I occupied the rear seat, and Count Bismarck-Bohlen - the nephew and aide-de-camp to the Chancellor - and Doctor Busch were seated facing us. The conveyance was strong, serviceable, and comfortable, but not specially prepossessing, and hitched to it were four stout horses - logy, ungainly animals, whose clumsy harness indicated that the whole equipment was meant for heavy work. Two postitions in uniform, in high military saddles on the nigh horse of each span, completed the establishment.

All being ready, we took one of the roads from Pont-à-Mousson to Rézonville, which is on the direct road from Metz to Chalons, and near the central point of the field where, on the 16th of August, the battle of Mars-la-Tour had been fought. It was by this road that the Pomeranians, numbering about 30,000 men, had been ordered to march to Gravelotte, and after proceeding a short distance we overtook the column. As this contingent came from Count Bismarcks own section of Germany, there greeted us as we passed along, first in the dim light of the morning, and later in the glow of the rising sun, continuous and most enthusiastic cheering for the German Chancellor.

On the way Count Bismarck again recurred to the state of public opinion in America with reference to the war. He also talked much about our form of government, and said that in early life his tendencies were all toward republicanism, but that family influence had overcome his preferences, and intimated that, after adopting a political career, he found that Germany was not sufficiently advanced for republicanism. He said, further, that he had been reluctant to enter upon this public career, that he had always longed to be a soldier, but that here again family opposition had turned him from the field of his choice into the sphere of diplomacy.

Not far from Mars-la-Tour we alighted, and in a little while an aide-de-camp was introduced, who informed me that he was there to conduct and present me to his Majesty, the King of Prussia. As we were walking along together, I inquired whether at the meeting I should remove my cap, and he said no; that in an out-of-door presentation it was not etiquette to uncover if in uniform. We were soon in presence of the King, where - under the shade of a clump of second-growth poplar-trees, with which nearly all the farms in the north of France are here and there dotted - the presentation was made in the simplest and most agreeable manner.

His Majesty, taking my hand in both of his, gave me a thorough welcome, expressing, like Count Bismarck, though through an interpreter, much interest as to the sentiment in my own country about the war. At this time William the First of Prussia was seventy-three years of age, and, dressed in the uniform of the Guards, he seemed to be the very ideal soldier, and graced with most gentle and courteous manners. The conversation, which was brief, as neither of us spoke the other's native tongue, concluded by his Majesty's requesting me in the most cordial way to accompany his headquarters during the campaign. Thanking him for his kindness, I rejoined Count Bismarck's party, and our horses having arrived meantime, we mounted and moved off to the position selected for the King to witness the opening of the battle.

This place was on some high ground overlooking the villages of Rézonville and Gravelotte, about the centre of the battle-field of Mars-la-Tour, and from it most of the country to the east toward Metz could also be seen. The point chosen was an excellent one for the purpose, though in one respect disagreeable, since the dead bodies of many of the poor fellows killed there two days before were yet unburied. In a little while the King's escort began to remove these dead, however, bearing them away on stretchers improvised with their rifles, and the spot thus cleared was much more acceptable. Then, when such unex-

ploded shells as were lying around loose had
been cautiously carried away, the King, his brother, Prince Frederick Charles Alexander, the chief-
of-staff, General von Moltke, the Minister of War,
General von Roon, and Count von Bismarck assembled on the highest point, and I being asked
to join the group, was there presented to General
von Moltke. He spoke our language fluently,
and Bismarck having left the party for a time to
go to a neighboring house to see his son, who had
been wounded at Mars-la-Tour, and about whom
he was naturally very anxious, General von Moltke
entertained me by explaining the positions of the
different corps, the nature and object of their
movements then taking place, and so on.

Before us, and covering Metz, lay the French
army, posted on the crest of a ridge extending
north, and about its centre curving slightly westward toward the German forces. The left of the
French position was but a short distance from
the Moselle, and this part of the line was separated from the Germans by a ravine, the slopes,
fairly well wooded, rising quite sharply; farther
north, near the centre, this depression disappeared,
merged in the general swell of the ground, and
thence on toward the right the ground over
which an approach to the French line must be
made was essentially a natural open glacis, that

could be thoroughly swept by the fire of the defenders.

The line extended some seven or eight miles. To attack this position, formidable everywhere, except perhaps on the right flank, the Germans were bringing up the combined forces of the First and Second armies, troops that within the past fortnight had already successfully met the French in three pitched battles. On the right was the First Army, under command of General Von Steinmetz, the victors, August 6, of Spicheren, near Saar, and, eight days later, of Colombey, to the east of Metz; while the centre and left were composed of the several corps of the Second Army, commanded by Prince Frederick Charles of Prussia, a part of whose troops had just been engaged in the sanguinary battle of Mars-la-Tour, by which Bazaine was cut off from the Verdun road, and forced back toward Metz.

At first the German plan was simply to threaten with their right, while the corps of the Second Army advanced toward the north, to prevent the French, of whose intentions there was much doubt, from escaping toward Chalons; then, as the purposes of the French might be developed, these corps were to change direction toward the enemy successively, and seek to turn his right flank. But the location of this vital turning-point was very uncertain, and until it was ascertained and carried, late in the afternoon, the action raged with more or less intensity along the entire line.

But as it is not my purpose to describe in detail the battle of Gravelotte, nor any other, I will speak of some of its incidents merely. About noon, after many preliminary skirmishes, the action was begun according to the plan I have already outlined, the Germans advancing their left while holding on strongly with their right, and it was this wing (the First Army) that came under my observation from the place where the King's headquarters were located. From here we could see, as I have said, the village of Gravelotte. Before it lay the German troops, concealed to some extent, especially to the left, by clumps of timber here and there. Immediately in front of us, however, the ground was open, and the day being clear and sunny, with a fresh breeze blowing (else the smoke from a battle between four hundred thousand men would have obstructed the view altogether), the spectacle presented was of unsurpassed magnificence and sublimity. The German artillery opened the battle, and while the air was filled with shot and shell from hundreds of guns along their entire line, the German centre and left, in rather open order, moved out to the attack, and as they went forward the reserves, in close column, took up positions within supporting distances, yet far enough back to be out of range.

The French artillery and mitrailleuses responded vigorously to the Krupps, and with deadly effect, but as far as we could see the German left continued its advance, and staff-officers came up frequently to report that all was going on well at points hidden from our view These reports were always made to the King first, and whenever anybody arrived with tidings of the fight we clustered around to hear the news, General Von Moltke unfolding a map meanwhile, and explaining the situation. This done, the chief of the staff, while awaiting the next report, would either return to a seat that had been made for him with some knapsacks, or would occupy the time walking about, kicking clods of dirt or small stones here and there, his hands clasped behind his back, his face pale and thoughtful. He was then nearly seventy years old, but because of his emaciated figure, the deep wrinkles in his face, and the crow's-feet about his eyes, he looked even older, his appearance being suggestive of the practice of church asceticisms rather than of his well-known ardent devotion to the military profession.

By the middle of the afternoon the steady progress of the German left and centre had driven the French from their more advanced positions from behind stone walls and hedges, through valleys and hamlets, in the direction of Metz, but as yet the German right had accomplished little except to get possession of the village of Gravelotte, forcing the French across the deep ravine I have mentioned, which runs north and south a little distance east of the town.

But it was now time for the German right to move in earnest to carry the Rozerieulles ridge, on which crest the French had evidently decided to make an obstinate fight to cover their withdrawal to Metz. As the Germans moved to the attack here, the French fire became heavy and destructive, so much so, indeed, as to cause General Von Steinmetz to order some cavalry belonging to the right wing to make a charge. Crossing the ravine before described, this body of horse swept up the slope beyond, the front ranks urged forward by the momentum from behind. The French were posted along a sunken road, behind stone walls and houses, and as the German cavalry neared these obstructions it received a dreadful fire without the least chance of returning it, though still pushed on till the front ranks were crowded into the deep cut of the road. Here the slaughter was terrible, for the horsemen could make no further headway; and because of the blockade behind, of dead and wounded men and animals, an orderly retreat was impossible, and disaster inevitable.

About the time the charge was ordered, the phase of the battle was such that the King concluded to move his headquarters into the village of Gravelotte; and just after getting there, we first learned fully of the disastrous result of the charge which had been entered upon with such spirit; and so much indignation was expressed against Steinmetz, who, it was claimed, had made an unnecessary sacrifice of his cavalry, that I thought he would be relieved on the spot; though this was not done.

Followed by a large staff, General Steinmetz appeared in the village presently, and approached the King. When near, he bowed with great respect, and I then saw that he was a very old man, though his soldierly figure, bronzed face, and short-cropped hair gave some evidence of vigor still. When the King spoke to him I was not close enough to learn what was said; but his Majesty's manner was expressive of kindly feeling, and the fact that in a few moments the veteran general returned to the command of his troops, indicated that, for the present at least, his fault had been overlooked.

The King then moved out of the village, and just a little to the east and north of it the headquarters were located on high, open ground, whence we could observe the right of the German infantry advancing up the eastern face of the ravine. The advance, though slow and irregular, resulted in gradually gaining ground, the French resisting stoutly with a stubborn musketry fire all along the slopes. Their artillery was silent, however; and from this fact the German artillery officers grew jubilant, confidently asserting that their Krupp guns had dismounted the French batteries and knocked their mitrailleuses to pieces. I did not indulge in this confidence, however; for, with the excellent field-glass I had, I could distinctly see long columns of French troops moving to their right, for the apparent purpose of making a vigorous fight on that flank; and I thought it more than likely that their artillery would be heard from before the Germans could gain the coveted ridge.

The Germans labored up the glacis slowly at the most exposed places; now crawling on their bellies, now creeping on hands and knees, but, in the main, moving with erect and steady bearing. As they approached within short range, they suddenly found that the French artillery and mitrailleuses had by no means been silenced - about two hundred pieces opening on them with fearful effect, while at the same time the whole crest

GENERAL GEORGE CROOK.

375

blazed with a deadly fire from the Chassepôt rifles. Resistance like this was so unexpected by the Germans that it dismayed them; and first wavering a moment, then becoming panic-stricken, they broke and fled, infantry, cavalry, and artillery coming down the slope without any pretence of formation, the French hotly following and pouring in a heavy and constant fire as the fugitives fled back across the ravine toward Gravelotte. With this the battle on the right had now assumed a most serious aspect, and the indications were that the French would attack the heights of Gravelotte; but the Pomeranian corps coming on the field at this crisis, was led into action by Von Moltke himself, and shortly after the day was decided in favor of the Germans.

When the French guns opened fire, it was discovered that the King's position was within easy range, many of the shells falling near enough to make the place extremely uncomfortable; so it was suggested that he go to a less exposed point. At first he refused to listen to this wise counsel, but yielded finally - leaving the ground with reluctance, however - and went back toward Rézonville. I waited for Count Bismarck, who did not go immediately with the King, but remained at Gravelotte, looking after some of the escort who had been wounded. When he had arranged for their care, we set out to rejoin the King, and before going far, overtook his Majesty, who had stopped on the Chalons road, and was surrounded by a throng of fugitives, whom he was berating in German so energetic as to remind me forcibly of the "Dutch" swearing that I used to hear in my boyhood in Ohio. The dressing down finished to his satisfaction, the King resumed his course toward Rézonville, halting, however, to rebuke in the same emphatic style every group of runaways he overtook.

Passing through Rézonville, we halted just beyond the village; there a fire was built, and the King, his brother, Prince Frederick Charles; and Von Roon were provided with rather uncomfortable seats about it, made by resting the ends of a short ladder on a couple of boxes. With much anxiety and not a little depression of spirits news from the battle-field was now awaited, but the suspense did not last long, for - presently came the cheering intelligence that the French were retiring, being forced back by the Pomeranian corps, and some of the lately broken right wing organizations, that had been rallied on the heights of Gravelotte. The lost ground being thus regained, and the French having been beaten on their right, it was not long before word came that Bazaines army was falling back to Metz, leaving the entire battle-field in possession of the Germans.

During the excitement of the day I had not much felt the want of either food or water, but now that all was over I was nearly exhausted, having had neither since early morning. Indeed, all of the party were in like straits; the immense armies had not only eaten up nearly everything in the country, but had drunk all the wells dry, too, and there seemed no relief for us till, luckily, a squad of soldiers came along the road with a small cask of wine in a cart. One of the staff-officers instantly appropriated the keg, and proceeded to share his prize most generously. Never had I tasted anything so refreshing and delicious, but as the wine was the ordinary sour stuff drunk by the peasantry of northern France, my appreciation must be ascribed to my famished condition rather than to any virtues of the beverage itself.

After I had thus quenched my thirst the King's brother called me aside, and drawing from his coat-tail pocket a piece of stale black bread, divided it with me, and while munching on this the Prince began talking of his son - General Prince Frederick Charles, popularly called the Red Prince - who was in command of the Second Army in this battle - the German left wing. In recounting his son's professional career the old man's face

was aglow with enthusiasm, and not without good
cause, for in the war between Prussia and Austria
in 1866, as well as in the present campaign, the
Red Prince had displayed the highest order of
military genius.

The headquarters now became the scene of
much bustle, despatches announcing the victory
being sent in all directions. The first one transmitted was to the Queen, the King directing
Count Bismarck to prepare it for his signature;
then followed others of a more official character,
and while these matters were being attended to I
thought I would ride into the village to find, if
possible, some water for my horse. Just as I entered the chief street, however, I was suddenly
halted by a squad of soldiers, who, taking me for
a French officer (my coat and forage cap resem-
bling those of the French), leveled their pieces at
me. They were greatly excited, so much so, indeed, that I thought my hour had come, for they
could not understand English, and I could not
speak German, and dare not utter explanations in
French. Fortunately a few disconnected German
words came to me in the emergency. With these
I managed to delay my execution, and one of the
party ventured to come up to examine the "suspect" more closely. The first thing he did was
to take off my cap, and looking it over carefully,

his eyes rested on the three stars above the visor, and, pointing to them, he emphatically pronounced me French. Then of course they all became excited again, more so than before, even, for they thought I was trying to practice a ruse, and I question whether I should have lived to recount the adventure had not an officer belonging to the King's headquarters been passing by just then, when, hearing the threatenings and imprecations, he rode up to learn the cause of the hubbub, and immediately recognized and released me. When he told my wrathy captors who I was, they were much mortified of course, and made the most profuse apologies, promising that no such mistake should occur again, and so on; but not feeling wholly reassured, for my uniform was still liable to mislead, I was careful to return to headquarters in company with my deliverer. There I related what had occurred, and after a good laugh all round, the King provided me with a pass which he said would preclude any such mishap in the future, and would also permit me to go wherever I pleased - a favor rarely bestowed.

CHAPTER XVII.

WHILE I was absent, as related in the preceding chapter, it had been decided that
the King's quarters should be established for the
night in the village of Rêzonville; and as it would
be very difficult, at such a late hour, to billet the
whole party regularly, Count Bismarck and I
went off to look for shelter for ourselves. Remembering that I had seen, when seeking to water
my horse, a partly burned barn with some fresh-
looking hay in it, I suggested that we lodge there.
He too thought it would answer our purpose, but
on reaching it we found the unburned part of the
barn filled with wounded, and this necessitating a
further search we continued on through the village in quest of some house not yet converted
into a hospital. Such, however, seemed impossible to come upon, so at last the Count fixed on

one whose upper floor, we learned, was unoccupied, though the lower one was covered with wounded.

Mounting a creaky ladder - there was no stairway - to the upper story, we found a good-sized room with three large beds, one of which the Chancellor assigned to the Duke of Mecklenburg and aide, and another to Count Bismarck-Bohlen and me, reserving the remaining one for himself. Each bed, as is common in Germany and northern France, was provided with a feather tick, but the night being warm, these spreads were thrown off, and discovering that they would make a comfortable shakedown on the floor, I slept there leaving Bismarck-Bohlen unembarrassed by companionship - at least of a human kind.

At daylight I awoke, and seeing that Count Bismarck was already dressed and about to go down the ladder, I felt obliged to follow his example, so I too turned out, and shortly descended to the ground-floor, the only delays of the toilet being those incident to dressing, for there were no conveniences for morning ablutions. Just outside the door I met the Count, who, proudly exhibiting a couple of eggs he had bought from the woman of the house, invited me to breakfast with him, provided we could beg some coffee from the king's escort. Putting the eggs under my charge, with many injunctions as to their safe-keeping, he went off to forage for the coffee, and presently returned, having been moderately successful. One egg apiece was hardly enough, however, to appease the craving of two strong men ravenous from long fasting. Indeed, it seemed only to whet the appetite, and we both set out on an eager expedition for more food. Before going far I had the good luck to meet a sutlers wagon, and though its stock was about all sold, there were still left four large bologna sausages, which I promptly purchased - paying a round sum for them too - and hastening back found the Count already returned, though without bringing anything at all to eat; but he had secured a couple of bottles of brandy, and with a little of this - it was excellent, too - and the sausages, the slim ration of eggs and coffee was amply reinforced.

Breakfast over, the Chancellor invited me to accompany him in a ride to the battle-field, and I gladly accepted, as I very much desired to pass over the ground in front of Gravelotte, particularly so to see whether the Krupp guns had really done the execution that was claimed for them by the German artillery officers. Going directly through the village of Gravelotte, following the causeway over which the German cavalry had passed to make its courageous but futile charge, we soon reached the ground where the fighting had been the most severe. Here the field was literally covered with evidences of the terrible strife, the dead and wounded strewn thick on every side.

In the sunken road the carnage had been awful; men and horses having been slaughtered there by hundreds, helpless before the murderous fire delivered from behind a high stone wall impracticable to mounted troops. The sight was sickening to an extreme, and we were not slow to direct our course elsewhere, going up the glacis toward the French line, the open ground over which we crossed being covered with thousands of helmets, that had been thrown off by the Germans during the fight and were still dotting the field, though details of soldiers from the organizations which had been engaged here were about to begin to gather up their abandoned headgear.

When we got inside the French works, I was astonished to observe how little harm had been done the defenses by the German artillery, for although I had not that serene faith in the effectiveness of their guns held by German artillerists generally, yet I thought their terrific cannonade must have left marked results. All I could perceive, however, was a disabled gun, a broken mitrailleuse, and two badly damaged caissons.

Everything else, except a little ammunition in the trenches, had been carried away, and it was plain to see, from the good shape in which the French left wing had retired to Metz, that its retreat had been predetermined by the disasters to the right wing.

By this hour the German cavalry having been thrown out to the front well over toward Metz, we, following it to get a look at the city, rode to a neighboring summit, supposing it would be a safe point of observation; but we shortly realized the contrary, for scarcely had we reached the crest when some of the French pickets, lying concealed about six hundred yards off, opened fire, making it so very hot for us that, hugging the necks of our horses, we incontinently fled. Observing what had taken place, a troop of German cavalry charged the French outpost and drove it far enough away to make safe our return, and we resumed possession of the point, but only to discover that the country to the east was so broken and hilly that no satisfactory view of Metz could be had.

Returning to Gravelotte, we next visited that part of the battle-field to the northeast of the village, and before long Count Bismarck discovered in a remote place about twenty men dreadfully wounded. These poor fellows had had no attention whatever, having been overlooked by the hospital corps, and their condition was most pitiful. Yet there was one very handsome man in the group-a captain of artillery - who, though shot through the right breast, was talkative and cheerful, and felt sure of getting well. Pointing, however, to a comrade lying near, also shot in the breast, he significantly shook his head; it was easy to see on this man's face the signs of fast approaching death.

An orderly was at once despatched for a surgeon, Bismarck and I doing what we could meanwhile to alleviate the intense sufferings of the maimed men, bringing them water and administering a little brandy, for the Count still had with him some of the morning's supply, When the surgeons came, we transferred the wounded to their care, and making our way to Rêzonville there took the Count's carriage to rejoin the King's headquarters, which in the mean time had been moved to Pont-à-Mousson. Our route led through the village of Gorze, and here we found the streets so obstructed with wagons that I feared it would take us the rest of the day to get through, for the teamsters would not pay the slightest heed to the cries of our postilions. The Count was equal to the emergency, however, for, taking a pistol from behind his cushion, and bidding me keep my seat,

he jumped out and quickly began to clear the
street effectively, ordering wagons to the right
and left. Marching in front of the carriage and
making way for us till we were well through the
blockade, he, then resumed his seat, remarking,
"This is not a very dignified business for the
Chancellor of the German Confederation, but its
the only way to get through."

At Pont-à-Mousson I was rejoined by my aide,
General Forsyth, and for the next two days our
attention was almost wholly devoted to securing
means of transportation. This was most difficult
to obtain, but as I did not wish to impose on the
kindness of the Chancellor longer, we persevered
till, finally, with the help of Count Bismarck-Bohl-
en, we managed to get tolerably well equipped
with a saddle-horse apiece, and a two-horse carriage. Here also, on the afternoon of August 21,
I had the pleasure of dining with the King. The
dinner was a simple one, consisting of soup, a
joint, and two or three vegetables; the wines
vin ordinaire and Burgundy. There were a good
many persons of high rank present, none of whom
spoke English, however, except Bismarck, who sat
next the King and acted as interpreter when his
Majesty conversed with me. Little was said of
the events taking place around us, but the King
made many inquiries concerning the war of the

rebellion, particularly with reference to Grant's campaign at Vicksburg; suggested, perhaps, by the fact that there, and in the recent movements of the German army, had been applied many similar principles of military science.

The French army under Marshal Bazaine having retired into the fortifications of Metz, that stronghold was speedily invested by Prince Frederick Charles. Meantime the Third Army, under the Crown Prince of Prussia - which, after having fought and won the battle of Worth, had been observing the army of Marshal MacMahon during and after the battle of Gravelotte - was moving toward Paris by way of Nancy, in conjunction with an army called the Fourth, which had been organized from the troops previously engaged around Metz, and on the 22d was directed toward Bar-le-Duc under the command of the Crown Prince of Saxony. In consequence of these operations the King decided to move to Commercy, which place we reached by carriage, traveling on a broad macadamized road lined on both sides with poplar-trees, and our course leading through a most beautiful country thickly dotted with prosperous-looking villages.

On reaching Commercy, Forsyth and I found that quarters had been already selected for us, and our names written on the door with chalk;

the quartermaster charged with the billeting of the officers at headquarters having started out in advance to perform this duty and make all needful preparations for the King before he arrived, which course was usually pursued thereafter, whenever the royal headquarters took up a new location.

Forsyth and I were lodged with the notary of the village, who over and over again referred to his good fortune in not having to entertain any of the Germans. He treated us most hospitably, and next morning, on departing, we offered compensation by tendering a sum - about what our bill would have been at a good hotel - to be used for the "benefit of the wounded or the Church." Under this stipulation the notary accepted, and we followed that plan of paying for food and lodging afterward, whenever quartered in private houses.

The next day I set out in advance of the headquarters, and reached Bar-le-Duc about noon, passing on the way the Bavarian contingent of the Crown Prince's army. These Bavarians were trim-looking soldiers, dressed in neat uniforms of light blue; they looked healthy and strong, but seemed of shorter stature than the North Germans I had seen in the armies of Prince Frederick Charles and General von Steinmetz. When, later in the day, the King arrived, a guard for him was detailed from this Bavarian contingent; a stroke of policy no doubt, for the South Germans were so prejudiced against their brothers of the North that no opportunity to smooth them down was permitted to go unimproved.

Bar-le-Duc, which had then a population of about 15,000, is one of the prettiest towns I saw in France, its quaint and ancient buildings and beautiful boulevards charming the eye as well as exciting deep interest. The King and his immediate suite were quartered on one of the best boulevards in a large building - the Bank of France - the balcony of which offered a fine opportunity to observe a part of the army of the Crown Prince the next day on its march toward Vitry. This was the first time his Majesty had had a chance to see any of these troops - as hitherto he had accompanied either the army of Prince Frederick Charles, or that of General Steinmetz - and the cheers with which he was greeted by the Bavarians left no room for doubting their loyalty to the Confederation, notwithstanding ancient jealousies.

While the troops were passing, Count Bismarck had the kindness to point out to me the different organizations, giving scraps of their history, and also speaking concerning the qualifications of the different generals commanding them. When the review was over we went to the Count's house, and there, for the first time in my life, I tasted kirschwasser, a very strong liquor distilled from cherries. Not knowing anything about the stuff, I had to depend on Bismarck's recommendation, and he proclaiming it fine, I took quite a generous drink, which nearly strangled me and brought on a violent fit of coughing. The Chancellor said, however, that this was in no way due to the liquor, but to my own inexperience, and I was bound to believe the distinguished statesman, for he proved his words by swallowing a goodly dose with an undisturbed and even beaming countenance, demonstrating his assertion so forcibly that I forthwith set out with Bismarck-Bohlen to lay in a supply for myself.

I spent the night in a handsome house, the property of an exceptionally kind and polite gentleman bearing the indisputably German name of Lager, but who was nevertheless French from head to foot, if intense hatred of the Prussians be a sign of Gallic nationality. At daybreak on the 26th word came for us to be ready to move by the Chalons road at 7 o'clock, but before we got off, the order was suspended till 2 in the afternoon. In the interval General von Moltke arrived and held a long conference with the King, and when we did pull out we traveled the remainder of the afternoon in company with a part of the Crown Prince's army, which after this conference inaugurated the series of movements from Bar-le-Duc northward, that finally compelled the surrender at Sedan. This sudden change of direction I did not at first understand, but soon learned that it was because of the movements of Marshal MacMahon, who, having united the French army beaten at Worth with three fresh corps at Chalons, was marching to relieve Metz in obedience to orders from the Minister of War at Paris.

As we passed along the column, we noticed that the Crown Prince's troops were doing their best, the officers urging the men to their utmost exertions, persuading weary laggards and driving up stragglers. As a general thing, however, they marched in good shape, notwithstanding the rapid gait and the trying heat, for at the outset of the campaign the Prince had divested them of all impedimenta except essentials, and they were therefore in excellent trim for a forced march.

The King traveled further than usual that day - to Clermont - so we did not get shelter till late, and even then not without some confusion, for the quartermaster having set out toward Chalons before the change of programme was ordered, was not at hand to provide for us. I had extreme good luck, though, in being quartered with a certain apothecary, who, having lived for a time in the United States, claimed it as a privilege even to lodge me, and certainly made me his debtor for the most generous hospitality. It was not so with some of the others, however; and Count Bismarck was particularly unfortunate, being billeted in a very small and uncomfortable house, where, visiting him to learn more fully what was going on, I found him, wrapped in a shabby old dressing-gown, hard at work. He was established in a very small room, whose only furnishings consisted of a table - at which he was writing - a couple of rough chairs, and the universal feather-bed, this time made on the floor in one corner of the room. On my remarking upon the limited character of his quarters, the Count replied, with great good-humor, that they were all right, and that he should get along well enough. Even the tramp of his clerks in the attic, and the clanking of his orderlies' sabres below, did not disturb him much; he said, in fact, that he would have no grievance at all were it not for a guard of Bavarian soldiers stationed about the house-for his safety, he presumed - the sentinels from which insisted on protecting and saluting the Chancellor of the North German Confederation in and out of season, a proceeding that led to embarrassment sometimes, as he was much troubled with a severe dysentery. Notwithstanding his trials, however, and in the midst of the correspondence on which he was so intently engaged, he graciously took time to explain that the sudden movement northward from Bar-le-Duc was, as I have previously recounted, the result of information that Marshal MacMahon was endeavoring to relieve Metz by marching along the Belgian frontier; "a blundering manœuvre," remarked the Chancellor, "which cannot be accounted for, unless it has been brought about by the political situation of the French."

CHAPTER XVIII.

AFTER MacMAHON - THE BATTLE AT BEAUMONT - THE
FRENCH SURPRISED - THE MARCHING OF THE GER-
MAN SOLDIERS - THE BATTLE OF SEDAN - GALLANT
CAVALRY CHARGES - DEFEAT OF THE FRENCH -
THE SURRENDER OF NAPOLEON - BISMARCK AND
THE KING - DECORATING THE SOLDIERS.

A LL night long the forced march of the army
went on through Clermont, and when I
turned out, just after daylight, the columns were
still pressing forward, the men looking tired and
much bedraggled, as indeed they had reason
to be, for from recent rains the roads were
very sloppy. Notwithstanding this, however, the
troops were pushed ahead with all possible vigor
to intercept MacMahon and force a battle before
he could withdraw from his faulty movement, for
which it has since been ascertained he was not at
all responsible. Indeed, those at the royal headquarters seemed to think of nothing else than to
strike MacMahon, for, feeling pretty confident that
Metz could not be relieved, they manifested not
the slightest anxiety on that score.

By 8 o'clock, the skies having cleared, the

headquarters set out for Grand Pré, which place
we reached early in the afternoon, and that evening I again had the pleasure of dining with the
King. The conversation at table was almost
wholly devoted to the situation, of course, everybody expressing surprise at the manœuvre of the
French at this time, their march along the Belgian
frontier being credited entirely to Napoleon. Up
to bed-time there was still much uncertainty as
to the exact positions of the French, but next
morning intelligence being received which denot-
ed the probability of a battle, we drove about ten
miles, to Buzancy, and there mounting our horses,
rode to the front.

The French were posted not far from Buzancy
in a strong position, their right resting near Stonne
and the left extending over into the woods beyond Beaumont. About 10 o'clock the Crown
Prince of Saxony advanced against this line, and
while a part of his army turned the French right,
compelling it to fall back rapidly, the German
centre and right attacked with great vigor and
much skill, surprising one of the divisions of General De Failly's corps while the men were in the
act of cooking their breakfast.

The French fled precipitately, leaving behind
their tents and other camp equipage, and on inspecting the ground which they had abandoned

so hastily, I noticed on all sides ample evidence that not even the most ordinary precautions had been taken to secure the division from surprise, The artillery horses had not been harnessed, and many of them had been shot down at the picket-rope where they had been haltered the night before, while numbers of men were lying dead with loaves of bread or other food instead of their muskets in their hands.

Some three thousand prisoners and nearly all the artillery and mitrailleuses of the division were captured, while the fugitives were pursued till they found shelter behind Douay's corps and the rest of De Failly's beyond Beaumont. The same afternoon there were several other severe combats along the Meuse, but I had no chance of witnessing any of them, and just before night-fall I started back to Buzancy, to which place the King's headquarters had been brought during the day.

The morning of the 31st the King moved to Vendresse. First sending our carriage back to Grand Pré for our trunks, Forsyth and I mounted our horses and rode to the battle-field accompanied by an English nobleman, the Duke of Manchester. The part of the field we traversed was still thickly strewn with the dead of both armies, though all the wounded had been collected in the hospitals. In the village of Beaumont, we stopped to take a look at several thousand French prisoners, whose worn clothing and evident dejection told that they had been doing a deal of severe marching under great discouragements.

The King reached the village shortly after, and we all continued on to Chémery, just beyond where his Majesty alighted from his carriage to observe his son's troops file past as they came in from the direction of Stonne. This delay caused us to be as late as 9 o'clock before we got shelter that night, but as it afforded me the best opportunity I had yet had for seeing the German soldiers on the march, I did not begrudge the time. They moved in a somewhat open and irregular column of fours, the intervals between files being especially intended to give room for a peculiar swinging gait, with which the men seemed to urge themselves over the ground with ease and rapidity. There was little or no straggling, and being strong, lusty young fellows, and lightly equipped - they carried only needle-guns, ammunition, a very small knapsack, a water-bottle, and a haversack - they strode by with an elastic step, covering at least three miles an hour.

It having been definitely ascertained that the demoralized French were retiring to Sedan, on the evening of August 31 the German army began the work of hemming them in there, so disposing the different corps as to cover the ground from Donchery around by Raucourt to Carignan. The next morning this line was to be drawn in closer on Sedan; and the Crown Prince of Saxony was therefore ordered to take up a position to the north of Bazeilles, beyond the right bank of the Meuse, while the Crown Prince of Prussia was to cross his right wing over the Meuse at Remilly, to move on Bazeilles, his centre meantime marching against a number of little hamlets still held by the French between there and Donchery. At this last-mentioned place strong reserves were to be held, and from it the Eleventh Corps, followed by the Fifth and a division of cavalry, was to march on St. Menges.

Forsyth and I started early next morning, September 1, and in a thick fog - which, however, subsequently gave place to bright sunshine - we drove to the village of Chevenges, where, mounting our horses, we rode in a northeasterly direction to the heights of Frénois and Wadelincourt, bordering the river Meuse on the left bank, where from the crest we had a good view of the town of Sedan with its circling fortifications, which, though extensive, were not so formidable as those around Metz. The King and his staff were already established on these heights, and at a point so well chosen that his Majesty could observe the movements of both armies immediately east and south of Sedan, and also to the northwest toward Floing and the Belgian frontier.

The battle was begun to the east and northeast of Sedan as early as half-past 4 o'clock by the German right wing - the fighting being desultory - and near the same hour the Bavarians attacked Bazeilles. This village, some two miles southeast of Sedan, being of importance, was defended with great obstinacy, the French contesting from street to street and house to house the attack of the Bavarians till near 10 o'clock, when, almost every building being knocked to pieces, they were compelled to relinquish the place. The possession of this village gave the Germans to the east of Sedan a continuous line, extending from the Meuse northward through La Moncelle and Daigny to Givonne, and almost to the Belgian frontier.

While the German centre and right were thus engaged, the left had moved in accordance with the prescribed plan. Indeed, some of these troops had crossed the Meuse the night before, and now, at a little after 6 o'clock, their advance could be seen just north of the village of Floing. Thus far these columns, under the immediate eye of the Crown Prince of Prussia, had met with no opposition to their march, and as soon as they got to the high ground above the village they began extending to the east, to connect with the Army of the Meuse. This juncture was effected at Illy without difficulty, and the French army was now completely encompassed.

After a severe fight, the Crown Prince drove the French through Floing, and as the ground between this village and Sedan is an undulating, open plain, everywhere visible, there was then offered a rare opportunity for seeing the final conflict preceding the surrender. Presently up out of the little valley where Floing is located came the Germans, deploying just on the rim of the plateau a very heavy skirmish-line, supported by a line of battle at close distance. When these skirmishers appeared, the French infantry had withdrawn within its intrenched lines, but a strong body of their cavalry, already formed in a depression to the right of the Floing road, now rode at the Germans in gallant style, going clear through the dispersed skirmishers to the main line of battle. Here the slaughter of the French was awful, for in addition to the deadly volleys from the solid battalions of their enemies, the skirmishers, who had rallied in knots at advantageous places, were now delivering a severe and effective fire. The gallant horsemen, therefore, had to retire precipitately, but re-forming in the depression, they again undertook the hopeless task of breaking the German infantry, making in all four successive charges. Their ardor and pluck were of no avail, however, for the Germans, growing stronger every minute by the accession of troops from Floing, met the fourth attack in such large force that, even before coming in contact with their adversaries, the French broke and retreated to the protection of the intrenchments, where, from the beginning of the combat, had been lying plenty of idle infantry, some of which at least, it seemed plain to me, ought to have been thrown into the fight. This action was the last one of consequence around Sedan, for, though with the contraction of the German lines their batteries kept cannonading more or less, and the rattle of musketry continued to be heard here and there, yet the hard fighting of the day practically ended on the plateau of Floing.

By 3 o'clock, the French being in a desperate and hopeless situation, the King ordered the firing to be stopped, and at once despatched one of his staff-Colonel von Bronsart - with a demand for a surrender. Just as this officer was starting off, I remarked to Bismarck that Napoleon himself would likely be one of the prizes, but the Count, incredulous, replied, "Oh no; the old fox is too cunning to be caught in such a trap; he has doubtless slipped off to Paris "- a belief which I found to prevail pretty generally about headquarters.

In the lull that succeeded, the King invited many of those about him to luncheon, a caterer having provided from some source or other a substantial meal of good bread, chops and peas, with a bountiful supply of red and sherry wines. Among those present were Prince Carl, Bismarck, Von Moltke, Von Roon, the Duke of Weimar, the Duke of Coburg, the Grand-Duke of Mecklenburg, Count Hatzfeldt, Colonel Walker, of the English army, General Forsyth, and I. The King was agreeable and gracious at all times, but on this occasion he was particularly so, being naturally in a happy frame of mind because this day the war had reached a crisis which presaged for the near future the complete vanquishment of the French.

Between 4 and 5 o'clock Colonel von Bronsart returned from his mission to Sedan, bringing word to the King that the commanding officer there, General Wimpffen, wished to know, in order that the further effusion of blood might be spared, upon what terms he might surrender. The Colonel brought the intelligence also that the French Emperor was in the town. Soon after Von Bronsart's arrival, a French officer approached from

Sedan, preceded by a white flag and two German officers. Coming up the road till within a few hundred yards of us, they halted; then one of the Germans rode forward to say that the French officer was Napoleon's adjutant, bearing an autograph letter from the Emperor to the King of Prussia. At this the King, followed by Bismarck, Von Moltke, and Von Roon, walked out to the front a little distance and halted, his Majesty still in advance, the rest of us meanwhile forming in a line some twenty paces to the rear of the group. The envoy then approached, at first on horseback, but when within about a hundred yards he dismounted, and uncovering, came the remaining distance on foot, bearing high up in his right hand the despatch from Napoleon. The bearer proved to be General Reille, and as he handed the Emperor's letter to the King, his Majesty saluted him with the utmost formality and precision. Napoleon's letter was the since famous one, running so characteristically, thus: "Not having been able to die in the midst of my troops, there is nothing left me but to place my sword in your Majesty's hands." The reading finished, the King returned to his former post, and after a conference with Bismarck, Von Moltke, and Von Roon, dictated an answer accepting Napoleon's surrender, and requesting him to designate an officer with power to treat for the capitulation of the army, himself naming Von Moltke to represent the Germans. The King then started for Vendresse, to pass the night.

It was after 7 o'clock now, and hence too late to arrange anything more where we were, so further negotiations were deferred till later in the evening; and I, wishing to be conveniently near Bismarck, resolved to take up quarters in Donchery. On our way thither we were met by the Count's nephew, who assuring us that it would be impossible to find shelter there in the village, as all the houses were filled with wounded, Forsyth and I decided to continue on to Chevenge. On the other hand, Bismarck-Bohlen bore with him one great comfort - some excellent brandy. Offering the flask to his uncle, he said: "You've had a hard day of it; won't you refresh yourself ?" The Chancellor, without wasting time to answer, raised the bottle to his lips, exclaiming: "Here's to the unification of Germany!" which sentiment the gurgling of an astonishingly long drink seemed to emphasize. The Count then handed the bottle back to his nephew, who, shaking it, ejaculated, "Why, we can't pledge you in return - there is nothing left!" to which came the waggish response, "I beg pardon; it was so dark I couldn't see"; nevertheless there was a little remaining, as I myself can aver.

Having left our carriage at Chevenge, Forsyth and I stopped there to get it, but a long search proving fruitless, we took lodging in the village at the house of the curé, resolved to continue the hunt in the morning.   But then we had no better success, so concluding that our vehicle had been pressed into the hospital service, we at an early hour on the 2d of September resumed the search, continuing on down the road in the direction of Sedan.   Near the gate of the city we came on the German picket-line, and one of the officers, recognizing our uniforms - he having served in the war of the rebellion - stepped forward and addressed me in good English.   We naturally fell into conversation, and in the midst of it there came out through the gate an open carriage, or landau, containing two men, one of whom, in the uniform of a general and smoking a cigarette, we recognized, when the conveyance drew near, as the Emperor Louis Napoleon.   The landau went on toward Donchery at a leisurely pace, and we, inferring that there was something more impor-tant at hand just then than the recovery of our trap, followed at a respectful distance. Not quite a mile from Donchery is a cluster of three or four cottages, and at the first of these the landau stopped to await, as we afterward ascertained, Count Bismarck, with whom the diplomatic negotiations were to be settled. Some minutes elapsed before he came, Napoleon remaining seated in his carriage meantime, still smoking, and accepting with nonchalance the staring of a group of German soldiers near by, who were gazing on their fallen foe with curious and eager interest.

Presently a clattering of hoofs was heard, and looking toward the sound, I perceived the Chancellor cantering down the road. When abreast of the carriage he dismounted, and walking up to it, saluted the Emperor in a quick, brusque way that seemed to startle him. After a word or two, the party moved perhaps a hundred yards further on, where they stopped opposite the weaver's cottage so famous from that day. This little house is on the east side of the Donchery road, near its junction with that to Frénois, and stands about twenty paces back from the highway. In front is a stone wall covered with creeping vines, and from a gate in this wall runs to the front door a path, at this time bordered on both sides with potato vines.

The Emperor having alighted at the gate, he and Bismarck walked together along the narrow path and entered the cottage. Reappearing in about a quarter of an hour, they came out and seated themselves in the open air, the weaver having brought a couple of chairs. Here they engaged in an animated conversation, if much gesticulation is any indication. The talk lasted fully an hour, Bismarck seeming to do most of it, but at last he arose, saluted the Emperor, and strode down the path toward his horse. Seeing me standing near the gate, he joined me for a moment, and asked if I had noticed how the Emperor started when they first met, and I telling him that I had, he added, "Well, it must have been due to my manners, not my words, for these were, I salute your Majesty just as I would my King." Then the Chancellor continued to chat a few minutes longer, assuring me that nothing further was to be done there, and that we had better go to the Chateau Bellevue, where, he said, the formal surrender was to take place. With this he rode off toward Vendresse to communicate with his sovereign, and Forsyth and I made ready to go to the Chateau Bellevue.

Before we set out, however, a number of officers of the King's suite arrived at the weaver's cottage, and from them I gathered that there were differences at the royal headquarters as to whether peace should be made then at Sedan, or the war continued till the French capital was taken. I further heard that the military advisers of the King strongly advocated an immediate move on Paris, while the Chancellor thought it best to make peace now, holding Alsace and Lorraine, and compelling the payment of an enormous levy of money; and these rumors were most likely correct, for I had often heard Bismarck say that France being the richest country in Europe, nothing could keep her quiet but effectually to empty her pockets; and besides this, he impressed me as holding that it would be better policy to preserve the Empire.

On our way to the château we fell in with a number of artillery officers bringing up their guns hurriedly to post them closer in to the beleaguered town on a specially advantageous ridge. Inquiring the cause of this move, we learned that General Wimpffen had not yet agreed to the terms of surrender; that it was thought he would not, and that they wanted to be prepared for any such contingency. And they were preparing with a vengeance too, for I counted seventy-two Krupp guns in one continuous line trained on the Chateau Bellevue and Sedan.

Napoleon went directly from the weaver's to the Château Bellevue, and about 10 o'clock the King of Prussia arrived from Frénois, accompanied by a few of his own suite and the Crown Prince with several members of his staff; and Von Moltke and Wimpffen having settled their points of difference before the two monarchs met, within the next half-hour the articles of capitulation were formally signed.

On the completion of the surrender - the occasion being justly considered a great one - the Crown Prince proceeded to distribute among the officers congregated in the chateau grounds the order of the Iron Cross - a generous supply of these decorations being carried in a basket by one of his orderlies, following him about as he walked along. Meantime the King, leaving Napoleon in the château to ruminate on the fickleness of fortune, drove off to see his own victorious soldiers, who greeted him with huzzas that rent the air, and must have added to the pangs of the captive Emperor.

CHAPTER XIX.

RIDING OVER THE BATTLE-FIELD - DESTRUCTION OF
BAZEILLES - MISTAKES OF THE FRENCH -- MARSHAL
BAZAINE - ON TO PARIS - A WEEK IN MEAUX-
RHEIMS - ON THE PICKET-LINE - UNDER FIRE -
A SURRENDER - AT VERSAILLES - GENERAL BURN-
SIDE AND MR. FORBES IN PARIS.

T HE Crown Prince having got to the bottom
of his medal basket - that is to say, having
finished his liberal distribution of decorations to
his officers - Forsyth and I rode off by way of
Wadelincourt to Bazeilles to see what had taken
place on that part of the field, and the sight that
met our eyes as we entered the village was truly
dreadful to look upon. Most of the houses had
been knocked down or burned the day before, but
such as had been left standing were now in flames,
the torch having been applied because, as it was
claimed, Frenchmen concealed in them had fired
on the wounded. The streets were still encum-
bered with both German and French dead, and it
was evident that of those killed in the houses the
bodies had not been removed, for the air was
loaded with odors of burning flesh. From Bazeil-

les we rode on toward the north about two miles, along where the fight had been largely an artillery duel, to learn what we could of the effectiveness of the Krupp gun. Counting all the French dead we came across killed by artillery, they figured up about three hundred - a ridiculously small number; in fact, not much more than one dead man for each Krupp gun on that part of the line. Although the number of dead was in utter disproportion to the terrific six-hour cannonade, yet small as it was the torn and mangled bodies made such a horrible sight that we turned back toward Bazeilles without having gone further than Givonne.

At Bazeilles we met the King, accompanied by Bismarck and several of the staff. They too had been riding over the field, the King making this a practice, to see that the wounded were not neglected. As I drew up by the party, Bismarck accosted me with, "Well, General, aren't you hungry? This is just the place to whet one's appetite - these burning Frenchmen - Ugh!" and shrugging his shoulders in evident disgust, he turned away to join his Majesty in further explorations, Forsyth and I continuing on to Chevenges. Here we got the first inkling of what had become of our carriage since leaving it two days before: it had been pressed into service to carry wounded officers from the field during the battle, but afterward released, and was now safe at the house in Vendresse where we had been quartered the night of the 31st, so, on hearing this, we settled to go there again to lodge, but our good friend, the curé, insisting that we should stay with him, we remained in Chevenges till next morning.

On September 3 the King removed from Vendresse to Rethel, where he remained two days; in the mean while the Germans, 240,000 strong, beginning their direct march to Paris. The French had little with which to oppose this enormous force, not more, perhaps, than 50,000 regular troops; the rest of their splendid army had been lost or captured in battle, or was cooped up in the fortifications of Metz, Strasburg, and other places, in consequence of blunders without parallel in history, for which Napoleon and the Regency in Paris must be held accountable. The first of these gross faults was the fight at Worth, where MacMahon, before his army was mobilized, accepted battle with the Crown Prince, pitting 50,000 men against 175,000; the next was Bazaine's fixing upon Metz as his base, and stupidly putting himself in position to be driven back to it, when there was no possible obstacle to his joining forces with MacMahon at Chalons; while the third and greatest blunder of all was MacMahon's move to relieve Metz, trying to slip 140,000 men along the Belgian frontier. Indeed, it is exasperating and sickening to think of all this; to think that Bazaine carried into Metz - a place that should have been held, if at all, with not over 25,000 men - an army of 180,000, because it contained, the excuse was, "an accumulation of stores." With all the resources of rich France to draw upon, I cannot conceive that this excuse was sincere; on the contrary, I think that the movement of Bazaine must have been inspired by Napoleon with a view to the maintenance of his dynasty rather than for the good of France.

As previously stated, Bismarck did not approve of the German army's moving on Paris after the battle of Sedan. Indeed, I think he foresaw and dreaded the establishment of a Republic, his idea being that if peace was made then, the Empire could be continued in the person of the Prince Imperial, who, coming to the throne under German influences, would be pliable in his hands. These views found frequent expression in private, and in public too; I myself particularly remember the Chancellor's speaking thus most unguardedly at a dinner in Rheims. But he could not prevent the march to Paris; it was impossible to stop the Germans, flushed with success. "On to Paris" was written by the soldiers on every door, and

every fence-board along the route to the capital,
and the thought of a triumphant march down the
Champs Elysées was uppermost with every German, from the highest to the lowest grade.

The 5th of September we set out for Rheims.
There it was said the Germans would meet with
strong resistance, for the French intended to die
to the last man before giving up that city. But
this proved all fudge, as is usual with these "last
ditch" promises, the garrison decamping immediately at the approach of a few Uhlans.   So far as
I could learn, but a single casualty happened; this
occurred to an Uhlan, wounded by a shot which it
was reported was fired from a house after the
town was taken; so, to punish this breach of
faith, a levy of several hundred bottles of champagne was made, and the wine divided about
headquarters, being the only seizure made in the
city, I believe, for though Rheims, the centre of
the champagne district, had its cellars well
stocked, yet most of them being owned by German firms, they received every protection.

The land about Rheims is of a white, chalky
character, and very poor, but having been terraced
and enriched with fertilizers, it produces the
champagne grape in such abundance that the region, once considered valueless, and named by the
peasantry the "land of the louse," now supports

a dense population. We remained in Rheims eight days, and through the politeness of the American Consul - Mr. Adolph Gill - had the pleasure of seeing all the famous wine cellars, and inspecting the processes followed in champagne making, from the step of pressing the juice from the grape to that which shows the wine ready for the market. Mr. Gill also took us to see everything else of special interest about the city, and there being much to look at - fine old churches, ancient fortifications, a Roman gateway, etc. - the days slipped by very quickly, though the incessant rains somewhat interfered with our enjoyment.

For three or four days all sorts of rumors were rife as to what was doing in Paris, but nothing definite was learned till about the 9th; then Count Bismarck informed me that the Regency had been overthrown on the 4th, and that the Empress Eugénie had escaped to Belgium. The Ming of Prussia offered her an asylum with the Emperor at Wilhelmshöhe, "where she ought to go," said the Chancellor, "for her proper place is with her husband," but he feared she would not. On the same occasion he also told me that Jules Favre - the head of the Provisional Government - had sent him the suggestion that, the Empire being gone, peace should be made and the Germans

withdrawn, but that he (Bismarck) was now compelled to recognize the impossibility of doing this
till Paris was taken, for although immediately
after the surrender of Sedan he desired peace, the
past few days had made it plain that the troops
would not be satisfied with anything short of
Paris, no matter what form of Government the
French should ultimately adopt.

The German army having met with no resistance whatever in its march on Paris, its advance
approached the capital rapidly, and by the 14th
of September the royal headquarters moved by a
fine macadamized road to the Chateau Thierry, and
on the 15th reached Meaux, about twenty-eight
miles from Paris, where we remained four days
awaiting the reconstruction of some railroad and
canal bridges. The town of Meaux has a busy population of about 10,000 souls, in peaceable times
principally occupied in manufacturing flour for the
Paris market, having a fine water-power for the
many mills. These were kept going day and night
to supply the German army; and it was strange
to see with what zeal Frenchmen toiled to fill the
stomachs of their inveterate enemies, and with
what alacrity the mayor and other officials filled
requisitions for wine, cheese, suits of livery, riding-
whips, and even squab pigeons.

During our stay at Meaux the British Minister,

Lord Lyons, endeavored to bring about a cessation of hostilities, to this end sending his secretary out from Paris with a letter to Count Bismarck, offering to serve as mediator. The Chancelior would not agree to this, however, for he conjectured that the action of the British Minister had been inspired by Jules Favre, who, he thought, was trying to draw the Germans into negotiations through the medium of a third party only for purposes of delay. So the next morning Lord Lyons's secretary, Mr. Edward Malet, returned to Paris empty-handed, except that he bore a communication positively declining mediation; which message, however, led no doubt to an interview between Bismarck and Favre a couple of days later.

The forenoon of September 19 the King removed to the Chateau Ferrières - a castle belonging to the Rothschild family, where Napoleon had spent many happy days in the time of his prosperity. His Majesty took up his quarters here at the suggestion of the owner, we were told, so that by the presence of the King the magnificent chateau and its treasures of art would be unquestionably protected from all acts of vandalism.

All of the people at headquarters except the King's immediate suite were assigned quarters at Lagny; and while Forsyth and I, accompanied

GENERAL SHERIDAN AND STAFF. DINWIDDIE COURT-HOUSE.

419

by Sir Henry Havelock, of the British army, were driving thither, we passed on the road the representative of the National Defense Government, Jules Favre, in a carriage heading toward Meaux. Preceded by a flag of truce and accompanied by a single companion, he was searching for Count Bismarck, in conformity, doubtless, with the message the Chancellor had sent to Paris on the 17th by the British secretary. A half-mile further on we met Bismarck. He too was traveling toward Meaux, not in the best of humor either, it appeared, for having missed finding the French envoy at the rendezvous where they had agreed to meet, he stopped long enough to say that the "air was full of lies, and that there were many persons with the army bent on business that did not concern them."

The armies of the two Crown Princes were now at the outskirts of Paris. They had come from Sedan mainly by two routes - the Crown Prince of Saxony marching by the northern line, through Laon and Soissons, and the Crown Prince of Prussia by the southern line, keeping his right wing on the north bank of the Marne, while his left and centre approached the French capital by roads between that river and the Seine.

The march of these armies had been unobstructed by any resistance worth mentioning, and as the routes of both columns lay through a region teeming with everything necessary for their support, and rich even in luxuries, it struck me that such campaigning was more a vast picnic than like actual war. The country supplied at all points bread, meat, and wine in abundance, and the neat villages, never more than a mile or two apart, always furnished shelter; hence the enormous trains required to feed and provide camp equipage for an army operating in a sparsely settled country were dispensed with; in truth, about the only impedimenta of the Germans was their wagons carrying ammunition, pontoon-boats, and the field telegraph.

On the morning of the 20th I started out accompanied by Forsyth and Sir Henry Havelock, and took the road through Boissy St. George, Boissy St. Martins and Noisy Le Grand to Brie. Almost every foot of the way was strewn with fragments of glass from wine bottles, emptied and then broken by the troops. There was, indeed, so much of this that I refrain from making any estimate of the number of bottles, lest I be thought to exaggerate, but the road was literally paved with glass, and the amount of wine consumed (none was wasted) must have been enormous, far more, even, than I had seen evidence of at any time before. There were two almost continuous lines of broken bottles along the roadsides all the way down from Sedan; but that exhibit was small compared with what we saw about Brie.

At Brie we were taken charge of by the German commandant of the place. He entertained us most hospitably for an hour or so, and then, accompanied by a lieutenant, who was to be our guide, I set out ahead of my companions to gain a point on the picket-line where I expected to get a good look at the French, for their rifle-pits were but a few hundred yards off across the Marne, their main line being just behind the rifle-pits. As the lieutenant and I rode through the village, some soldiers warned us that the adventure would be dangerous, but that we could probably get to the desired place unhurt if we avoided the French fire by forcing our horses to a run in crossing some open streets where we would be exposed. On getting to the first street my guide galloped ahead to show the way, and as the French were not on the lookout for anything of the kind at these dangerous points, only a few stray shots were drawn by the lieutenant, but when I followed, they were fully up to what was going on, and let fly a volley every time they saw me in the open. Fortunately, however, in their excitement they overshot, but when I drew rein alongside of my guide under protection of the bluff where the German picket was posted, my hair was all on end, and I was about as badly scared as ever I had been in my life. As soon as I could recover myself I thought of Havelock and Forsyth, with the hope that they would not follow; nor did they, for having witnessed my experience, they wisely concluded that, after all, they did not care so much to see the French rifle-pits.

When I had climbed to the top of the bluff I was much disappointed, for I could see but little-only the advanced rifle-pits across the river, and Fort Nogent beyond them, not enough, certainly, to repay a non-combatant for taking the risk of being killed. The next question was to return, and deciding to take no more such chances as those we had run in coming out, I said we would wait till dark, but this proved unnecessary, for to my utter astonishment my guide informed me that there was a perfectly safe route by which we might go back. I asked why we had not taken it in coming, and he replied that he had thought it "too long and circuitous." To this I could say nothing, but I concluded that that was not quite the correct reason; the truth is that early that morning the young fellow had been helping to empty some of the many wine bottles I saw around Brie, and consequently had a little more

"Dutch courage" - was a little more rash-than would have been the case under other conditions.

I rode back to Brie by the "long and circui-tous " route, and inquiring there for my compan-ions, found Havelock waiting to conduct me to the village of Villiers, whither, he said, Forsyth had been called to make some explanation about his passport, which did not appear to be in satis-factory shape. Accordingly we started for Vil-liers, and Havelock, being well mounted on an English "hunter," and wishing to give me an exhibition of the animal's training and power, led the way across ditches and fences, but my horse, never having followed "the hounds," was unsafe to experiment with, so, after trying a low fence or two, I decided to leave my friend alone in his diversion, and a few moments later, seeing both horse and rider go down before a ditch and high stone wall, I was convinced that my resolution was a discreet one. After this mishap, which luckily resulted in no harm, I hoped Sir Henry would give up the amusement, but by failure be-coming only the more determined, in a second effort he cleared the wall handsomely and rode across-country to the villages. Following the road till it passed under a railway bridge, I there thought I saw a chance to gain Villiers by a short cut, and changing my course accordingly, I struck into a large vineyard to the left, and proceeding a few hundred yards through the vines, came suddenly upon a German picket-post. The guard immediately leveled their rifles at me, when, remembering my Rêzonville experience of being taken for a French officer because of my uniform, I hastily flung myself from the saddle in token of surrender. The action being rightly interpreted, the men held their fire, and as my next thought was the King's pass I reached under my coat-skirt for the document, but this motion being taken as a grab for my pistol, the whole lot of them-some ten in number - again aimed at me, and with such loud demands for surrender that I threw up my hands and ran into their ranks. The officer of the guard then coming up, examined my credentials, and seeing that they were signed by the King of Prussia, released me and directed the recovery of my horse, which was soon caught, and I was then conducted to the quarters of the commandant, where I found Forsyth with his pass properly *viséd,* entirely ignorant of my troubles, and contentedly regaling himself on cheese and beer. Havelock having got to the village ahead of me, thanks to his cross-country ride, was there too, sipping beer with Forsyth; nor was I slow to follow their example, for the ride of the day, though rather barren in other results, at any rate had given me a ravenous appetite.

Late that evening, the 20th, we resumed our old quarters at Lagny, and early next day I made a visit to the royal headquarters at Ferrières, where I observed great rejoicing going on, the occasion for it being an important victory gained near Mendon, a French corps of about 30,000 men under General Ducrot having been beaten by the Fifth Prussian and Second Bavarian corps. Ducrot had been stubbornly holding ground near Mendon for two or three days, much to the embarrassment of the Germans too, since he kept them from closing a gap in their line to the southwest of Paris; but in the recent fight he had been driven from the field with such heavy loss as to render impossible his maintaining the gap longer. The Crown Prince of Prussia was thus enabled to extend his left, without danger, as far as Bougival, north of Versailles, and eventually met the right of the Crown Prince of Saxony, already at Denil, north of St. Denis. The unbroken circle of investment around Paris being wellnigh assured, news of its complete accomplishment was momentarily expected; therefore everybody was jubilant on account of the breaking up of Ducrot, but more particularly because word had been received the same morning that a correspondence had begun

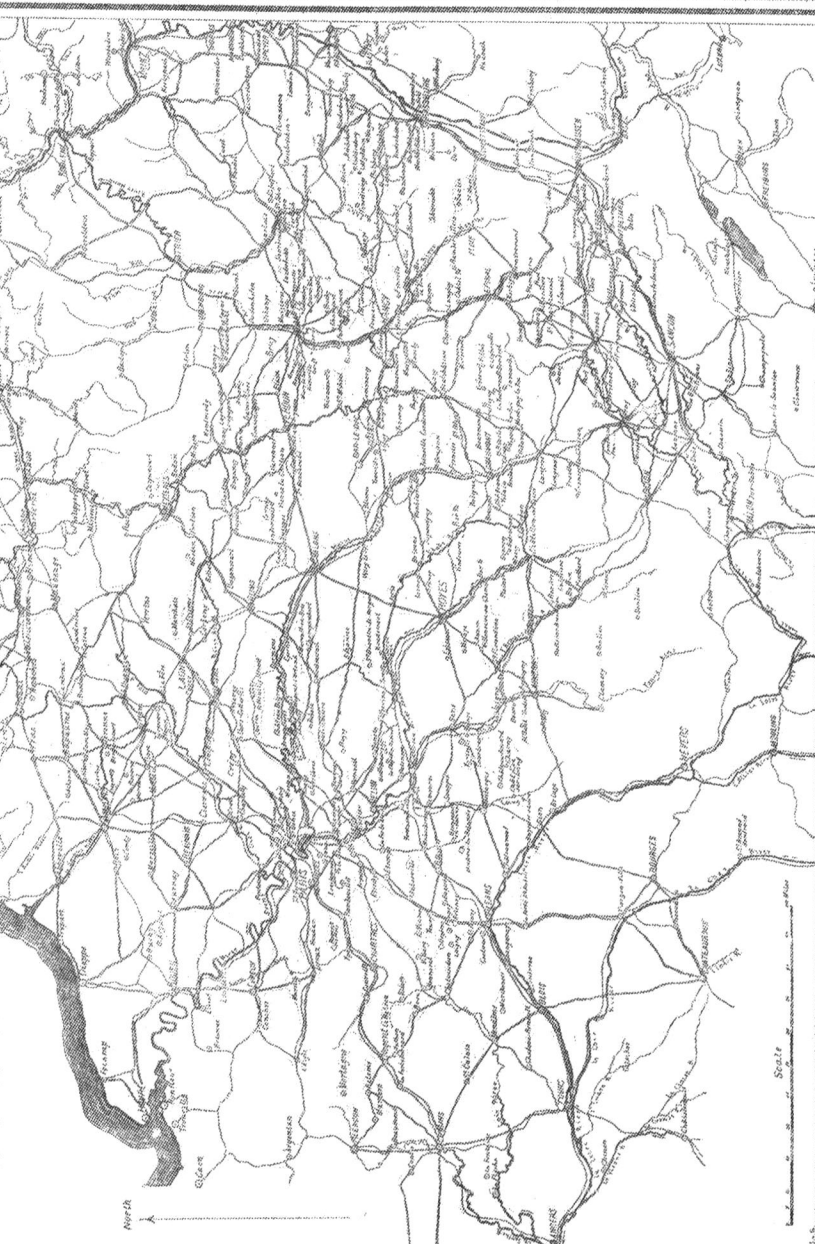

MAP
showing parts of
FRANCE, BELGIUM, & GERMANY

between Bazaine and Prince Frederick Charles, looking to the capitulation of Metz, for the surrender of that place would permit the Second Army to join in the siege of Paris.

Learning all this, and seeing that the investment was about completed, I decided to take up my quarters at Versailles, and started for that place on the 22d, halting at Noisy le Grand to take luncheon with some artillery officers, whose acquaintance we had made the day of the surrender at Sedan. During the meal I noticed two American flags flying on a couple of houses near by. Inquiring the significance of this, I was told that the flags had been put up to protect the buildings-the owners, two American citizens, having in a bad fright abandoned their property, and, instead of remaining outside, gone into Paris - "very foolishly," said our hospitable friends, "for here they could have obtained food in plenty, and been perfectly secure from molestation."

We arrived at Versailles about 7 o'clock that evening and settled ourselves in the Hotel Reservoir, happy to find there two or three American families, with whom, of course, we quickly made acquaintance. This American circle was enlarged a few days later by the arrival of General Wm. B. Hazen, of our army, General Ambrose E. Burnside, and Mr. Paul Forbes. Burnside and Forbes were hot to see, from the French side, something of the war, and being almost beside themselves to get into Paris, a permit was granted them by Count Bismarck, and they set out by way of Sèvres, Forsyth and I accompanying them as far as the Palace of St. Cloud, which we proposed to see, though there were strict orders against its being visited generally. After much trouble we managed, through the "open sesame" of the King's pass, to gain access to the palace; but to our great disappointment we found that all the pictures had been cut from the frames and carried off to Paris, except one portrait, that of Queen Victoria, against whom the French were much incensed. All other works of art had been removed, too - a most fortunate circumstance, for the palace being directly on the German line, was raked by the guns from the fortress of Mont Valérien, and in a few days burned to the ground.

In less than a week Burnside and Forbes returned from Paris. They told us their experience had been interesting, but were very reticent as to particulars, and though we tried hard to find out what they had seen or done, we could get nothing from them beyond the general statement that they had had a good time, and that General Trochu had been considerate enough to postpone a sortie, in order to let them return; but this we did not quite swallow. After a day or two they went into Paris again, and I then began to suspect that they were essaying the rôle of mediators, and that Count Bismarck was feeding their vanity with permits, and receiving his equivalent by learning the state of affairs within the beleaguered city.

From about the 1st of October on, the Germans were engaged in making their enveloping lines impenetrable, bringing up their reserves, siege guns, and the like, the French meanwhile continuing to drill and discipline the National Guard, and relieving the monotony occasionally by a more or less spirited, but invariably abortive, sortie. The most notable of these was that made by General Vinoy against the heights of Clamart, the result being a disastrous repulse by the besiegers. After this, matters settled down to an almost uninterrupted quietude, only a skirmish here and there; and it being plain that the Germans did not intend to assault the capital, but would accomplish its capture by starvation, I concluded to find out from Count Bismarck about when the end was expected, with the purpose of spending the interim in a little tour through some portions of Europe undisturbed by war, returning in season for the capitulation. Count Bismarck having kindly advised me as to the possible date,

Forsyth and I, on the 14th of October, left Versailles, going first direct to the Chateau Ferrières to pay our respects to the King, which we did, and again took luncheon with him. From the château we drove to Meaux, and there spent the night; resuming our journey next morning, we passed through Epernay, Rheims, and Rethel to Sedan, where we tarried a day, and finally, on October 18, reached Brussels.

CHAPTER XX.

ON reaching Brussels, one of the first things to do was to pay my respects to the King of Belgium, which I did, accompanied by our Minister, Mr. Russell Jones. Later I dined with the King and Queen, meeting at the dinner many notable people, among them the Count and Countess of Flanders. A day or two in Brussels sufficed to mature our plans for spending the time up to the approximate date of our return to Paris; and deciding to visit eastern Europe, we made Vienna our first objective, going there by way of Dresden.

At Vienna our Minister, Mr. John Jay, took charge of us - Forsyth was still with me - and the few days' sojourn was full of interest. The Emperor being absent from the capital, we missed seeing him; but the Prime Minister, Count von Beust, was very polite to us, and at his house we had the pleasure of meeting at dinner Count Andrassy, the Prime Minister of Hungary.

From Vienna we went to Buda-Pesth, the Hungarian capital; and thence, in a small, crowded, and uncomfortable steamboat, down the Danube to Rustchuck, whence we visited Bucharest - all who travel in eastern Europe do so - and then directing our course southward, we went first to Varna, and from that city by steamer through the Black Sea to Constantinople.

We reached the Turkish capital at the time of Ramadan, the period of the year (about a month) during which the Mohammedans are commanded by the Koran to keep a rigorous fast every day from sunrise till sunset. All the followers of the Prophet were therefore busy with their devotions - holding a revival, as it were; hence there was no chance whatever to be presented to the Sultan, Abdul Aziz, it being forbidden during the penitential season for him to receive unbelievers, or in fact any one except the officials of his household. However, the Grand Vizier brought me many messages of welcome, and arranged that I should be permitted to see and salute his Serene Highness on the Esplanade as he rode by on horseback to the mosque.

So, the second day after arrival, the Grand
Vizier drove me in a barouche to the Esplanade,
where we took station about midway of its
length an hour or so before the Sultan was to
appear. Shortly after we reached the Esplanade,
carriages occupied by the women of the Sultan's
harem began to appear, coming out from the
palace grounds and driving up and down the road-
way. Only a few of the women were closely
veiled, a majority of them wearing an apology
for veiling, merely a strip of white lace covering
the forehead down to the eyebrows. Some were
yellow, and some white-types of the Mongolian
and Caucasian races. Now and then a pretty face
was seen, rarely a beautiful one. Many were
plump, even to corpulence, and these were the
closest veiled, being considered the greatest beau-
ties I presume, since with the Turk obesity is the
chief element of comeliness. As the carriages
passed along in review, every now and then an
occupant, unable or unwilling to repress her natural promptings, would indulge in a mild flirtation,
making overtures by casting demure side-glances,
throwing us coquettish kisses, or waving strings
of amber beads with significant gestures, seeming
to say: "Why don't you follow?" But this we could
not do if we would, for the Esplanade throughout
its entire length was lined with soldiers, put there

especially to guard the harem first, and later, the Sultan on his pilgrimage to the mosque.

But as it was now time for His Serene Highness to make his appearance, the carriages containing his wives drove off into the palace grounds, which were inclosed by a high wall, leaving the Esplanade wholly unencumbered except by the soldiers. Down between the two ranks, which were formed facing each other, came the Sultan on a white steed-a beautiful Arabian - and having at his side his son, a boy about ten or twelve years old, who was riding a pony, a diminutive copy of his father's mount, the two attended by a numerous body-guard, dressed in gorgeous Oriental uniforms. As the procession passed our carriage, I, as pre-arranged, stood up and took off my hat, His Serene Highness promptly acknowledging the salute by raising his hand to the forehead. This was all I saw of him, yet I received every kindness at his hands, being permitted to see many of his troops, to inspect all the ordnance, equipment, and other military establishments about Constantinople, and to meet numbers of the high functionaries of the Empire.

Among other compliments tendered through his direction, and which I gladly accepted, was a review of all the troops then in Stamboul - about 6,000 - comprising infantry, cavalry, and artillery.

They were as fine looking a body of soldiers as I ever saw - well armed and well clothed, the men all large and of sturdy appearance.

After the review we attended a grand military dinner given by the Grand Vizier. At the hour set for this banquet we presented ourselves at the palace of the Grand Vizier, and being ushered into a large drawing-room, found already assembled there the guests invited to meet us. Some few spoke French, and with these we managed to exchange an occasional remark; but as the greater number stood about in silence, the affair, thus far, was undeniably a little stiff. Just before the dinner was announced, all the Turkish officers went into an adjoining room, and turning their faces to the east, prostrated themselves to the floor in prayer. Then we were all conducted to a large salon, where each being provided with a silver ewer and basin, a little ball of highly perfumed soap and a napkin, set out on small tables, each guest washed his hands. Adjacent to this salon was the dining-room, or, rather, the banqueting room, a very large and artistically frescoed hall, in the centre of which stood a crescent-shaped table, lighted with beautiful silver candelabra, and tastefully decorated with flowers and fruits. The viands were all excellent; cooked, evidently, by a French *chef,* and full justice was done the dishes, especially by the Turks, who, of course, had been fasting all day.

At the close of the banquet, which consisted of not less than fifteen courses, we withdrew to a smoking-room, where the coffee was served and cigarettes and chibouks offered us - the latter a pipe having a long flexible stem with an amber mouthpiece. I chose the chibouk, and as the stem of mine was studded with precious stones of enormous value, I thought I should enjoy it the more; but the tobacco being highly flavored with some sort of herbs, my smoke fell far short of my anticipations. The coffee was delicious, however, and I found this to be the case wherever I went in Constantinople, whether in making calls or at dinner, the custom of offering coffee and tobacco on these occasions being universal.

The temptations to linger at Constantinople were many indeed, not the least being the delightful climate; and as time pressed, we set out with much regret on the return journey, stopping a few days at Athens, whence we made several short excursions into the interior. King George and Queen Olga made our stay in Athens one of extreme interest and exceeding pleasure. Throwing aside all ceremony, they breakfasted and dined us informally, gave us a fine ball, and in addition to these hospitalities showed us much personal attention, his Majesty even calling upon me, and the Queen sending her children to see us at our hotel.

Of course we visited all that remained of the city's ancient civilization - the Acropolis, temples, baths, towers, and the like; nor did we omit to view the spot where St. Paul once instructed the Athenians in lessons of Christianity. We traveled some little through the country districts outside of Athens, and I noticed that the peasantry, in point of picturesqueness of dress and color of complexion, were not unlike the gypsies we see at times in America. They had also much of the same shrewdness, and, as far as I could learn, were generally wholly uneducated, ignorant, indeed, except as to one subject - politics - which I was told came to them intuitively, they taking to it, and a scramble for office, as naturally as a duck to water. In fact, this common faculty for politics seems a connecting link between the ancient and modern Greek.

Leaving Athens with the pleasantest recollections, we sailed for Messina, Sicily, and from there went to Naples, where we found many old friends; among them Mr. Buchanan Reed, the artist and poet, and Miss Brewster, as well as a score or more of others of our countrymen, then or since distinguished in art and letters at home and abroad. We remained some days in Naples, and during the time went to Pompeii to witness a special excavation among the ruins of the buried city, which search was instituted on account of our visit. A number of ancient household articles were dug up, and one, a terra cotta lamp bearing upon its crown in bas-relief the legend of "Leda and the Swan," was presented to me as a souvenir of the occasion, though it is usual for the Government to place in its museums everything of such value that is unearthed.

From Naples to Rome by rail was our next journey.   In the Eternal City we saw picture-galleries, churches, and ruins in plenty, but all these have been so well described by hundreds of other travelers that I shall not linger even to name them. While at Rome we also witnessed an overflow of the Tiber, that caused great suffering and destroyed much property. The next stage of our tour took us to Venice, then to Florence - the capital of Italy - for although the troops of the King of Italy had taken possession of Rome the preceding September, the Government itself had not yet removed thither.

At Florence, our Minister, Mr. Marsh, though suffering with a lame foot, took me in charge, and in due course of time I was presented to King Victor-Emmanuel.   His Majesty received me informally at his palace in a small, stuffy room - his office, no doubt - and an untidy one it was too. He wore a loose blouse and very baggy trousers; a comfortable suit, certainly, but not at all conducing to an ideal kingliness of appearance.

His Majesty's hobby was hunting, and no sooner had I made my bow than he began a conversation on that subject, thrusting his hands nearly up to the elbows into the pockets of his trousers. He desired to learn about the large game of America, particularly the buffalo, and when I spoke of the herds of thousands and thousands I had seen on the plains of western Kansas, he interrupted me to bemoan the fate which kept him from visiting America to hunt, even going so far as to say that he "didn't wish to be King of Italy, anyhow," but would much prefer to pass his days hunting than "be bedeviled with the cares of state." On one of his estates, near Pisa, he had several large herds of deer, many wild boars, and a great deal of other game. Of this preserve he was very proud, and before we separated invited me to go down there to shoot deer, adding that he would be there himself if he could, but feared that a trip which he had to take to Milan would interfere, though he wished me to go in any event.

I gladly accepted the invitation, and in two or three days was notified when I would be expected at the estate. At the designated time I was escorted to Pisa by an aide-de-camp, and from there we drove the few miles to the King's chateau, where we fortified ourselves for the work in hand by an elaborate and toothsome breakfast of about ten courses. Then in a carriage we set out for the King's stand in the hunting-grounds, accompanied by a crowd of mounted game-keepers, who with great difficulty controlled the pack of sixty or seventy hounds, the dogs and keepers together almost driving me to distraction with their, yelping and yelling. On reaching the stand, I was posted within about twenty yards of a long, high picket fence, facing the fence and covered by two trees very close together. It was from behind these that the King usually shot, and as I was provided with a double-barreled shot-gun, I thought I could do well, especially since close in rear of me stood two game-keepers to load and hand me a second gun when the first was emptied.

Meantime the huntsmen and the hounds had made a circuit of the park to drive up the game. The yelps of the hounds drawing near, I cautiously looked in the direction of the sound, and the next moment saw a herd of deer close in to the fence, and coming down at full speed. Without a miss, I shot the four leading ones as they tried to run the gauntlet, for in passing between the stand and the fence, the innocent creatures were not more than ten to fifteen paces from me. At the fourth I stopped, but the game-keepers insisted on more butchery, saying, "No one but the King ever did the like" (I guess no one else had ever had the chance), so, thus urged, I continued firing till I had slaughtered eleven with eleven shots-an easy task with a shot-gun and buck-shot cartridges.

The "hunt" being ended - for with this I had had enough, and no one else was permitted to do any shooting - the aide-de-camp directed the game to be sent to me in Florence, and we started for the chateau. On the way back I saw a wild boar - the first and only one I ever saw - my attention being drawn to him by cries from some of the game-keepers. There was much commotion, the men pointing out the game and shouting excitedly, "See the wild boar!" otherwise I should not have known what was up, but now, looking in the indicated direction, I saw scudding over the plain what appeared to me to be nothing but a half-grown black pig, or shoat. He was not in much of a hurry either, and gave no evidence of ferocity, yet it is said that this insignificant-looking animal is dangerous when hunted with the spear - the customary way. After an early dinner at the chateau we returned to Florence, and my venison next day arriving, it was distributed among my American friends in the city.

Shortly after the hunt the King returned from Milan, and then honored me with a military dinner, his Majesty and all the guests, numbering eighty, appearing in full uniform. The banqueting hall was lighted with hundreds of wax candles, there was a profusion of beautiful flowers, and to me the scene altogether was one of unusual magnificence. The table service was entirely of gold - the celebrated set of the house of Savoy - and behind the chair of each guest stood a servant in powdered wig and gorgeous livery of red plush. I sat at the right of the King, who - his hands resting on his sword, the hilt of which glittered with jewels - sat through the hour and a half at table without once tasting food or drink, for it was his rule to eat but two meals in twenty-four hours - breakfast at noon, and dinner at midnight. The King remained silent most of the time, but when he did speak, no matter on what subject, he inevitably drifted back to hunting. He never once referred to the France-Prussian war, nor to the political situation in his own country, then passing through a crisis. In taking leave of his Majesty I thanked him with deep gratitude for honoring me so highly, and his response was that if ever he came to America to hunt buffalo, he should demand my assistance.

From Florence I went to Milan and Geneva, then to Nice, Marseilles, and Bordeaux. Assembled at Bordeaux was a convention which had been called together by the government of the National Defense for the purpose of confirming or rejecting the terms of an armistice of twenty-one days, arranged between Jules Favre and Count Bismarck in negotiations begun at Versailles the latter part of January. The convention was a large body, chosen from all parts of France, and was unquestionably the most noisy, unruly and unreasonable set of beings that I ever saw in a legislative assembly. The frequent efforts of Thiers, Jules Favre, and other leading men to restrain the more impetuous were of little avail. When at the sittings a delegate arose to speak on some question, he was often violently pulled to his seat and then surrounded by a mob of his colleagues, who would throw off their coats and gesticulate wildly, as though about to fight.

But the bitter pill of defeat had to be swallowed in some way, so the convention delegated M. Thiers to represent the executive power of the country, with authority to construct a ministry. Three commissioners were appointed by the Executive, to enter into further negotiations with

Count Bismarck at Versailles and arrange a peace, the terms of which, however, were to be submitted to the convention for final action. Though there had been so much discussion, it took but a few days to draw up and sign a treaty at Versailles, the principal negotiators being Thiers and Jules Favre for France, and Bismarck on the part of the Germans. The terms agreed upon provided for the occupation of Paris till ratification should be had by the convention at Bordeaux; learning of which stipulation from our Minister, Mr. Washburn, I hurried off to Paris to see the conquerors make their triumphal entry

In the city the excitement was at fever heat, of course; the entire population protesting with one voice that they would never, never look upon the hated Germans marching through their beloved city. No; when the day arrived they would hide themselves in their houses, or shut their eyes to such a hateful sight. But by the 1st of March a change had come over the fickle Parisians, for at an early hour the sidewalks were jammed with people, and the windows and doors of the houses filled with men, women, and children eager to get a look at the conquerors. Only a few came in the morning, however - an advance-guard of perhaps a thousand cavalry and infantry. The main column marched from the Arc-de-Triomphe toward the middle of the afternoon. In its composition it represented united Germany - Saxons, Bavarians, and the Royal Guard of Prussia - and, to the strains of martial music, moving down the Champ Elysées to the Place de la Concorde, was distributed thence over certain sections of the city agreed upon beforehand. Nothing that could be called a disturbance took place during the march; and though there was a hiss now and then, and murmurings of discontent, yet the most noteworthy mutterings were directed against the defunct Empire. Indeed, I found everywhere that the national misfortunes were laid at Napoleon's door - he, by this time, having become a scapegoat for every blunder of the war.

The Emperor William (he had been proclaimed German Emperor at Versailles the 18th of January) did not accompany his troops into Paris, though he reviewed them at Long Champs before they started. After the occupation of the city he still remained at Versailles, and as soon as circumstances would permit, I repaired to the Imperial headquarters to pay my respects to his Majesty under his new title and dignities, and to say good-bye.

Besides the Emperor, the only persons I met at Versailles were General von Moltke and Bismarck. His Majesty was in a very agreeable frame of mind, and as bluff and hearty as usual. His increased rank and power had effected no noticeable change of any kind in him, and by his genial and cordial ways he made me think that my presence with the German army had contributed to his pleasure. Whether this was really so or not, I shall always believe it true, for his kind words and sincere manner could leave no other conclusion.

General von Moltke was, as usual, quiet and reserved, betraying not the slightest consciousness of his great ability, nor the least indication of pride on account of his mighty work. I say this advisedly, for it is an undoubted fact that it was his marvelous mind that perfected the military system by which 800,000 men were mobilized with unparalleled celerity and moved with such certainty of combination that, in a campaign of seven months, the military power of France was destroyed and her vast resources sorely crippled.

I said good-bye to Count Bismarck, also, for at that busy time the chances of seeing him again were very remote. The great Chancellor manifested more joy over the success of the Germans than did anyone else at the Imperial headquarters. Along with his towering strength of mind and body, his character partook of much of the enthusiasm and impulsiveness commonly restricted to younger men, and now in his frank, free way he plainly showed his light-heartedness and gratification at success. That which for years his genius had been planning and striving for - permanent unification of the German States, had been accomplished by the war. It had welded them together in a compact Empire which no power in Europe could disrupt, and as such a union was the aim of Bismarck's life, he surely had a right to feel jubilant.

Thanks to the courtesies extended me, I had been able to observe the principal battles, and study many of the minor details of a war between two of the greatest military nations of the world, and to examine critically the methods followed abroad for subsisting, equipping, and manœuvring vast bodies of men during a stupendous campaign. Of course I found a great deal to interest and instruct me, yet nowadays war is pretty much the same everywhere, and this one offered no marked exception to my previous experiences. The methods pursued on the march were the same as we would employ, with one most important exception. Owing to the density of population throughout France it was always practicable for the Germans to quarter their troops in villages, requiring the inhabitants to subsist both officers and men. Hence there was no necessity for camp and garrison equipage, nor enormous provision trains, and the armies were unencumbered by these impedimeta, indispensable when operating in a poor and sparsely settled country. As I have said before, the only trains were those for ammunition, pontoon-boats, and the field telegraph, and all these were managed by special corps. If transportation was needed for other purposes, it was obtained by requisition from the invaded country, just as food and forage were secured. Great celerity of combination was therefore possible, the columns moving in compact order, and as all the roads were broad and macadamized, there was little or nothing to delay or obstruct the march of the Germans, except when their enemy offered resistance, but even this was generally slight and not very frequent, for the French were discouraged by disaster from the very outset of the campaign

The earlier advantages gained by the Germans may be ascribed to the strikingly prompt mobilization of their armies, one of the most noticeable features of their perfect military system, devised by almost autocratic power; their later successes were greatly aided by the blunders of the French, whose stupendous errors materially shortened the war, though even if prolonged it could, in my opinion, have had ultimately no other termination.

As I have previously stated, the first of these

blunders was the acceptance of battle by Mac-
Mahon at Worth; the second in attaching too
much importance to the fortified position of Metz,
resulting in three battles - Colombey, Mars-la-
Tour, and Gravelotte - all of which were lost;
and the third, the absurd movement of MacMahon
along the Belgian frontier to relieve Metz, the
responsibility for which, I am glad to say, does
not belong to him.

With the hemming in of Bazaine at Metz and
the capture of MacMahon's army at Sedan the
crisis of the war was passed, and the Germans
practically the victors. The taking of Paris was
but a sentiment - the money levy could have been
made and the Rhine provinces held without mo-
lesting that city, and only the political influences
consequent upon the changes in the French Government caused peace to be deferred.

I did not have much opportunity to observe the
German cavalry, either on the march or in battle.
The only time I saw any of it engaged was in the
unfortunate charge at Gravelotte. That proved
its mettle good and discipline fair, but answered
no other purpose. Such of it as was not attached
to the infantry was organized in divisions, and
operated in accordance with the old idea of covering the front and flanks of the army, a duty which
it thoroughly performed. But thus directed it

was in no sense an independent corps, and hence cannot be said to have accomplished anything in the campaign, or have had a weight or influence at all proportionate to its strength. The method of its employment seemed to me a mistake, for, being numerically superior to the French cavalry, had it been massed and manœuvred independently of the infantry, it could easily have broken up the French communications, and done much other work of weighty influence in the prosecution of the war.

The infantry was as fine as I ever saw, the men young and hardy in appearance, and marching always with an elastic stride. The infantry regiment, however, I thought too large - too many men for a colonel to command unless he has the staff of a general - but this objection may be counterbalanced by the advantages resulting from associating together thus intimately the men from the same district, or county as we would call it; the celerity of mobilization, and, in truth, the very foundation of the German system, being based on this local or territorial scheme of recruiting.

There was no delay when the call sounded for the march; all turned out promptly, and while on the road there was very little straggling, only the sick falling out. But on such fine, smooth roads, and with success animating the men from the day they struck the first blow, it could hardly be expected that the columns would not keep well closed up. Then, too, it must be borne in mind that, as already stated, campaigning in France - that is, the marching, camping, and subsisting of an army - is an easy matter, very unlike anything we had during the war of the rebellion. To repeat: the country is rich, beautiful, and densely populated, subsistence abundant, and the roads all macadamized highways; thus the conditions are altogether different from those existing with us. I think that under the same circumstances our troops would have done as well as the Germans, marched as admirably, made combinations as quickly and accurately, and fought with as much success. I can but leave to conjecture how the Germans would have got along on bottomless roads - often none at all - through the swamps and quicksands of northern Virginia, from the Wilderness to Petersburg, and from Chattanooga to Atlanta and the sea.

Following the operations of the German armies from the battle of Gravelotte to the siege of Paris, I may, in conclusion, say that I saw no new military principles developed, whether of strategy or grand tactics, the movements of the different armies and corps being dictated and governed by the same general laws that have so long obtained, simplicity of combination and manœuvre, and the concentration of a numerically superior force at the vital point.

After my brief trip to Versailles, I remained in Paris till the latter part of March. In company with Mr. Washburn, I visited the fortifications for the defense of the city, and found them to be exceptionally heavy; so strong, indeed, that it would have been very hard to carry the place by a general assault. The Germans, knowing the character of the works, had refrained from the sacrifice of life that such an attempt must entail, though they well knew that many of the forts were manned by unseasoned soldiers. With only a combat here and there, to tighten their lines or repulse a sortie, they wisely preferred to wait till starvation should do the work with little loss and absolute certainty.

The Germans were withdrawn from Paris on the 3d of March, and no sooner were they gone than factional quarrels, which had been going on at intervals ever since the flight of the Empress and the fall of her regency on the 4th of September, were renewed with revolutionary methods that eventually brought about the Commune. Having witnessed one or two of these outbreaks, and concluding that while such turbulence reigned in the city it would be of little profit for me to tarry there, I decided to devote the rest of the time I could be away from home to travel in England, Ireland, and Scotland. My journeys through those countries were full of pleasure and instruction, but as nothing I saw or did was markedly different from what has been so often described by others, I will save the reader this part of my experience. I returned to America in the fall, having been absent a little more than a year, and although I saw much abroad of absorbing interest, both professional and general, yet I came back to my native land with even a greater love for her, and with increased admiration for her institutions.

THE END.

INDEX

455

456 INDEX

466

478   *INDEX.*

Bringing the Past into the Future

More Great Books Brought Back by DSI

Series 1: Lincoln
Special Series 1 includes a total of nine volumes: *The Life of Abraham Lincoln* by Ida Tarbell, a four-volume set; *Debates of Lincoln and Douglas; Six Months at the White House with Lincoln* by F. B. Carpenter; and *Herndon's Lincoln: The True Story of a Great Life*, three volumes unabridged, written by Lincoln's law partner of more than twenty years.
CD-ROM ISBN 1-58218-084-9

The Life of Abraham Lincoln
By Ida M. Tarbell. Illustrations and maps. 4 vols. Originally published by the Lincoln Historical Society in 1900.
Discover the incredible facts of the life of Abraham Lincoln, a man who changed the fabric of America forever. Read in his own words his views on equality and ending slavery. This work details Lincoln's entire life including the origins of the Lincoln family, his entry into the military during the Black Hawk War, his important law cases, his entire political career, the Civil War, his personal life with Mary Todd, the devastating loss of one of their children, and his constant battles with depression.
CD-ROM ISBN 1-58218-017-2
Softcover ISBN 1-58218-002-4

Debates of Lincoln and Douglas
Carefully prepared by the reporters of each party at the times of their delivery. Originally published by Follett & Foster in 1860.
Perhaps the most consequential artifact of American election campaigning and its political arguments. Political debates between Hon. Abraham Lincoln and Hon. Stephen A. Douglas, in the celebrated campaign of 1858 in Illinois. Included are the preceding speeches of each at Chicago, Springfield, etc., as well as the two great speeches of Lincoln in Ohio in 1859, published at the times of their delivery.
CD-ROM ISBN 1-58218-009-1
Softcover ISBN 1-58218-000-8

Series 2: Custer
Special Series 2 includes both *A Life of Major Gen'l George A. Custer* by Frederick Whittaker and *Tenting on the Plains* by Custer's wife, Elizabeth. Also included are the National Archives' transcripts concerning the Court Martial of Custer (1867) and the Court of Inquiry of Reno (1879) for his actions at Little Big Horn.
CD-ROM ISBN 1-58218-081-4

A Life of Major Gen'l George A. Custer
By Frederick Whittaker. Originally published in 1876.
With no marked advantages of education or wealth to command his situation, Custer yet passed through a career so brilliant that his deeds are household words, his "Last Stand" against Sioux and Cheyenne warriors at Little Big Horn an enduring legend in American history. Truth and sincerity, honor and bravery, tenderness and sympathy, unassuming piety and temperance were the mainspring of Major Gen'l Custer, the man.
CD-ROM ISBN 1-58218-042-3
Softcover ISBN 1-58218-040-7

Tenting on the Plains
By Elizabeth Custer. Includes illustrations by Frederic Remington. Originally published in 1889.
Elizabeth Custer was just a young girl when she fell in love with one of the most controversial Indian fighters of the late 1800s, and barely a woman when she defied her father to marry him. She went on to earn literary fame as well as financial independence with her entertaining tales of frontier life as the wife of General George Custer. Her stories of life on the Plains are as colorful today as when they first appeared over a century ago.
CD-ROM ISBN 1-58218-052-0
Softcover ISBN 1-58218-050-4

Series 3: Generals
Special Series 3 includes *Personal Memoirs of U. S. Grant, Memoirs of General W. T. Sherman, Personal Memoirs of P. H. Sheridan*, and *McClellan's Own Story.*
CD-ROM ISBN 1-58218-082-2

Personal Memoirs of U. S. Grant
Illustrations, Maps, and Facsimiles of Handwriting. 2 vols. Originally published in 1885.
Published by Mark Twain under the Charles L. Webster Company imprint, this memoir is widely admired as one of the finest military autobiographies ever written. Grant recounts the failings and triumphs of his leadership in strong, clear prose including his boyhood in Ohio, his graduation from West Point, his marriage to Julia Dent, his brilliant military campaigns, and his presidency.
CD-ROM ISBN 1-58218-029-6
Softcover ISBN 1-58218-005-9

Memoirs of General W. T. Sherman
With a map showing the marches of U.S. forces under his command. 2 vols. Originally published in 1890.
General William Tecumseh Sherman, a great man both in his gifts and his achievements, was altogether a solider in the habits of mind. A natural student of the topography of the countryside, this characteristic of true military genius served Sherman well in planning his devastating march from Atlanta, across Georgia to the sea, the most striking achievement of the Civil War. The memoirs of this courageous, patient, and self-sacrificing "Old Warrior" are certain of a permanent place in literature.
CD-ROM ISBN 1-58218-025-3
Softcover ISBN 1-58218-004-0

Personal Memoirs of P. H. Sheridan
Illustrated. Twenty-six maps, prepared specially for this book by the War Department. 2 vols. Originally published in 1888.
General Phil Sheridan revolutionized the handling of mounted men in this country and abroad as commander of America's army. A hell-for-leather cavalryman, Sheridan was as deliberate and careful as he was brave. His memoirs vividly depict the brilliant campaigns he masterminded, including his victory at Appomattox where his men blocked Lee's retreat to force his surrender, ending the Civil War.
CD-ROM ISBN 1-58218-033-4
Softcover ISBN 1-58218-006-7

Digital Scanning, Inc. • 344 Gannett Road, Scituate, MA 02066 • www.digitalscanning.com • toll-free 1-888-349-4443

McClellan's Own Story

Illustrations from sketches drawn on the field of battle by A. R. Waud, the great war artist. Originally published in 1886.

After Bull Run, Lincoln appointed 34-year-old Gen. George B. McClellan as commander of the newly created Army of the Potomac. An able administrator and drillmaster, McClellan proceeded to reorganize the army for what he expected to be an overwhelming demonstration of Northern military superiority. "Our George," as his soldiers lovingly called him, was one of the ablest commanders which the United States has ever produced.

CD-ROM ISBN 1-58218-037-7
Softcover ISBN 1-58218-007-5

History of Massachusetts in the Civil War

By William Schouler, Late Adjutant-General of the Commonwealth. Originally published in 1868.

Massachusetts played a prominent part in the Civil War, from the beginning to the end; not only in furnishing soldiers for the army, sailors for the navy, and financial aid to the government, but in advancing ideas, which though scoffed at in the early months of the war, were afterwards accepted by the nation, before the war could be brought to a successful end.

CD-ROM ISBN 1-58218-013-X
Softcover ISBN 1-58218-001-6

Series 4: Indians

Special Series 4 includes George Catlin's *North American Indians* and *Indian Tribes of North America*. Also included are Indian Treaties from the National Archives.

CD-ROM ISBN 1-58218-083-0

North American Indians

By George Catlin. Illustrations and maps. 2 vols. Originally published in 1903.

Explore the territories of the North American Indian with the historical text, illustrations, and maps of George Catlin. Catlin gave up the practice of law to pursue his self-taught art, travelling throughout the American West from 1832 to 1840, painting portraits and writing on his encounters with various Indian tribes. Scholars and researchers alike will delight in the descriptions and portraits that portray this moment in history with such vivid detail.

CD-ROM ISBN 1-58218-021-0

Civil War Prison Stories

Daring and Suffering: A History of the Great Railroad Adventure

By Lieut. William Pittenger, One of Andrews' Raiders. Originally published in 1863.

This courageous raid into Georgia ranks high among the striking and novel incidents of the Civil War. Pittenger and his comrades embarked on a secret raid deep into Confederate territory to cut the rail link between Marietta and Chattanooga, only to run out of fuel after a long and dangerous chase. Those that survived the mission were the first soldiers at rank of private to be awarded the Congressional Medal of Honor.

CD-ROM ISBN 1-58218-077-6
Softcover ISBN 1-58218-075-X

Beyond the Lines: A Yankee Loose in Dixie

By Capt. J. J. Geer. Originally published in 1864.

Geer narrates the suffering endured as a prisoner in the Southern Confederacy. After being captured at the battle of Shiloh, Geer was tried on the most frivolous charges and subsequently chained with slaves' chains and cast into military prisons and common jails. He managed to escape, overcoming malarious marshes and bloodhounds only to be recaptured!

CD-ROM ISBN 1-58218-085-7
Softcover ISBN 1-58218-088-1

Prison Life in Dixie

By Sergeant Oats. Originally published in 1880.

The author describes his harrowing capture and imprisonment by the Rebels at Sumter Prison a.k.a. "Andersonville Prison Pen". Renowned as one of the worst prisons of the Civil War, the Andersonville pen spread over only 11 acres, with a 12-foot wall surrounding over 33,000 Union soldiers. The writer endeavors to furnish such descriptions and incidents that give the reader a true picture of Rebel prisons and the means and methods of either surviving or dying in them.

CD-ROM ISBN 1-58218-101-2
Softcover ISBN 1-58218-100-4

Forthcoming Titles

Herndon's Lincoln: The True Story of a Great Life
By William H. Herndon, Lincoln's friend and law partner

Six Months at the White House with Lincoln
By F. B. Carpenter

Reminiscences of Winfield Scott Hancock
By his wife, A. R. Hancock

The Battle of Gettysburg
By Comte de Paris

Sheridan's Troopers on the Border
By De B. Randolph Keim

Genesis of the Civil War
By Samuel Wylie Crawford

Following the Guidon
By Elizabeth Custer

The Indian Tribes of North America
By McKenney and Hall

The History of Philip's War
By Thomas Church

Book of the Indians of North America
By Samuel G. Drake

Digital Scanning, Inc. • 344 Gannett Road, Scituate, MA 02066 • www.digitalscanning.com • toll-free 1-888-349-4443

www.ingramcontent.com/pod-product-compliance
Lightning Source LLC
Chambersburg PA
CBHW020408100426
42812CB00001B/250